CHRISTIAN
ETHICS
IN PLAIN
LANGUAGE

NELSON'S PLAIN LANGUAGE™ SERIES

CHRISTIAN ETHICS IN PLAIN LANGUAGE

KERBY ANDERSON

NELSON REFERENCE & ELECTRONIC
A Division of Thomas Nelson Publishers
Since 1798

For other life-changing resources, visit us at:
www.thomasnelson.com

CHRISTIAN ETHICS IN PLAIN LANGUAGE

LIBRARY OF CONGRESS CATALOGING-IN-PUBLICATION DATA IS AVAILABLE UPON REQUEST

ISBN 1-4185-0003-8

Printed in the United States of America

2 3 4 5 6 7—10 09 08 07 06

*Dedicated to
my beloved wife of thirty years,
Susanne Elise Anderson,
and my three adult children,
Amy, Jonathan, and Catherine.*

TABLE OF CONTENTS

CHAPTER TWENTY-TWO: GOVERNMENT AND CIVIL DISOBEDIENCE

PREFACE

WHY IS CHRISTIAN ETHICS IMPORTANT? First, we make ethical decisions every day. It is nearly impossible to go for a very long period of time without being forced to make a decision that has moral consequences. Second, we confront ethical issues in society. Many people (in certain fields like medicine and government) deal with moral dilemmas on a regular basis.

This is a book about ethics from a Christian worldview. Christian ethics seeks to integrate philosophy with theology. But it is much more than a book on philosophy. In a sense, the premise of the book is that ethics is too important to be left to philosophers. Christian ethics has challenged philosophers, theologians, and lay people for centuries.

The challenge of Christian ethics today is significant. We live in a postmodern world where values are inverted: evil is called good, and good is called evil (Isaiah 5:20). Consider that in this postmodern world, even our philosophical foundations are reversed. As one wag put it, we live in a world where the theory of relativity is considered an absolute value and where biblical absolutes are considered relative.

Christian Ethics in Plain Language attempts to bring the facts and resources of Christian research to bear on Christian decision-making. Ethics, philosophy, and Christian ethical foundations are presented in a logical and practical way. The book is intentionally broad in its scope of subjects. Topics as diverse as bioethics (abortion, euthanasia, genetic engineering), social problems (race, drugs, crime, gambling, pornography), sexual ethics (adultery, cohabitation, homosexuality), media, and government are covered in this book.

We need a clear understanding of the moral issues of our age, and we need a consistent and coherent application of biblical principles to those important personal and social issues. It is my hope that this book will inform and challenge those attempting to find answers to our personal questions as well as the complex issues we face in the 21st century.

—Kerby Anderson

KERBY ANDERSON

KERBY ANDERSON serves as the National Director of Probe Ministries and is the host of Point of View (USA Radio Network). He holds master's degrees from Yale University (science) and Georgetown University (government).

He is the author of the seven books including *Moral Dilemmas* and *Signs of Warning, Signs of Hope*. He has served as editor and contributor to other books including *Marriage, Family & Sexuality* and *Technology, Spirituality & Social Trends*.

He has spoken on university campuses around the country and has been a visiting professor at Dallas Theological Seminary, Philadelphia Biblical University, and Temple Baptist Seminary.

His editorials have appeared in the *Dallas Morning News*, the *Miami Herald*, the *San Jose Mercury*, and the *Houston Post*. He is a regular commentator on "Prime Time America" (Moody Broadcasting Network) and "Today's Issues" (American Family Radio). He has appeared on numerous radio and TV talk shows including the "MacNeil/Lehrer News Hour," "Focus on the Family," and "The 700 Club."

CHRISTIAN
ETHICS
IN PLAIN
LANGUAGE

1

ETHICS AND SOCIETY

DAILY we are confronted with ethical choices and moral complexity. Society is awash in controversial issues such as abortion, euthanasia, cloning, race, drug abuse, homosexuality, gambling, pornography, and capital punishment. Life may have been simpler in a previous age, but now the rise of technology and the fall of ethical consensus have brought us to a society full of moral dilemmas.

The premise of this book is that Christians can embrace the scientific and social changes in our world and still be true to biblical principles. These chapters are written to equip you with biblical guidelines to navigate the rough waters of morality in modern society.

Never has society needed biblical perspectives to evaluate contemporary moral issues. And never have Christians been less equipped to address these topics from a biblical perspective.

CHRISTIAN WORLDVIEW

The Barna Research Group conducted a national survey of adults and concluded that only 4 percent of adults have a biblical worldview as the basis of their decision making. The survey also discovered that only 9 percent of born again Christians have such a perspective on life.[1]

Everyone has a worldview, but relatively few people (even religious people) have a biblical worldview. This explains a great deal about behavior. The reason so few people act like Christians is that they do not think like Christians. Behavior results from our values and beliefs. Thinking biblically about the issues of life should ultimately result in living biblically in society. Conversely, not thinking biblically should result in not living biblically within society.

Part of the problem is the lack of sound biblical teaching about a biblical worldview. The Barna Research Group found in a nationwide survey of senior

1

pastors that only half of the country's Protestant pastors have a biblical world-view. The gap among churches is reflected in the outcomes from the nation's two largest denominations. Southern Baptists had the highest percentage of pastors with a biblical worldview (71 percent), while the Methodists were lowest (27 percent).[2]

Absolute Truth

Biblical ethics rests on the belief in absolute truth. Yet surveys show that a minority of born-again adults (44 percent) and an even smaller proportion of born-again teenagers (9 percent) are certain of the existence of absolute moral truth.[3] By a three-to-one margin adults say truth is always relative to the person and his or her situation. This perspective is even more lopsided among teenagers who over-whelmingly believe moral truth depends on the circumstances.[4]

Social scientists as well as pollsters have been warning that American society is becoming more and more dominated by moral anarchy. Writing in the early 1990s, James Patterson and Peter Kim said in *The Day America Told the Truth* that there was no moral authority in America: "We choose which laws of God we believe in. There is absolutely no moral consensus in this country as there was in the 1950s, when all our institutions commanded more respect."[5]

Ten years after the publication of *The Day America Told the Truth*, George Barna and Mark Hatch, writing in their book *Boiling Point*, concluded that moral anarchy has arrived and dominates our culture today.[6] Their argument hinged on a substantial amount of attitudinal and behavioral evidence, such as rapid growth of the pornography industry, highway speeding as the norm, income tax cheating, computer hacking, rampant copyright violations (movies, books, recordings), increasing rates of cohabitation and adultery, and Internet-based plagiarism.[7]

When asked the basis on which they form their moral choices, nearly half of all adults cited their desire to do whatever will bring them the most pleasing or satisfying results. Although the Bible should be the basis of our moral decision-making, the survey showed that only four out of every ten born-again Christian adults relied on the Bible or church teaching as their primary source of moral guidance.[8] The survey also found that the younger generation was even more inclined to support behaviors that conflict with traditional Christian morals: "Among the instances in which young adults were substantially more likely than their elders to adopt a nouveau moral view were in supporting homosexuality, cohabitation, the non-medicinal use of marijuana, voluntary exposure to pornography, profane language, drunkenness, speeding and sexual fantasizing."[9]

Christian Commitment

A person's faith commitment definitely affects his or her perspective on moral issues. More than four out of five adults say they are concerned about the moral condition of the nation. Yet a large portion of these same people hold to views that conflict with the moral teachings of their professed faith.[10]

The single exception to this general rule are committed evangelicals (who would be considered a subset of the broader term "born-again Christians"). Apparently, faith commitment makes a difference in one's perspective on moral issues within society.

By contrast, only a minority of born-again teenagers (44 percent) claim that they are "absolutely committed to the Christian faith." Even more disturbing was a representative nationwide survey among born-again adults. In the survey, none of the individuals interviewed said that the single, most important goal in their life is to be a committed follower of Jesus Christ.[11]

Barna noted that the church is struggling to influence the nation's culture because "believers think of themselves as individuals first, Americans second, and Christians third. Until that prioritization is rearranged, the Church will continue to lose influence, and biblical principles will represent simply one more option among the numerous worldviews that Americans may choose from."[12]

ETHICS AND EDUCATION

Ethics is sometimes taught in the public schools. Frequently, however, teachers avoid discussing ethical issues in the classroom. And when ethics is taught, teachers usually instruct students that one's ethics are relative and situational. Students learn that ethics depends on the person and on the situation. They learn concepts like values clarification which teach that each student must make up his or her mind about what is right and wrong.

Students also learn that they are not to judge another person's actions by assuming that ethics are absolute and therefore binding on the behavior of others. Professor Robert Simon (Hamilton College, New York) said that he has never met a student who denied the Holocaust happened. But he also reported that 10 to 20 percent of his students cannot bring themselves to say that killing millions of people is wrong. "Of course, I dislike the Nazis," one student told him, "but who is to say they are morally wrong?"[13]

Professor Kay Haugaard (Pasadena City College, California) wrote that her current students have trouble expressing any moral reservations about human sacrifice. The subject came up when she taught her class Shirley Jackson's *The Lottery*. The short story deals with a small American farm town where one person is killed each year to make the crops grow. In the story, a woman is ritually stoned to death by her husband, her twelve-year-old daughter, and her four-year-old son.

In the past, the message of blind conformity always caused students to raise questions about right and wrong. No longer. When Haugaard asked one woman in the class if she believed in human sacrifice, the student said, "I really don't know. If it was a religion of long standing. . . ." Haugaard wrote, "I was stunned. This was the woman who wrote so passionately of saving the whales, of concern for the rain forests, of her rescue and tender care of a stray dog."[14]

Even when college professors attempt to teach ethics, the evidence suggests that such attempts have been unsuccessful. For example, a Zogby International poll of American college seniors found that 97 percent said that they believed that their professors gave them a good education in ethics. But when asked what those professors taught them, 73 percent chose the item "what is right and wrong depends on differences in individual values and cultural diversity." Only one-fourth chose "there are clear and uniform standards of right and wrong by which everyone should be judged."[15]

Forbes magazine found that business schools are "talking up their ethics programs, but there's no evidence that all the studying will prevent" further corporate scandals. A reporter for the magazine observed an ethics class at Harvard Business School in which the professor and students discussed case studies but avoided coming to any moral conclusions. The reporter concluded that students "develop skills enabling them to rationalize anything this side of cannibalism."[16]

There is a need to teach and study ethics based upon something more than personal preference and nonjudgmentalism. Our society confronts difficult moral dilemmas which need keen ethical evaluation based upon an ethical system that provides clear direction and a basis for decisive moral commitment.

2

ETHICS AND PHILOSOPHY

THE PRIMARY FOCUS of this book is on ethics. Quite simply, the study of ethics considers what ought to be, not what is. We do not need to evaluate what we ought to do if we always did it in the course of our daily lives. Ethics describes normative behavior: what we should do in a particular situation.

In modern society, the words *ethics* and *morality* are used interchangeably. However, there are distinctions between the two. *Ethics* comes from the Greek word *ethos*, meaning a "stall" for horses, a place of stability and permanence. *Morality* comes from *mores*, which describes the shifting behavioral patterns of society.

Put another way, ethics is what is normative or absolute; it is a set of standards we use to organize our lives. Ethics is more concerned with what people ought to do, whereas morality is more concerned with what people are already doing.

Various theories on ethics use normative ethical principles to evaluate or justify particular actions and behavior. In order to be useful and practical, ethical discussions must use procedures and criteria that all people accept and understand. Ethical principles must be the ground rules for our moral decision-making.

CATEGORIES OF ETHICS

Ethics as an academic discipline can be listed under a number of categories. These various categories of moral philosophy help organize and systematize the various views and concepts. Philosophers divide ethical theories into three general subject areas: metaethics, normative ethics, and applied ethics. In this book, our primary focus will be on the last two areas.

Metaethics investigates the meaning of moral language. This discipline is called the epistemology of ethics. It asks where our ethical principles come from, and what they mean. Metaethics seeks to understand *the nature of* ethical evaluations. Examples of meta-ethical questions include: What is the meaning of words like

5

right, good, and just? Do these words have intrinsic meaning or are they merely social inventions? How do we know what is right and wrong?

Normative ethics is a more practical look at ethics. The goal is to arrive at moral principles that govern human conduct. Arriving at this goal involves describing good habits that we should acquire and duties that we should follow. Put another way, normative ethics prescribes moral behavior, while descriptive ethics describes moral behavior. Normative ethics seeks to answer these types of questions: What actions are good and bad? What should we do?

Applied ethics applies normative ethics to specific controversial issues, such as abortion, euthanasia, pornography, homosexuality, and capital punishment. Ethical conclusions result from applying the principles derived from of metaethics and normative ethics. Most of these ethical problems deal with social ethics and therefore deal directly or indirectly with public policy.

HISTORY OF ETHICS

Ethics must be applied to reality, and numerous worldviews exist in the real world. In his book *The Universe Next Door*, James Sire described eight basic worldviews but also acknowledges that there are many more than those documented in his basic worldview catalog.[1] Thus, Christian ethics must be able to interact with the different philosophies and worldviews in the world today.

In the past, Christianity has been forced to interact with various religions and philosophies. Christian theologians and philosophers have had to defend their positions as well as critique the ethical positions of others. In many cases, Christian ethics has been the better for this interaction as new information (from academic disciplines) and rigorous critique have sharpened Christians' moral analysis of contemporary moral dilemmas.

Christian philosophers such as Augustine and Aquinas attempted to interact with secular philosophies and even synthesize them with Christian theology. The apostle Paul used the Bible and the writings of secular philosophers to make his case before the Epicurean and Stoic philosophers at the Areopagus (Acts 17:16–34). To be effective, Christians and a Christian ethic must be willing to interact with the secular world and the ideas of secular philosophers. The following is a brief look at a few of the major figures in philosophy who proposed ethical systems.

Classical Greek Philosophers

Plato was born around 428–426 B.C. and lived to 346 B.C. When he was twenty, he became an eager disciple of Socrates and later was Aristotle's teacher. He was the greatest student of Socrates and pulled together the teachings of Socrates in his academy, which he founded at the age of forty.

Plato taught four things: a theory of knowledge (epistemology), a theory of conduct (ethics), a theory of government (political science), and a theory of the universe (cosmology). Most of his writings consist of approximately two dozen dialogues. The one most read is *The Republic*.

Plato's ethics is not so much a moral philosophy as it is a discourse on virtue. Like all Greeks, Plato believed the greatest good of man is happiness. And the means by which this highest good is attained is through the practice of virtue and acquisition of wisdom.

Plato was not concerned about whether an action was right or wrong; rather, he focused more on whether someone was a good person. This holistic view in essence was a blending of philosophy and psychology.

The central entity in *The Republic* is the state. The state, he maintained, should have unlimited authority. In this governmental system, there should be no private property or even family institutions. Children belong to the state and should be educated by officials appointed by the state according to the measure of their ability.

Plato's theory of ethics contrasts sharply from Christian ethics because it is a man-centered view of morality. He taught that what was right and wrong were to be judged by whatever was reasonable to the individual. In other words, if someone can provide a rational justification for his or her actions, then the action was ethical. But Christians understand that our hearts are deceitful (Jer. 17:9) and our minds are unregenerate, so we can always find a way to justify even immoral actions. Just because we can find a way to justify our actions does not make them right.

Aristotle lived from 384 B.C. to 322 B.C. From his eighteenth to his thirty-seventh year he lived in Athens as a pupil of Plato. King Philip of Macedon later summoned him to become the tutor of Alexander the Great, who was thirteen.

Aristotle accepted Plato's concept of the universe as an ideal world and an interrelated whole. He extended Plato's concept of the virtuous person by describing the specific virtues of moral behavior. He also produced a wide variety of essays on subjects including logic, metaphysics, physics, biology, psychology, ethics, and politics.

Aristotle's method is both inductive and deductive, while Plato's is essentially deductive. In other words, Plato tended to idealize reality in light of intuition of a higher world, whereas Aristotle used science and logic to examine the real world. He extended Plato's thought by providing an important connection between knowing the good and producing it in one's life.

Aristotle's ethic rests on the Greek word *telos*, meaning end or goal. All of life should be directed toward goodness. The chief good is goodness or happiness, and happiness comes from self-realization. This understanding of life contrasts with Christian theology, which teaches that loving and obeying God is the highest goal for human beings, not personal happiness.

His moral theory also moves from the idea of goodness (happiness as an end) to the concept of being a good person (virtue). Many of Aristotle's virtues come from the concept of the "golden mean." He taught that virtue often is found between two extremes of behavior. For example, temperance can be seen as the mean between gluttony (an excess) and asceticism (a denial).

While the golden mean may often be an accurate perspective on morality, the Bible also teaches that what is moral is sometimes not the mean between two extremes. Biblical virtues such as abstinence, purity, and holiness are just a few examples of morality that do not derive from finding the mean of two extremes.

Aristotle's ethic also assumes the goodness of human beings. Classical Greek thought placed great faith in reason and rationality, believing that they would help humans be good people who could live in peace. Both the Bible (Rom. 3:23) and the history of civilization contradict such faith.

Medieval Philosophers

St. Augustine, bishop of Hippo from 396 to 430, was the dominant philosopher of the Western Church of his time. He wove together the New Testament teachings with the Platonic tradition of Greek philosophy and transmitted these ideas into the Medieval period. He struggled with the Pelagian heresy (which denied the doctrine of original sin) as well as the heresy known as Manicheanism (which is characterized by a dualism of good and evil). He rejected these ideas and put forth a Christian theology and ethics that have been influential to our day. His two best-known works are the *Confessions* and *The City of God.*

Augustine shifted the emphasis from happiness and goodness to doing good and following biblical commands. Unlike Aristotle, Augustine did not believe we could acquire virtue on our own because of the effect of sin on the human race. Instead, he believed in the necessity of God's grace.

Augustine also developed a social ethic in *The City of God.* He taught that there were two different communities (the city of God and the city of man), and he formalized the concept of separating church and state. Augustine also developed the foundation for the idea of a just war, which later theologians and philosophers have expanded and developed further.

St. Thomas Aquinas (1224/1225–1274) systematized Latin theology by including the writings of Aristotle that were "rediscovered" and translated into Latin in the thirteenth century. These translations became a key part of his writings, which include the *Summa Theologica* and the *Summa Contra Gentiles.*

Aquinas was attempting to address the philosophy of Aristotle with the theology of Augustine. At the same time, he and other theologians were confronting the rigorous demands of scientific rationalism. The world was changing from an agrarian society, and technology and scientific progress were changing society's perspectives.

Aquinas proposed that law and society can achieve the common good. Unlike Augustine, Aquinas argued that the purpose of law was to mold good people, not merely to restrain evil. He also distinguished between four different kinds of law:

1. *eternal law*—by which Divine Reason governs the whole community and which can be found in the mind of God (gravity and other physical laws)

2. *natural law*—in which good is to be done and promoted, and evil is to be avoided, and whose principles are self evident (views on contraception)

3. *human law*—which involves those civil laws that govern communities (civil and criminal laws)

4. *divine law*—which pertain to God's special plans for humanity and is revealed through the Bible (God's grace revealed in Scripture)

Aquinas believed that human beings innately live together because they are created in the image of God (Gen. 1:27–28). This understanding of humanity differed from Augustine's, who focused on human sinfulness and the need for society to restrain evil. Aquinas, however, believed that social institutions could encourage the development of good people.

Modern Philosophers

David Hume (1711–1776) lived during the Scottish Enlightenment and took the empiricism of John Locke and George Berkeley to the logical extreme of radical skepticism. Empiricism is the belief that our theories should be based only on matters of fact that we perceive through our senses.

Hume rejected the idea of certain knowledge since he believed that the mind is nothing but a series of sensations. He even claimed that cause-and-effect in the natural world is merely the conjunction of two sense impressions. He also argued that moral facts and morality itself are merely sense impressions. Thus, vice and virtue are merely perceptions in the mind.

Hume noted that many moral philosophers would talk about *what ought to be* on the basis of statements about *what is*. He believed that descriptive statements (what is) and prescriptive statements (what ought to be) differ significantly. The question he asked was how someone could derive an 'ought' from an 'is.' Hume argued that such a derivation is impossible. Instead, he suggested that one can derive moral sense from its usefulness (or what later philosophers called utility). As we will see in the next chapter dealing with utilitarianism, Hume's philosophy has led to the idea of "If it feels good, do it."

Immanuel Kant (1724–1804) is one of the great figures in philosophy and lived during the height of the Enlightenment. He argued in his *Critique of Pure Reason* that objective reality conforms to the structure of the knowing mind. Only objects of experience (phenomena) may be known. Objects beyond our experience (noumena) are unknowable.

In the *Metaphysics of Ethics*, Kant described an ethical system where reason is the final authority for morality. Enlightenment ethics attempted to construct an ethical system not based upon religious values but resting on reason alone. The foundation of Kant's ethical system is his categorical imperative, or absolute moral law.

Actions, he believed, must be done from a sense of duty dictated by reason. No action performed for expediency or solely in obedience to law or custom can be regarded as moral. Moral imperatives based on desire are what Kant called "hypothetical imperatives." A true moral imperative must be categorical and not based upon some desire; therefore, a maxim, which is a plan of action for an individual in a particular set of circumstances, determines actions. He maintained, "Act as if the maxim from which you act were to become through your will a universal law."[2] In other words, a person should be willing to regard his or her action as a moral principle that is equivalent to a law of nature. For example, people should never lie because if lying became a universal law, society would plunge into chaos.

The preceding examples are just a few of the major philosophers who have written on the subject of ethics. Obviously there are many more who have made a contribution to this field, but these are some of the key philosophers in this field. The next chapter will focus on some of the most popular secular ethical systems in modern society.

3

SECULAR ETHICAL SYSTEMS

THE CENTRAL PREMISE of this book is that ethics should be rooted in the Bible and biblical principles. But many philosophical systems of ethics do not start with this biblical presupposition. The following is a brief summary of the more popular contemporary ethical systems that rest on secular assumptions rather than a biblical foundation.

CULTURAL RELATIVISM

Any student in a class on anthropology cannot help but notice the differences between various cultures of the world. Differences in dress, diet, and social norms are readily apparent. Such diversity in terms of ethics and justice are also easily seen and apparently shaped by the culture in which we live.

If there is no transcendent ethical standard, then culture often becomes the ethical norm for determining whether an action is right or wrong. This ethical system is known as *cultural relativism*. Cultural relativism is the view that all ethical truth is relative to a specific culture. Whatever a cultural group approves is considered right within that culture. Conversely, whatever a cultural group condemns is wrong.

The key to cultural relativism is that right and wrong can only be judged relative to a specified society. No ultimate standard of right and wrong exists by which to judge culture.

A famous proponent of this view was John Dewey, often considered the father of American education. He taught that moral standards were like language and therefore the result of custom. Language evolved over time and eventually became organized by a set of principles known as grammar. But language also changes over time to adapt to the changing circumstances of its culture. Likewise, Dewey said, ethics were also the product of an evolutionary process. No fixed ethical norms exist. Rather, ethics are merely the result of particular cultures attempting to organize a set of moral principles. But these principles can also change over time to adapt to the changing circumstances of the culture. This would also mean that different forms of morality evolved in different communities. Thus, there are no universal ethical principles. What may be right in one culture would be wrong in another culture, and vice versa.

Although it is hard for us in the modern world to imagine, a primitive culture might value genocide, treachery, deception, and even torture. While we may not like these traits, a true follower of cultural relativism could not say that these acts are wrong since they are merely the product of cultural adaptation.

A key figure who expanded on Dewey's ideas was William Graham Sumner of Yale University. He argued that what our conscience tells us depends solely upon our social group. The moral values we hold are not part of our moral nature, according to Sumner. They are part of our training and upbringing.

Sumner argued in his book *Folkways*: "World philosophy, life policy, right, rights, and morality are all products of the folkways."[1] In other words, what we perceive as conscience is merely the product of culture upon our minds through childhood training and cultural influence. There are no universal ethical principles, merely different cultural conditioning.

Sumner studied all sorts of societies (primitive and advanced) and was able to document numerous examples of cultural relativism. Although many cultures promoted the idea, for example, that a man could have many wives, Sumner discovered that in Tibet a woman was encouraged to have many husbands. He also described how some Eskimo tribes allowed deformed babies to die by being exposed to the elements. In the Fiji Islands, aged parents were killed.

Sumner believed that this diversity of moral values clearly demonstrated that culture is the sole determinant of our ethical standards. In essence, culture determines what is right and wrong. And different cultures come to different ethical conclusions.

Proponents of cultural relativism believe that this cultural diversity proves that culture alone is responsible for our morality. There is no soul or spirit or mind or conscience. Moral relativists say that what we perceive as moral convictions or conscience are the by-products of culture.

The strength of cultural relativism is that it allows us to withhold moral judgments about the social practices of another culture. In fact, proponents of cultural relativism would say that to pass judgment on another culture would be ethnocentric. This strength, however, is also a major weakness. Cultural relativism excuses us from judging the moral practices of another culture. Yet we all feel compelled to condemn such actions as the Holocaust or ethnic cleansing. Cultural relativism as an ethical system, however, provides no foundation for doing so.

Melville J. Herskovits wrote in *Cultural Relativism*: "Judgments are based on experience, and experience is interpreted by each individual in terms of his own enculturation."[2] In other words, a person's judgment about what is right and wrong is determined by his or her cultural experiences, which would include everything from childhood training to cultural pressures to conform to the majority views of the group. Herskovits further argued that even the definition of what is normal and abnormal is relative to culture.

Herskovits believed that because cultures are flexible, ethical norms change over time to meet new cultural pressures and demands. When populations are unstable and infant mortality is high, cultures value life and develop ethical systems to protect it. When a culture is facing overpopulation, that culture redefines ethical systems and even the value of life. Life is valuable and sacred in the first society. Mercy killing might become normal and acceptable in the second society.

Polygamy might be a socially acceptable standard for society. But later, that society might change its perspective and believe that it is wrong for a man to have more than one wife. Herskovits believed that whatever a society accepted or rejected became the standard of morality for the individuals in that society.

Herskovits contended that "the need for a cultural relativistic point of view has become apparent because of the realization that there is no way to play this game of making judgment across cultures except with loaded dice."[3] Ultimately, he believed, culture determines our moral standards and attempting to compare or contrast cultural norms is futile.

In a sense, the idea of cultural relativism has helped encourage such concepts as multiculturalism and postmodernism. After all, if truth is created, not discovered, then all truths created by a particular culture are equally true, meaning that cultural norms and institutions should be considered equally valid if they are useful to a particular group of people within a culture. And this is one of the major problems with a view of cultural relativism: you cannot judge the morality of another culture. If no objective standard exists, then someone in one culture does not have a right to evaluate the actions or morality of another culture. Yet in our hearts we know that certain things like racism, discrimination, and exploitation are wrong.

Foundational to the view of cultural relativism is the theory of evolution. Since social groups experience cultural change with the passage of time, changing customs and morality evolve differently in different places and times. For example, Anthony Flew, author of *Evolutionary Ethics*, stated his perspective this way: "All morals, ideas and ideals have been originated in the world; and that, having thus in the past been subject to change, they will presumably in the future too, for better or worse, continue to evolve."[4] He denied the existence of God and therefore an objective, absolute moral authority. But he also believed in the authority of a value system.

Flew's theory is problematic because it does not adequately account for the origin, nature, and basis of morals. Flew suggests that morals somehow originated in this world and are constantly evolving. Even if we concede his premise, we must still ask: Where and when did the first moral value originate? Essentially, Flew is arguing that a value came from a non-value. In rejecting the biblical idea of a Creator whose character establishes a moral standard for values, Flew is forced to attempt to derive an *ought* from an *is*.

Evolutionary ethics rests upon the assumption that values are by nature constantly changing or evolving. It claims that changing values are valuable. But is *this* value changing? If it is not, then moral values do not have to be constantly changing. And if that is the case, then there could be unchanging values (known as absolute standards). However, if the value that values change is itself unchanging, then evolutionary ethics is self-contradictory.

Another form of evolutionary ethics is *sociobiology*. E. O. Wilson of Harvard University has been a major advocate of sociobiology and has claimed that scientific materialism will eventually replace traditional religion and other ideologies.[5]

According to sociobiology, human social systems have been shaped by an evolutionary process. Human societies exist and survive because they work and because they have worked in the past. One key principle of sociobiology is the reproductive imperative.[6] The ultimate goal of any organism is to survive and reproduce. Moral systems exist because they ultimately promote human survival and reproduction. Another key principle is that all behavior is selfish at the most basic level. We love our children, according to this view, because love is an effective means of raising effective reproducers.

At the very least, sociobiology is a very cynical view of human nature and human societies. Are we really to believe that all behavior is selfish? Is there no altruism?

In attempting to evaluate cultural relativism, we should acknowledge that we could indeed learn many things from other cultures. We should never fall into the belief that our culture has all the answers. No culture has a complete monopoly on the truth. Likewise, Christians must guard against the assumption that their Christian perspective on their cultural experiences should be normative for every other culture.

However, as we have already seen, the central weakness of cultural relativism is its unwillingness to evaluate another culture. Such reluctance may seem satisfactory when we talk about language, customs, or even forms of worship. But this nonjudgmental mindset breaks down when confronted by real evils such as slavery or genocide. The Holocaust, for example, cannot be merely explained away as an appropriate cultural response for Nazi Germany.

Cultural relativism faces other philosophical problems. For example, stating that morals originated in the world and that they are constantly changing is insufficient. Cultural relativists need to answer how value originated out of non-value. How did the first value arise?

Fundamental to cultural relativism is a belief that values change. But if the value that values change is itself unchanging, then this theory claims an unchanging value that all values change and evolve. The position is self-contradictory.

Another important concern is conflict. If no absolute values exist trans-culturally or externally to the group, how are different cultures to get along when values collide? How are we to handle these conflicts?

Moreover, is there ever a place for courageous individuals to challenge the cultural norm and fight against social evil? Cultural relativism seems to leave no place for social reformers. The abolition movement, the suffrage movement, and the civil rights movement are all examples of social movements that ran counter to the social circumstances of the culture. Abolishing slavery and providing rights to citizens are good things even if many people within society oppose them.

The Bible provides a true standard by which to judge attitudes and actions. Christians can use biblical standards to judge individual sin as well as corporate sin institutionalized within a culture. By contrast, people cannot use culture to judge right and wrong because a changing culture cannot provide a fixed standard for morality. Only God's character, revealed in the Bible, provides a reliable measure for morality.

UTILITARIANISM

You have probably heard a politician say that he passed a piece of legislation because it provided the greatest good for the greatest number of citizens. Perhaps you have heard someone justify her actions because it was for the greater good. This philosophy is known as *utilitarianism*, which claims that the sole standard of morality is determined by its usefulness.

Philosophers refer to utilitarianism as a "teleological" system. The Greek word *telos* means "end" or "goal." Consequently, this ethical system determines morality by the end result. Whereas Christian ethics is based on rules, utilitarianism is based on results.

Utilitarianism began with the philosophies of Jeremy Bentham (1748–1832) and John Stuart Mill (1806–1873). Utilitarianism gets its name from Bentham's test question, "What is the use of it?" He conceived the idea when he ran across the words "the greatest happiness of the greatest number" in Joseph Priestly's *Treatise of Government*.

Bentham was a leading theorist in Anglo-American philosophy of law and one of the founders of utilitarianism. He developed his ethical system around the idea of pleasure, and he built that system on ancient hedonism, which pursued physical pleasure and avoided physical pain. According to Bentham, the most moral acts are those that maximize pleasure and minimize pain, which has sometimes been called the "utilitarian calculus." An act would be moral if it brings the greatest amount of pleasure and the least amount of pain.

Bentham developed his idea of utility and a utilitarian calculus in his *Introduction to the Principles of Morals and Legislation* (1781). In the beginning of that work he wrote: "Nature has placed mankind under the governance of two sovereign masters, *pain* and *pleasure*. It is for them alone to point out what we ought to do, as well as to determine what we shall do. On the one hand the standard of right and wrong, on the other the chain of causes and effects, are fastened to their throne. They govern us in all we do, in all we say, in all we think: every effort we can make to throw off our subjection, will serve but to demonstrate and confirm it."[7]

Bentham believed that pain and pleasure not only explain our actions but also help us define what is good and moral. He believed that this foundation could provide a basis for social, legal, and moral reform in society.

Key to Bentham's ethical system is the principle of utility. That is, what is the greatest good for the greatest number? Bentham wrote: "By the principle of utility is meant that principle which approves or disapproves of every action whatsoever, according to the tendency which it appears to have to augment or diminish the happiness of the party whose interest is in question: or, what is the same thing in other words, to promote or to oppose that happiness."[8]

Mill was a brilliant scholar who was subjected to a rigid system of intellectual discipline and shielded from boys his own age. When Mill was a teenager, he read Bentham's works. Mill said that the feeling "that all previous moralists were superseded" rushed upon him. He believed that the principle of utility "gave unity to my conception of things. I now had opinions: a creed, a doctrine, a philosophy; in one among the best senses of the word, a religion; the inculcation and diffusion of what could be made the principle outward purpose of a life."[9]

Mill modified Bentham's utilitarianism, developing it apart from Bentham's hedonistic foundation. Mill used the same utilitarian calculus but instead focused on maximizing the general happiness by calculating the greatest good for the greatest number. Bentham used the calculus in a quantitative sense and established an *act* utilitarianism. In Bentham's ethic, a particular act is right only in a particular situation. In another situation, that act might be wrong. Mill, however, used the calculus in a qualitative sense. He believed, for example, that some pleasures were of higher quality than others. Mill's utilitarianism was a *rule* utilitarianism. According to Mill, we can develop rules to determine what is right based on what has produced the best consequences for the most people in the past.

Many people have embraced utilitarianism simply because it seems to make a good deal of sense and seems relatively simple to apply. However, when it was first proposed, utilitarianism was a radical philosophy. It attempted to set forth a moral system apart from divine revelation and biblical morality. Utilitarianism focused on results rather than rules. Ultimately the focus on the results demolished the rules.

Utilitarianism is appealing for several reasons. First, it is a relatively simple ethical system to apply. To determine whether an action is moral, you merely have to calculate the good and bad consequences that will result from a particular action. If the good outweighs the bad, then the action is moral.

Second, utilitarianism avoids the need to appeal to divine revelation. Many adherents to this ethical system are looking for a way to live a moral life apart from the Bible and a belief in God. The system replaces revelation with reason. Logic rather than an adherence to biblical principles guides the ethical decision-making of a utilitarian.

Third, most people already use a form of utilitarianism in their daily decisions. We make many non-moral decisions every day based upon consequences. At the checkout line, we try to find the shortest line so we can get out the door more quickly. We make most of our financial decisions (writing checks and buying merchandise) on a utilitarian calculus of cost and benefits. So making moral decisions using utilitarianism seems like a natural extension of our daily decision-making procedures.

Nevertheless, utilitarianism contains a number of problems. One problem is that it leads to an "end justifies the means" mentality. If any worthwhile end can justify the means to attain it, a true ethical foundation is lost. But we all know that the end does *not* justify the means. If that were so, then Hitler could have justified the Holocaust because the end was to purify the human race, and Stalin could have de fended his slaughter of millions because he was trying to achieve a communist utopia.

The end never justifies the means. The means must justify themselves. A particular act cannot be judged as good simply because it may lead to a good consequence. The means must be judged by some objective and consistent standard of morality.

Second, utilitarianism cannot protect the rights of minorities if the goal is the greatest good for the greatest number. Americans in the eighteenth century could have justified slavery on the basis that it provided a good consequence for a majority of Americans. Certainly the majority benefited from cheap slave labor even though the lives of black slaves were much worse.

A third problem with utilitarianism is predicting the consequences. If morality is based on results, then we would have to be omniscient in order to accurately predict the consequence of any action. But at best we can only guess at the future, and often these educated guesses are wrong.

A fourth problem with utilitarianism is that consequences themselves must be judged. When results occur, we must still ask whether they are good or bad results. Utilitarianism provides no objective and consistent foundation to judge results because results are the mechanism used to judge the action itself.

SITUATION ETHICS

A popular form of utilitarianism is *situation ethics,* first proposed by Joseph Fletcher (1905–1991) in his book by the same name.[10] Fletcher acknowledged that situation ethics is essentially utilitarianism, but he modified the pleasure principle and called it the *agape* (love) principle.

Fletcher developed his ethical system as an alternative to two extremes: legalism and antinomianism. Legalist are like the Pharisees in the time of Jesus who had all sorts of laws and regulations but no heart. They emphasized the law over love. Antinomians are like the libertines in Paul's day who promoted their lawlessness.

The foundation of situation ethics is what Fletcher calls the law of love. Love replaces the law. Fletcher said, "We follow law, if at all, for love's sake."[11] He even quoted certain biblical passages to make his case. For example, he quoted Romans 13:8 which says, "Let no debt remain outstanding, except the continuing debt to love one another, for he who loves his fellow man has fulfilled the law." Another passage he quoted is Matthew 22:37–40: "Jesus replied: 'Love the Lord your God with all your heart and with all your soul and with all your mind. . . . Love your neighbor as yourself.' All the Law and the Prophets hang on these two commandments."

Proponents of situation ethics would argue that these summary verses require only one absolute (the law of love). No other universal laws can be derived from this commandment to love. Even the Ten Commandments are subject to exceptions based upon the law of love.

Situation ethics also accepts the view that the end justifies the means. Only the ends can justify the means; the means cannot justify themselves. Fletcher contended that "no act apart from its foreseeable consequences has any ethical meaning whatsoever."[12]

Fletcher told the story of Lenin, the Russian revolutionary who had become weary of being told that he had no ethics. Yet he maintained that he used a very pragmatic and utilitarian philosophy to force communism on the people. So some of those around Lenin accused him of believing that the end justifies the means. Finally, Lenin shot back, "If the end does not justify the means, then in the name of sanity and justice, *what does?*"[13]

Like utilitarianism, situation ethics attempts to define morality with an "end justifies the means" philosophy. According to Fletcher, the law of love requires the greatest love for the greatest number of people in the long run. But as we will see in the next section, we do not always know how to define love, and we do not always know what will happen in the long run.

Perhaps the biggest problem with situation ethics is that the law of love is too general. People are going to have different definitions of what love is. What some may believe is a loving act, others might feel is an unloving act.

Moreover, the context of love varies from situation to situation and certainly varies from culture to culture. So deriving moral principles that can be known and applied universally is extremely difficult. In other words, it is impossible to say that to follow the law of love is to do such and such in every circumstance. Situations and circumstances change, and so the moral response may change as well.

The admonition to do the loving thing is even less specific than to do what is the greatest good for the greatest number. It has about as much moral force as to say to do the "good thing" or the "right thing." Without a specific definition, "doing the loving thing" is nothing more than a moral platitude.

Second, situation ethics suffers from the same problem of utilitarianism in predicting consequences. In order to judge the morality of an action, we have to know the results of the action we are about to take. Often we cannot know the consequences. Fletcher acknowledged this problem when he said, "We can't always guess the future, even though we are always being forced to try."[14] But according to his ethical system, we have to know the results in order to make a moral choice. In fact, we should be relatively certain of the consequences, otherwise our action would by definition be immoral.

Situation ethics also assumes that the situation will determine the meaning of love. Yet love is not determined by the particulars of our circumstance but merely conditioned by them. The situation does not determine what is right or wrong. The situation instead helps us determine which biblical command applies in that particular situation.

From the biblical perspective, the problem with utilitarianism and situation ethics is that they ultimately provide no consistent moral framework. Situation ethics also permits us to do evil to achieve good, which is totally contrary to the Bible. For example, Proverbs 14:12 says that "There is a way *that seems* right to a man, but its end is the way of death." The road to destruction is paved with good intentions, which is a fundamental flaw with an "ends justifies the means" ethical system.

In Romans 6:1 Paul asked, "Shall we continue sinning so that grace may increase?" His response was, "By no means!" Utilitarianism attempts to provide a moral system apart from God's revelation in the Bible, but in the end, it does not succeed.

In the next chapter we will consider a Christian view of morality. What is Christian ethics? How do Christians make moral decisions? What are some key foundations of Christian ethics?

4

CHRISTIAN ETHICS

WHAT IS CHRISTIAN ETHICS? Christian ethics seeks to integrate philosophy with theology. But this attempt to bring these two disciplines together must also be mindful of the apostle Paul's warning to believers in the first century: "See to it that no one takes you captive through philosophy and empty deception, according to the tradition of men, according to the elementary principles of the world, rather than according to Christ" (Col. 2:8). Understanding ethics and philosophy is helpful but only when the Bible is used as the foundation and the filter for the philosophical ideas and principles.

BIBLICAL MORALITY

A Christian understanding of ethics and philosophy begins with the assumption that God exists and has revealed Himself to the human race. He has chosen to reveal Himself in nature (Psalm 19; Romans 1) and in human conscience (Rom. 2:14–15). He has also revealed Himself through the Bible (Psalm 119; 2 Tim. 3:16) and in the person of Jesus Christ (John 10:30; Heb. 1:1–4).

God's character is the ultimate standard of right and wrong. And even though the Bible was written long before the development of genetic engineering or modern media, it nevertheless provides useful principles to evaluate the morality of social, scientific, and technological issues.

Biblical morality can be developed from learning to live God's way according to biblical principles. Though the Christian life is much more than a set of rules or principles, these principles do provide moral boundaries for behavior. The following chapters set forth these principles and moral boundaries.

Biblical morality is also based upon love, which has its source in God. Some teachers of the law asked Jesus which was the most important commandment. Jesus responded: "The most important one is this: 'Hear, O Israel, the Lord our God, the Lord is one. Love the Lord your God with all your heart and with all your soul and with all your mind and with all your strength.' The second is this: 'Love your neighbor as yourself.' There is no commandment greater than these" (Mark 12:29–31).

The two most important commandments are to love God and to love your neighbor. Essentially all biblical principles rest upon this foundation. And these principles can be found in God's revelation in the Bible. God's character as expressed in God's Word should be diligently applied to every area of life.

OLD TESTAMENT ETHICS

The primary emphasis in the Old Testament is on social ethics, while the primary emphasis in the New Testament is on personal ethics. The reason for the Old Testament emphasis on social ethics is that the Old Testament is the story of the covenant God made with Israel through Moses (Exodus 24), and the Old Testament's principles provided the structure of the Jewish theocracy.

The foundation of Old Testament ethics is the law, which can be found in the Pentateuch (the first five books of the Bible). The Old Testament principles can be found primarily in Exodus 20—40, Leviticus, and Deuteronomy 5—30. The law in the Old Testament consists of three parts: ceremonial law, civil law, and moral law. All three are important in the Old Testament, but some become less important in the New Testament. The relationship of these three aspects of Old Testament law to the New Testament era will be discussed in the next section.

Although the primary emphasis in the Old Testament is on social ethics, some sections of the Old Testament contain commands concerning personal ethics. For example, Proverbs provides many principles that apply to individual morality and that are addressed to a broader audience than the specific Old Testament commands to the nation of Israel.

Justice is a primary moral foundation in the Old Testament and governs how the nation of Israel was to execute justice and treat those less fortunate. Strangers were to be treated with kindness (Lev. 19:33–34). This kindness included such things as the gleaning laws (Lev. 19:9–10) that allowed the needy and the stranger in the land to glean the corners of the field not to be harvested.

The Old Testament provided protection for private property (Leviticus 19, 25). It also prohibited usury (Ex. 22:25; Lev. 25:35–37) and any perversion of the legal system (Ex. 23:1–2; Deut. 18–20).

Old Testament prophets frequently spoke out against social evil in the land. Amos condemned those who "sell the righteous for silver and the needy for a pair of sandals" (2:6) and those who "oppress the poor" (4:1) as well as those "who oppress the righteous and take bribes" (5:12). Micah spoke out against those who take the fields and houses of others (2:2) and those who used "dishonest scales and a bag of false weights" (6:11). Hosea stripped off the religious hypocrisy of those who hide their moral failures behind a false veneer of religious observance (6:6).

Individual sin and corporate sin in the nation of Israel overwhelmed the prophets (Hab. 1:13; Is. 6:3–5) as they saw the enormous chasm between a holy God and sinful humans. The prevelance of sin caused them to look to the Messiah when God would write a new covenant (Jer. 31:31).

THE RELATIONSHIP BETWEEN THE OLD AND NEW TESTAMENTS

What is the relationship between the Old Testament and the New Testament in terms of ethics? As we will see in the chapters on homosexuality and government, this relationship is an important issue. Is there continuity or discontinuity between the Old and New Testaments? The answer to this question needs to be addressed to the three parts of the Old Testament law: ceremonial law, civil law, and moral law.

Nearly all Christians would agree that there is a discontinuity between the Old and New Testaments in terms of ceremonial law. The apostle Paul taught that Christians were no longer under the Old Testament law (Rom. 10:4; Gal. 3:21–25; 5:18; and 1 Cor. 9:20–21). The Book of Hebrews makes it clear that Old Testament ceremonial law no longer applies in the New Testament era. Jesus Christ's sacrifice ended the need for ceremonial law. Christians do not follow the Mosaic sacrificial system within their churches, nor do they follow the practices of the Jewish theocracy.

On the other hand, Christians would agree that there is continuity between the Old and New Testaments in terms of moral law. The moral perspective in Ten Commandments and other Old Testament moral principles certainly apply to the New Testament era.

What about the application of civil law? Here, there is some debate, but most Christians would agree that a discontinuity exists between the Old and New Testaments. The Old Testament laws were directly applied to those who lived under the Jewish theocracy. But the New Testament assumes that believers will be governed by both believers and non-believers who are to be obeyed (Rom. 13:1–7; 1 Pet. 2:13–15). These New Testament principles apply to a diversity of social and ethnic groups (and not just to Jews living in a theocracy). Paul and Peter command believers to submit to those in governing authority. The government they were talking about was a secular government (Roman Empire) that was not run by principles of the Old Testament civil code. Nevertheless, they command obedience to a government that was neither a theocracy nor a government run by Old Testament civil law.

NEW TESTAMENT ETHICS

The primary emphasis in the New Testament is on personal ethics, particularly morality within the church. As we have noted, that fact does not invalidate the Old Testament moral law. Jesus showed great respect for the Old Testament moral law and said that He came not to abolish it but to fulfill it (Matt. 5:17–19). The Sermon on the Mount (Matthew 5—7) primarily criticizes the Pharisees' misuse and misinterpretation of the Old Testament law.

Jesus' teaching went beyond the outward manifestations of obedience to the law and focused on inward motives. For example, the Old Testament forbids murder, but Jesus taught that "anyone who is angry with his brother" is also guilty (Matt. 5:21–22). Likewise, the Old Testament forbids adultery, but Jesus taught that "anyone who looks at a woman lustfully" is also guilty (Matthew 5:27–28). Moral obedience goes beyond our actions by focusing on our motives.

While the New Testament focuses primarily on personal ethics, a number of passages also provide a foundation for social ethics. In particular, various passages that command believers to submit to those in civil authority (Rom. 13:1–2; Titus 3:1; 1 Pet. 2:13) relate to our obedience to government and our social and political involvement.

Jesus' teaching also contained a social dimension. When asked what is the greatest commandment, Jesus replied that there were two great commandments: "Love the Lord" and "Love your neighbor" (Matt. 22:37–39). The second commandment about loving your neighbor provides a foundation for social ethics. Jesus further illustrated the extent of neighbor love through the parable of the "Good Samaritan" (Luke 10:30–37). Such love is a key moral foundation that will be discussed in the following chapter.

MAKING MORAL DECISIONS

How do we make proper moral choices based upon biblical principles? The Bible does provide biblical guidelines on a vast array of issues. Christians also have the liberty to make individual moral choices in areas of moral neutrality. Ultimately, making moral choices involves discerning the will of God in one's life.

Whole books have been written on how we can know the will of God, so the following principles will be a mere summary of what has been discussed at length in other places. Various Christian groups and denominations also disagree about particular points concerning how we discern the will of God. Therefore, the following are a summary of those points that are held in common agreement by most Christians.

First, we can know God's will through the Bible. Before considering any other way to discern God's will, one should ask whether the Bible has already provided guidance in a particular area. The Bible is full of God's specific commands and principles. For example, a teenager does not have to ask if he should get drunk because the Bible has already addressed that issue (Eph. 5:18). Nor does a businessman have to ask if he should cheat on his income taxes, for the Bible has spoken to that question (Rom. 13:7). An unmarried couple does not need to ask if they should live together before they marry. Again, the Bible has addressed that issue (1 Cor. 6:18).

The Bible provides boundaries and barriers to our moral actions. We are to stay within those moral boundaries. Paul, writing to the church in Corinth, told them, "Do not go beyond what is written" (1 Cor. 4:6).

A second way we discern God's will is through prayer. We are commanded to bring our requests before God. In Philippians 4:6 we are told: "Do not be anxious about anything, but in everything, by prayer and petition, with thanksgiving, present your requests to God."

If we are earnestly reading the Bible and seeking God's will, He will reveal it to us, often through the work of the Holy Spirit in our lives. We read in Romans 8:27 that "The Spirit intercedes for the saints in accordance with God's will."

A third way we discern God's will is through our conscience. If our conscience is troubling us about a particular action or behavior, then we should refrain from that activity. Paul said that each person "should be fully convinced in his own mind" (Rom. 14:5). He added that "everything that does not come from faith is sin" (Rom. 14:23).

The opposite is not necessarily true. In other words, conscience is a good stop sign but not a green light. A troubled conscience is sufficient justification to refrain, and a guilty conscience is reason enough to stop a particular action or behavior.

A clear conscience, however, is no justification for proceeding. The Bible teaches that "The heart is deceitful above all things and beyond cure. Who can understand it?" (Jer. 17:9). We can easily deceive ourselves into sin.

Christians should strive to have a good conscience before God and man (Acts 24:16). A troubled conscience is reason to avoid an action, but a clear conscience may not be sufficient justification to proceed.

CHRISTIAN LIBERTY

While the Bible provides absolute moral commands for much human behavior, many areas of conduct are not specifically prohibited. These areas of moral neutrality are still governed by biblical principles that guide our Christian liberty.

Even though a particular action may not be prohibited in Scripture, it still may be offensive to others because of their social, ethnic, or religious background. Another person's family background or spiritual maturity is also a consideration Christians must make.

Before we look at the principles governing our Christian liberty, we must consider some examples. The Bible clearly teaches that we should not become drunk with wine (Eph. 5:18). But the decision about whether a Christian will or will not drink any alcoholic beverage falls under the principles of Christian liberty.

These principles could also be applied to the morality of birth control. Methods of birth control that destroy human life in the womb are wrong (Ps. 139), but other methods that merely prevent fertilization from taking place are not murder. Christians may come to different conclusions about using methods of birth control that do not kill an unborn child.

Watching pornography is wrong. But the decision about watching other types of television programs and movies falls under the principles of Christian liberty.

In Romans 14—15 the apostle Paul articulated the principles guiding our liberty. The specific example that he used involves the eating of meat sacrificed to idols. While this issue is of no moral concern today, it does provide key biblical principles that we can apply in determining our response to issues not specifically addressed in the Bible.

The first principle is that Christians should not have a judgmental attitude toward one another in regard to issues that are morally neutral. Paul said in Romans 14:3 that the "man who eats everything must not look down on him who does not," nor should the "man who does not eat . . . condemn the man who does." In other words, whether you participate in or refrain from a morally neutral activity, you should not be judgmental of the other person.

No one has the right to force their moral conclusions on others when the Bible does not provide clear principles on the matter. Paul asked in Romans 14:4, "Who are you to judge someone else's servant?" Christians are instructed to decide these matters for themselves as they consult the Bible and their conscience.

Second, each Christian must decide what is right or wrong for him or her. Paul taught that if you believe a particular action to be wrong for you, then it is wrong. He said in Romans 14:14, "I am fully convinced that no food is unclean in itself. But if anyone regards something as unclean, then for him it is unclean." Paul taught that all things were clean. In other words, eating meat sacrificed to idols was not a sin because it was morally neutral. But he also taught that if a person believes that eating such meat is sinful, then it is indeed sinful for him or her.

Each person "must be fully convinced in his own mind" (Rom. 14:5). If a person has doubt, then she should refrain from participating rather than engaging in what has become a sinful action for her. Doubt or uncertainty is a sufficient reason to refrain from a particular activity or behavior.

A key test of Christian obedience is whether a person can do something "to the Lord" (Rom. 14:6). Christians are to "live for the Lord" because "we belong to the Lord" (Rom. 14:8). If one cannot participate in an activity while serving the Lord, then he or she should refrain. Paul said that "everything that does not come from faith is sin" (Rom. 14:23).

A third principle is whether a morally neutral activity would be "a stumbling block or obstacle" to another believer (Rom. 14:13). Christians should be aware of their actions on the Christian walk of others around them. While we may have liberty in Christ to participate in an action or behavior, another believer might be offended or adversely affected by what we do.

Paul teaches that we have a moral responsibility to other believers. He said, "We who are strong ought to bear with the failings of the weak" (Rom. 15:1). In order to do so, we may have to limit our Christian liberty.

At the same time we must balance enjoying our liberty in Christ and trying not to give offense. If one believes that he or she can participate in an activity, then one should do so with that firm conviction before God (Rom. 14:22). But it would be wise not to participate publicly but privately for the sake of a believer who might be hurt by one's actions (Rom. 14:15).

A final principle is how a particular action or behavior will affect the individual believer's walk with the Lord. Paul said in 1 Corinthians 6:12 that "Everything is permissible for me—but not everything is beneficial. Everything is permissible for me—but I will not be mastered by anything."

Although these morally neutral practices are lawful, they may not be profitable and could actually master (or enslave) a person. The Bible does not contain anything about such things as poor nutrition, addiction to caffeine, or watching lots of television, yet most would agree that such behaviors are not profitable. In fact, they are frequently debilitating to the individual. Concerning such things, Paul's reminder in 1 Corinthians 10:31 is applicable: "So whether you eat or drink or whatever you do, do it all to the glory of God."

5

CHRISTIAN ETHICAL FOUNDATIONS

CHRISTIAN ETHICS roots upon a number of biblical principles. Some of these moral foundations are love, justice, honesty, integrity, and civility. Christians are called to love God and have "integrity of heart." Anyone who is called will always try to do what is right and strive to live moral and upright lives. Living godly lives is the very foundation of personal moral ethics. Those who attempt to "love their neighbor" will apply these biblical principles in a loving way to society. And loving one's neighbor is the foundation of social ethics.

LOVE

Christian ethics rests upon many moral foundations, but one of the most important is the moral foundation of love. God loves us and desires that we love Him too. Such love is a mutual love and is seen in the love between God the Father and God the Son. And we are to both love God and each other.

The Bible has many words that we translate into the one English word love:

- *Agapē* is sacrificial love and means to love other persons unconditionally, despite their reaction to you or your love for them.

- *Philia* is a spontaneous natural affection and is also used in the word *philadelphia* (brotherly love) and *philia* (friendship).

- *Hesed* is found in the Old Testament to describe unselfish love and is sometimes translated as "loyalty" or "steadfast love."

The most frequently used word for love in the New Testament is *agapē*. Agape love is an unselfish love that is based upon principle and therefore spontaneous and not motivated by any value or benefit. Christians are to love others despite disappointment and rejection from others. This agape love is a special kind of unselfish love, a religious love for others. This sacrificial love can redeem our usual selfish kind of loving.

We can also define love as equal regard. Love means we value all persons equally, regardless of their situation or circumstances or race. In our chapters on bioethics, we will see how we are to love those whose medical and physical circumstances may be different than our own. In our chapter on race and race relations, we are reminded to love others who are different from us in their racial and ethnic characteristics.

The agape love we are to have for one another also applies to another moral foundation we will consider: justice. Justice is based upon equal rights and responsibilities for each person. If we love others and treat them with equal regard, then we will be applying a foundational aspect of justice to them.

Jesus also demonstrated *hesed* love in His care for others and in His call for Christians to demonstrate love for others. He taught that the kingdom of God offered good news to the poor and freedom to the oppressed, while providing sight to the blind and hearing to the deaf (Matt. 11:2–5; Luke 4:18).

Jesus taught that the two great commandments in God's law were to love God and to love your neighbor (Matt. 22:37–40):

> "Love the Lord your God with all your heart and with all your soul
> and with all your mind." This is the first and greatest commandment.
> And the second is like it: "Love your neighbor as yourself." All the
> Law and the Prophets hang on these two commandments.

Jesus provided the model for the expression of love to God and others. His own habits of religious activities (prayer, worship, obedience) provide a model to Christians to follow. His parable of the Good Samaritan provides insight in how we are to treat others even if we do not think of them as our neighbors.

The Good Samaritan parable provides a clear example of how Christians are to love their neighbor (Luke 10:30–37) and demonstrate compassion for others. Jesus began the parable by telling what happened when a man "fell among robbers" who "stripped him and beat him" and left him half dead. A priest saw the man and passed by the other side. A Levite saw him and also passed by on the other side. But it was a Samaritan who saw him and felt *compassion* for him. The Greek word for compassion literally means he had a gut-feeling for him and his needs.

The contrast is clear. Notice that the Samaritan not only met his initial needs (bandaged his wounds and brought him to an inn) but also provided for his continuing needs (took out two denarii and gave them to the innkeeper and promised to repay him for other needs). Though most parables are fairly short, Jesus spent time emphasizing the deeds done by the Samaritan who showed compassion to his neighbor. He was teaching that compassion is a verb and demands action from us.

Jesus also taught Christians to love their enemies: "Love your enemies and pray for those who persecute you, that you may be sons of your Father in heaven. He causes his sun to rise on the evil and the good, and sends rain on the righteous and the unrighteous" (Matt. 5:44–45). As his opening phrase suggests, loving one's enemies was not the common practice of the day. In fact, it was completely contrary to the concept of love practiced in that day or even in our day.

The apostle Paul taught that love is "the law of Christ" and thereby supreme and sufficient (Gal. 5:14; 6:2). He also instructed that love is the foundation of Christian obedience. Even if we manifest the gifts of the Spirit and do good works, they do not profit us unless they are done in love (1 Cor. 13:1–3).

Paul also taught that God shows His love to us in that Christ died for us (Rom. 5:8) and that nothing will separate us from the love of Christ (Rom. 8:37–39). Such love is not just a theological truth; it is a love that "compels us" (2 Cor. 5:14) and provides us with an ability to live the Christian life.

JUSTICE

Justice is another moral foundation of the Bible, though it may not be readily apparent because some words for justice are often translated as "righteousness" and "judgment." The four words for justice (two in Hebrew and two in Greek) can be found over 1,000 times in the Bible.

Justice is the standard by which privileges and penalties are distributed within a society. Ultimately, justice is the moral standard by which God measures human actions and attitudes. Justice is one of the chief attributes of God, and human beings who are created in God's image (Gen. 1:27–28) must also do justice (Gen. 18:19).

God is the defender of the poor and the oppressed (Jer. 22:15–16; Ps. 10:17–18). Likewise, God's special regard for the poor and the weak in society must also characterize God's people (Deut. 10:18–19). Specific focus is placed on the poor, widows, the fatherless, slaves, resident aliens, wage earners, and those with disabilities (Job 29:12–17; Ps. 146:7–9; Mal. 3:5).

Many Old Testament prophets called for justice. Amos (6:4) pled for the poor and criticized those who "lie on beds inlaid with ivory" and "lounge on couches" in drunken stupor while "eating lambs from their flock." Rather than heed the prophet's warnings of judgment, the leaders of Samaria pursued a decadent hedonism (wooden bed inlaid with ivory, gourmet food of lambs and calves) and ignored the poor.

Ezekiel (34:2–3) condemned the rulers of Israel, whom he described as shepherds who had been feeding themselves instead of the flock. These leaders ate "the curds" and clothed themselves with wool. They only took care of themselves and exploited those whom they were supposed to serve.

In the New Testament, Jesus continued this prophetic stance especially as he confronted the religious leaders of His day. He warned them not to neglect "the more important matters of the law—justice, mercy and faithfulness" (Matt. 23:23).

Likewise, Paul admonished Christians not to be just hearers, but also doers of the law (Rom. 2:13).

A biblical perspective on justice is a crucial moral foundation. In later chapters, we will consider how justice applies to crime, punishment, and government.

HONESTY

Another moral foundation is honesty. Honesty includes being honest in our dealings with others and being honest and truthful in what we say.

The Old Testament calls upon the people of God to deal honestly with one another. Leviticus 19:35 says, "Do not use dishonest standards when measuring length, weight, or quantity." Likewise, Proverbs 11:1 warns that "The Lord abhors dishonest scales." Believers are to use honest weights and be honest in their dealings with others.

A righteous person does not "accept a bribe against the innocent" (Ps. 15:5). Isaiah (5:23) pronounced judgment on those "who acquit the guilty for a bribe, but deny justice to the innocent."

The New Testament admonishes Christians to "have a good conscience" and desire to conduct themselves "honorably in every way" (Heb. 13:18). Paul said that he always attempted to maintain "a blameless conscience *both* before God and before men" (Acts 24:16). Christians should "do what is right, not only in the eyes of the Lord but also in the eyes of men" (2 Cor. 8:21).

The Bible also provides many examples of people being honest. These examples would include Jacob returning money placed in the sacks (Gen. 43:12), the overseers of the temple repairs (2 Kin. 12:15; 22:4–7), and the treasurers of the temple (Neh. 13:13).

Honesty also requires telling the truth. The Third Commandment forbids the swearing of false oaths, and the Ninth Commandment prohibits the bearing of false testimony (Ex. 20:7, 16; Deut. 5:11, 20; cf. Lev. 19:12; Jer. 7:9). In the Old Testament, false witnesses were to suffer the same punishment that they had hoped to inflict upon the others (Deut. 19:16–21).

Telling the truth also involved more than false testimony in a court. Believers are not to spread false reports (Prov. 12:17; 14:5, 25) or report the truth maliciously or engage in slander (Lev. 19:16; Prov. 26:20).

Speaking evil is prohibited (Ps. 34:13; Prov. 24:28; Eph. 4:31; James 4:11; 1 Pet. 3:10), and it disqualifies a person from God's favor (Ps. 15:3) and from a leadership position in the church (1 Tim. 3:8; Titus 2:3).

Jesus taught that we must tell the truth and let our yes, be yes (Matt. 5:33–37):

> Again, you have heard that it was said to the people long ago, "Do not break your oath, but keep the oaths you have made to the Lord." But I

tell you, Do not swear at all: either by heaven, for it is God's throne; or by the earth, for it is his footstool; or by Jerusalem, for it is the city of the Great King. And do not swear by your head, for you cannot make even one hair white or black. Simply let your "Yes" be "Yes," and your "No," "No"; anything beyond this comes from the evil one.

In the Old Testament oaths and vows were used many times. Abraham (Gen. 21:22–34), Jacob (Gen. 25:33; 28:20), Joseph (Gen. 50:5), Joshua (Josh. 6:26), Hannah (1 Sam 1:11), Saul (1 Sam. 14:24), David (1 Sam. 20:17), Ezra (Ezra 10:5), and Nehemiah (Neh. 13:25) all swore oaths or vows. The swearing of these oaths and vows underscores the seriousness of telling the truth and following up on one's commitment.

We need truth telling today like never before. Perhaps the greatest battle in society today is a battle over truth. Voters are skeptical of politicians. Proponents of various biomedical procedures (abortion, cloning) often redefine terms and mislead the public about the true nature of the procedures they advocate.

One study of high school students found that 71 percent of them admitted to cheating on an exam at least once in the last 12 months. And 92 percent of them said that they lied to their parents in the last 12 months while 79 percent said that they did so two or more times.[1]

We live in an environment where truth is no longer based upon objective reality but instead upon subjective feelings. By a three-to-one margin, adults said that truth is always relative to the person and his or her situation. And this perspective is even more lopsided among teenagers, with 83 percent saying that moral truth depends upon the circumstances.[2]

INTEGRITY

Integrity is a character quality that we often talk about but do not see quite as regularly in the lives of public officials or even in the lives of the people with whom we live and work. The word *integrity* comes from the same Latin root as *integer* and implies a wholeness of person. Just as we would talk about a whole number, so also we can talk about a whole person who is undivided.[3] A person of integrity is living rightly, not divided, nor being a different person in different circumstances. A person of integrity is the same person in private that he or she is in public.

In the Sermon on the Mount, Jesus talked about those who were "pure in heart" (Matt. 5:8), implying an undividedness in following God's commands. Integrity, therefore, not only implies an undividedness, but a moral purity as well.

The Bible is full of references to integrity, good character, and moral purity. Consider just a few Old Testament references to integrity. In 1 Kings 9:4, God instructed Solomon to walk with "integrity of heart and uprightness" as his father did. David proclaimed in 1 Chronicles 29:17, "I know, my God, that you test the heart and are pleased with integrity." And in Psalm 78: 72 we read that "David shepherded them [Israel] with integrity of heart, with skillful hands."

The Book of Proverbs provides an abundance of verses on integrity. Proverbs 10:9 says, "The man of integrity walks securely, but he who takes crooked paths will be found out." A person of integrity will have a good reputation and not have to fear that he or she will be exposed or found out. Integrity provides a safe path through life.

Proverbs 11:3 says, "The integrity of the upright guides them, but the the unfaithful are destroyed by their duplicity." Proverbs is a book of wisdom. The wise man or woman will live a life of integrity, which is a part of wisdom. Those who follow corruption or falsehood will be destroyed by the decisions and actions of their lives.

Proverbs 20:7 says, "The righteous man leads a blameless life [of integrity]; blessed are his children after him." Integrity leaves a legacy. A righteous man or woman walks in integrity and provides a path for his or her children to follow.

All of these verses imply a sense of duty and a recognition that we must have a level of discernment of God's will in our lives. Knowing God's will would certainly require that people of integrity be students of the Word, and then diligently seek to apply God's Word to their lives. The Book of James admonishes us to be doers of the word, and not merely hearers who delude themselves (James 1:22).

The opposite of integrity is the corruption. We claim to be a nation that demands integrity, but do we really? We say that we want politicians to be honest. But we really do not expect them to be, perhaps because often we are not as honest as we should be. We say that we are a nation of laws, but often we break some of those same laws—like speed limits and jaywalking—and try to justify our actions.

James Patterson and Peter Kim's book *The Day America Told the Truth* illustrates Americans' lack of integrity.[4] Using a survey technique that guaranteed the privacy and anonymity of the respondents, the authors documented what Americans really believe and do. The results were startling.

First, Patterson and Kim found that Americans lacked a moral authority: "Americans are making up their own moral codes. Only 13 percent of us believe in all the Ten Commandments. Forty percent of us believe in five of the Ten Commandments. We choose which laws of God we believe in. There is absolutely no moral consensus in this country as there was in the 1950s, when all our institutions commanded more respect."[5]

Second, they found Americans are not honest: "Lying has become an integral part of American culture, a trait of the American character. We lie and don't even think about it. We lie for no reason."[6] The authors estimated that 91 percent of us lie regularly.

Third, marriage and family are no longer sacred institutions: "While we still marry, we have lost faith in the institution of marriage. A third of married men and women confessed to us that they've had at least one affair. Thirty percent aren't really sure that they still love their spouse."[7]

Fourth, they found that the "Protestant [work] ethic is long gone from today's American workplace. Workers around America frankly admit that they spend more than 20 percent (7 hours a week) of their time at work totally goofing off. That amounts to a four-day work week across the nation."[8]

The authors concluded by suggesting that we have a new set of commandments for America:[9]

- I don't see the point in observing the Sabbath (77 percent).

- I will steal from those who won't really miss it (74 percent).

- I will lie when it suits me, so long as it doesn't cause any real damage (64 percent).

- I will cheat on my spouse; after all, given the chance, he or she will do the same (53 percent).

- I will procrastinate at work and do absolutely nothing about one full day in every five (50 percent).

We may say that we are a nation that wants integrity, but apparently a majority of us lack it in our own personal lives.

FOUR KEY TRAITS OF INTEGRITY

A person of integrity has at least four key traits. One of those traits is honesty. Patterson and Kim found that nearly everyone in America lies and does so on a fairly regular basis. Truth telling apparently is no longer a virtue people try to adopt for their lives. We may say we want people to tell the truth, but we do not do it ourselves. The problem with corruption is its corrosiveness. We believe that we can be dishonest just a little bit. We say that we want people to be honest, but then we cheat on our taxes. We say that we want people to obey the laws, but then we go "just a little" over the speed limit. We want to be honest just enough to ease our conscience.

Another characteristic of a person of integrity is trustworthiness. A person of integrity is unimpeachable. He or she stands by principles no matter what the consequences. A person of integrity realizes that moral absolutes exist even in a world of relative values.

When the book of Proverbs talks of the "integrity of the upright," it implies that we adhere to God's will and God's Laws. We have a duty to obey God's absolute commands in our lives and become men and women of integrity.

A popular book on the market is *Who Are You When Nobody's Looking?*[10] Who are you when nobody's looking? Will I see the same person that I see when you are in a group of people? Do you do the right thing no matter what the circumstances?

When the apostle Paul listed the qualifications for an elder in the church, he said that an elder "must have a good reputation with outsiders, so that he will not fall into disgrace and into the devil's trap" (1 Tim. 3:7). An impeccable reputation is not only a desirable quality for church elders; it is a quality all Christians should all aspire to have. Christians should be "above reproach" in their public testimony before the watching world.

Finally, what is the importance of integrity in our daily lives? According to an old saying, *we* may be the only Bible some people ever read. In other words, people around us often judge the truthfulness of Christianity by its affect in our lives. If they see Christians as hypocrites, they may not go any further in their investigation of the gospel.

Every day we rub shoulders with people who are watching us. Our lives will demonstrate to them whether Christianity is true or false. They make value judgments about us by our attitudes and actions. Have we made the right choices?

Being a person of integrity is a life-long process. All of us have to begin somewhere. Our lives are the collection of choices we have made in the past: both good choices and bad choices. The following poem illustrates the importance of making good choices:

> Sow a thought, reap an act.
> Sow an act, reap a habit.
> Sow a habit, reap a character.
> Sow a character, reap a destiny.

CIVILITY

The word *civilité* shares the same etymology with words like *civilized* and *civilization*. Quite simply, the root word means to be "a member of the household." Just as there are certain rules that allow family members to live peacefully within a household, so there are rules of civility that allow us to live peacefully within a society. We have certain moral responsibilities to one another.

While there have been many philosophical discussions on what civility is and how it should be practiced, I believe Jesus simply expressed the goal of civility when he taught that you should "love your neighbor as yourself" (Matt. 22:39). If we truly love our neighbors, then we should be governed by moral standards that express concern for others and limit our own freedom. Perhaps the reason that civility is on the decline is that more and more people live for themselves and do not feel morally accountable to anyone (even God) for their actions or behavior.

Civility also acknowledges the value of another person. Politeness and manners are not merely to make social life easier. Stephen Carter, in his book on *Civility*, said that our actions and sacrifice are a "signal of respect for our fellow citizens, marking them as full equals, both before the law and before God. Rules of civility are thus also rules of morality; it is morally proper to treat our fellow citizens with respect, and morally improper not to. Our crisis of civility is part of a larger crisis of morality."[11]

Carter's statement may help answer why civility is on the decline. An increasing majority in our society no longer believes in moral absolutes. These people deny that absolutes of any kind exist, much less moral absolutes. So as our crisis of morality unfolds, so does barbarism and decadence. Civility is what is lost from society. If this is so, then the rise of rudeness and incivility cannot be easily altered. Miss Manners and others have written books about how our nation can regain its civility. But if the crisis is greater than a lack of manners, its solution must be found in a greater social change than merely teaching manners or character. Ultimately, an increase in civility must flow out of a moral and religious change. Spiritual revival and reformation are the ultimate solutions to the current problem of incivility. And Christians should lead the way by exemplary behavior. In essence, Christians must be the best citizens and the best examples of civility in society.

Often when we talk about the need for civility, we focus on the political arena. Character assassination and negative political advertisements are on the increase. Many commentators lament what they call the "politics of personal destruction." And savvy candidates have tried to tap into this growing concern by calling for greater civility in our public discourse.

At the outset, we should acknowledge that politics has always been a dirty business. More than two centuries ago, the founders of this country often had harsh and critical things to say about each other during political campaigns. Yet we also have some very positive examples of civil discussions of major social ills.

According to Carter, one shining example of civility is the Civil Rights Movement: "The leaders of the Southern Christian Leadership Conference (SCLC) knew that the protests would be met with violence, because they were challenging a violently oppressive system. But they also knew that success would be found not through incivility, but through the display of moral courage."[12]

Martin Luther King Jr. and other civil rights leaders trained their protestors to remain civil and even loving in the face of repression. He called this the "process of purification," which "involved both prayer and repeated reminders that the Biblical injunction to love our neighbors is not a command to love only the nice ones." It is instructive to remember that the stated purpose of the Southern Christian Leadership Conference was "to save the soul of the nation."[13]

Those involved in social action today should be mindful of the examples of King and others as they fight against social ills in our society. Christians should be good citizens and models of civility, but that does not mean that we should not be passionate about trying to rectify social problems. And we can disagree with those who do not hold to a biblical view of morality. But we should learn to disagree without being disagreeable. We should make our case with logic and compassion. And I believe we will be more successful if we do so.

Consider the abortion debate. A majority of citizens have a great deal of ambivalence about abortion. They do not feel good about abortion on demand, but they also fear what might happen if abortion was totally banned in this country. Will Christians attract these millions of people by being angry, vociferous Bible-thumpers? Or will they attract them by being thoughtful, compassionate Christians who demonstrate their love for both mother and child at crisis pregnancy centers? I think the answer should be obvious, and that is the power of civility in the public arena.

CIVILITY: A BIBLICAL FRAMEWORK

At the heart of civility is the biblical command to love your neighbor as yourself. While loving people who are your friends or people who are nice to you is relatively easy, the real test of Christian love comes when we are with strangers or with people who are not civil to you. When we find ourselves in the presence of strangers, we should treat them with dignity and respect even if they are not civil to us. Even if they are not gracious toward us, we should not repay them with incivility. Romans 12:21 says, "Do not be overcome by evil, but overcome evil with good."

Our duty to be civil to others should not depend on whether we like them or agree with their moral or political perspectives. They may be disagreeable, and we are free to disagree with them, but we should do so by giving grace. Often such a gentle response can change a discussion or dialogue. Proverbs 15:1 reminds us that "A gentle answer turns away wrath."

Civility also requires humility. A civil person acknowledges that he or she does not possess all wisdom and knowledge. Therefore, one should listen to others and consider the possibility that they might be right and that he is wrong. Philippians 2:3 says, "Do nothing out of selfish ambition or vain conceit, but in humility consider others better than yourselves."

Civility also requires that we watch what we say. The Bible clearly warns us of the danger of the tongue (James 3:5–8). We should work to cleanse our language of harsh, critical, and condemning words. We should rid ourselves of nasty and vulgar language. Ephesians 4:29 says, "Do no let any unwholesome talk come out of your mouths, but only what is helpful for building others up according to their needs, that it may benefit those who listen."

If Christians want to reform society and return to civility, one excellent model is William Wilberforce (1759–1833). Most people know Wilberforce as the man who brought an end to the British slave trade. He served for half a century in the House of Commons. And led by his Christian faith, he tirelessly worked for the abolition of slavery. But that was only one of the "two great objects" of his life. The other, even more daunting object was his attempt to transform the civil and moral climate of his times. Although Wilberforce is best known as an abolitionist, the other great accomplishment of his life was in the reformation of manners. He provides a positive example of how Christians should engage the world. We should do so with courage, compassion, character, and civility.

6

ABORTION

ABORTION is one of the most controversial and divisive issues of our day, and it affects millions of Americans. Abortion is also the most frequently performed surgery on adults in America. In fact, one out of three babies conceived in the United States is deliberately aborted. Forty-nine percent of pregnancies among American women are unintended, and half of these are terminated by abortion.[1]

HISTORY OF ABORTION

Contrary to popular belief, debate and polarization over abortion is not a recent phenomenon. The practice of abortion was common even in the ancient world. Many cultures (Assyrians, Babylonians, Sumerians, Hittites) considered abortion a serious crime. In this tradition was the Hippocratic Oath, which stated, "I will not give a woman a pessary to produce an abortion." Other cultures, such as classical Greece, condoned the practice of abortion. Plato even wrote that ill-conceived embryos should not be brought to birth, and both Plato and Aristotle thought the deformed children should be exposed and left to die.[2] The Jewish historian Josephus also wrote against abortion: "The Law has commanded to raise all children and prohibited women from aborting or destroying seed; a woman who does so shall be judged a murderess of children, for she has caused a soul to be lost and the family of man to be diminished."[3]

The consensus of the early church was that abortion and infanticide were murder. The *Didache* (also known as the "Teaching of the Twelve Apostles") was a compilation of apostolic moral teachings at the end of the first century. It commanded, "Do not murder a child by abortion or kill a newborn infant."[4] The *Epistle of Barnabas*, an early second-century theological collection, also laid down a strong admonition against abortion and infanticide: "You shall love your neighbor more than your own life. You shall not slay a child by abortion. You shall not kill that which has already been generated."[5]

Athenagoras, a second-century apologist, wrote in a letter to Emperor Marcus Aurelius: "We say that women who induce abortions are murderers, and will have to give an account of it to God. . . . The fetus in the womb is a living being and therefore the object of God's care."[6] Clement of Alexandria wrote that "our whole life can proceed according to God's perfect plan only if we gain dominion over our desires, practicing continence from the beginning instead of destroying through perverse and pernicious arts human offspring, who are given birth by Divine Providence. Those who use abortifacient medicines to hide their fornication cause not only the outright murder of the fetus, but of the whole human race as well."[7] Tertullian also wrote in his *Apology* that "murder is forbidden once and for all. We may not destroy even the fetus in the womb."[8] Augustine condemned abortion and criticized married couples who attempted to avoid having children: "Sometime this lustful cruelty or cruel lust comes to this, that they even procure poisons of sterility, and if these do not work, they extinguish and destroy the fetus in some way in the womb, preferring that their offspring die before it lives, or if it was already alive in the womb, to kill it before it was born."[9]

Modern laws against abortion came in the nineteenth century with the discovery of the human ovum in the 1820s. This discovery led to the realization that a distinct human life was created through the fertilization of the ovum so that the woman was "with child" from the moment of conception.

These laws against abortion were in effect until 1967 when a few states began to liberalize their abortion laws. By the end of 1970, eighteen states had passed abortion statutes that allowed abortion in exceptional circumstances. Soon there was a backlash to the liberalization of these laws, and it appeared as if many of the laws would be overturned. However, on January 22, 1973, the Supreme Court handed down its *Roe v. Wade* decision which went even further than the most permissive abortion laws passed by the various states.

ABORTION PROCEDURES

Although most people are aware of the existence of abortion, many do not know how abortions are performed. Here are at least seven ways they are performed.

Dilation and curettage is commonly called D & C. The physician dilates the cervix with a series of instruments to allow the insertion of a curette—a loop-shaped knife—into the womb. The instrument is used to scrape the placenta from the uterus and then cut the baby apart. The pieces are then pulled through the cervix. The tiny body must then be reassembled by an attending nurse to make sure no parts remain in the womb to cause infection.

Suction aspiration is used in 80 percent of the abortions up to the twelfth week of pregnancy. The mouth of the cervix is dilated. A hollow tube with a knife-like edged tip is inserted into the womb. A suction force twenty-eight times stronger than a vacuum cleaner literally tears the developing baby and the placenta to pieces. These pieces are sucked into a container.

Saline injection is also known as salt-poisoning. A strong salt solution is injected through the mother's abdominal wall into the amniotic fluid surrounding the baby. The baby then breathes and swallows the solution causing internal poisoning and burning. In a few hours the unborn child dies from salt poisoning, dehydration, and hemorrhaging. The mother goes into labor and delivers a dead (or dying) baby.

Prostaglandin involves the use of prostaglandin hormones that are injected into the womb or released in a vaginal suppository. This causes the uterus to contract and deliver the child prematurely. A saline solution is sometimes injected first, killing the baby before birth, in order to make the procedure less distressful for the mother and medical staff.

Dilation and evacuation is commonly called a D & E and is used after the twelfth week of pregnancy. The doctor dilates the mother's cervix and uses forceps to reach into the uterus. He grasps the arms and legs, dismembers the body, and crushes the skull to remove it. The placenta and smaller pieces are removed by suction and sharp curetting.

Hysterotomy, similar to a Caesarean section, is performed in the last three months of pregnancy. This procedure involves opening the womb surgically and removing the baby. Unlike a C-section, the purpose of this procedure is to end the infant's life.

Dilation and extraction is also known as D & E or "partial birth abortion." The physician dilates the cervix and pulls the baby's body out except for the head. Leaving the head inside, the doctor inserts scissors in the skull of the baby and sucks out the brains. The head collapses and the baby is brought out to die. The American Medical Association has documented that partial birth abortion is never a medically necessary procedure.[10]

BIBLICAL ARGUMENTS AGAINST ABORTION

Any student of the Bible knows that the Scriptures say nothing directly about abortion. So why do most Christians oppose abortion? What biblical principles can be used to come to a pro-life perspective on the issues? Is an unborn baby of equal value to the life of a child that is born? These questions must be addressed.

First, what about the silence of the Bible on abortion? The answer is simple. Abortion was so unthinkable to an Israelite woman that there was no need to even mention it in the criminal code. Why was abortion an unthinkable act? First, children were viewed as a gift or "heritage from the Lord" (Ps. 127:3). Second, God opens and closes the womb and is sovereign over conception (Gen. 29:31, 33;

30:22; 1 Sam. 1:19–20). Third, childlessness was seen as a curse (Deut. 25:6; Ruth 4:5). Barrenness would mean the extinction of the family name (cf. Jer. 11:19). Therefore, abortion was so abhorrent to the Israelite mind that it was unnecessary to have a specific prohibition to deal with it in the law.

One of the key passages giving a biblical view of the sanctity of human life is Psalm 139, which is the inspired record of David's praise for God's sovereignty in his life. David began by acknowledging that God is omniscient and knows what David is doing (vv. 1–3). God was aware of David's thoughts before he expressed them (v. 4). Wherever David might go, he could not escape from God, whether he traveled to heaven (v. 8) or ventured into Sheol (v. 9). God is in the remotest part of the sea (v. 9) and even in the darkness (vv. 11–12). David contemplated the origin of his life and confessed that God was there forming him in the womb:

> For you created my inmost being;
>> you knit me together in my mother's womb.
> I praise you because I am fearfully
>> and wonderfully made;
>> your works are wonderful,
> I know that full well.
> My frame was not hidden from you when I was made in the secret place.
> When I was woven together in the depths of the earth,
>> your eyes saw my unformed body.
> All the days ordained for me
>> were written in your book
>> before one of them came to be (vv. 13–16).

Here David described God's relationship with him while he was growing and developing before birth. The Bible does not speak of fetal life as mere biochemistry. Fetal life is not a piece of protoplasm that became David because he was already being cared for by God while in the womb.

Verse 13 speaks of God as the Master Craftsman fashioning David into a living person. In verses 14–15 David reflected on the fact that he was a product of God's creative work within his mother's womb, and he praised God for how wonderfully God had woven him together. David drew a parallel between his development in the womb and Adam's creation from the earth. Using figurative language in verse 15, he referred to his life before birth when he "was made in secret, and skillfully wrought in the depths of the earth." This poetic allusion hearkens back to Genesis 2:7, which says that Adam was made from the dust of the earth.

David also noted that "your eyes saw my unformed body" (v. 16). This statement shows that God knew David even before he was known to others. The term translated "unformed body" derives from the verb "to roll up." When David was forming as a fetus, God's care and compassion were already extended to him. The reference to "God's eyes" is an Old Testament term connoting divine oversight of God in the life of an individual or a group of people.

Other verses show divine involvement in the formation of the unborn baby. God is active in the event of conception (Gen. 29:31–35; 30:17–24; Ruth 4:13; 1 Sam. 1:19–20), and also in the formation of the human baby in the mother's womb. Jeremiah 1:5 says, "Before I formed you in the womb I knew you, before you were born I set you apart; / I appointed you as a prophet to the nations." The word translated "formed" is used in Genesis 2:7–8 to describe God's special creation of Adam. It is also used of a potter fashioning clay into a vase or other piece of pottery. In essence God fashioned Jeremiah in the womb for his prophetic ministry.

Similar verses describe how God called out various servants of God while they were still in their mother's womb. God called Isaiah to serve: "Before I was born the LORD called me" (Is. 49:1). God created Samson for his ministry and put his mother under that same dietary regimen as he would undergo. The angel of the LORD said to Samson's mother, "'You will conceive and give birth to a son. Now then, drink no wine or other fermented drink and do not eat anything unclean, because the boy will be a Nazirite of God before birth until the day of his death.' Then Manoah [Samson's father] prayed to the Lord: 'O Lord, I beg you, let the man of God you sent to us come again to teach us how to bring up the boy who is to be born'" (Judg. 13:7–8).

Another significant passage is Psalm 51, which David wrote after his sin of adultery with Bathsheba and which records his repentance. David confessed that his sinful act demonstrated the original sin that was within him: "Surely I have been a sinner from birth, sinful from the time my mother conceived me" (Ps. 51:5). David concluded that from his conception that he had a sin nature, which implies that he carried the image of God from the moment of conception, including the marred image scarred from sin.

Human beings are created in the image and likeness of God (Gen. 1:26–27; 5:1; 9:6). Bearing the image of God is the essence of humanness. And though God's image in man was marred at the Fall, it was not erased (1 Cor. 11:7; James 3:9). Thus, unborn babies are made in the image of God and therefore are fully human in God's sight.

Psalm 51:5 also supports the *traducian* view of the origin of the soul. According to this perspective human beings were potentially in Adam (Rom. 5:12; Heb. 7:9–10) and thus participated in his original sin. The "soulish" part of humans is transferred through conception. Therefore, an unborn baby is morally accountable and thus is fully human.

A key passage that points to the humanness of the unborn child is Luke 1:41–44: "When Elizabeth heard Mary's greeting, the baby leaped in her womb, and Elizabeth was filled with the Holy Spirit. In a loud voice she exclaimed: 'Blessed are you among women, and blessed is the child you bear! But why am I so favored, that the mother of my Lord should come to me? As soon as the sound of your greeting reached my ears, the baby in my womb leaped for joy.'" John the Baptist's prenatal ability to recognize Mary by leaping "for joy" illustrates his mental and spiritual capacity. Also of note is that the term used to describe John in his prenatal state is "baby." The same Greek word is used for a baby inside the womb and outside the womb (cf. Luke 2:12, 16; 18:15; 2 Tim. 3:15).[11] Like Psalm 51:5, these verses also describe an unborn baby as a spiritual, rational, moral being (in essence a human being in the "image of God").

Another argument against abortion can be found in the Old Testament legal code, specifically Exodus 21:22–25: "If men who are fighting hit a pregnant woman and she gives birth prematurely but there is no serious injury, the offender must be fined whatever the woman's husband demands and the court allows. But if there is serious injury, you are to take life for life, eye for eye, tooth for tooth, hand for hand, foot for foot, burn for burn, wound for wound, bruise for bruise."

These verses seem to teach that if a woman gives birth prematurely, but the baby is not injured, then only a fine is appropriate. However, if the child dies, then the law of retaliation (*lex talionis*) should be applied. In other words, killing an unborn baby carried the same penalty as killing a born baby. A baby inside the womb had the same legal status as a baby outside the womb.

Some commentators have come to a different conclusion because they believe verses 22–23 refer only to a case of accidental miscarriage. Since only a fine is levied, they argue that an unborn baby is merely potential life and does not carry the same legal status as a baby that has been born. There are at least two problems with this interpretation. First, the normal Hebrew word for "miscarry" is not used in this passage (cf. Gen. 31:38; Ex. 23:26; Job 3:16; Hos. 9:14). Most commentators now believe that the action described in verse 22 is a premature birth, not an accidental miscarriage. Second, even if the verses do describe a miscarriage, the passage cannot be used to justify abortion. The injury was accidental, not intentional (as an abortion would be). Also the action was a criminal offense and punishable by law.

OTHER ARGUMENTS AGAINST ABORTION

In addition to various biblical arguments against abortion, a number of other arguments speak against abortion. The medical arguments against abortion are compelling. For example, at conception the embryo is genetically distinct from the mother. To say, as many people do, that the developing baby is no different from the mother's appendix is scientifically inaccurate. A developing embryo is genetically different from the mother. A developing embryo is also genetically different from the sperm and egg that created it. A human being has forty-six chromosomes (sometimes forty-seven chromosomes). Sperm and egg each have twenty-three chromosomes. A trained geneticist can distinguish between the DNA of an embryo and sperm and egg. But that same geneticist could not distinguish between the DNA of a developing embryo and a full-grown human being.

Another set of medical arguments against abortion surrounds the definition of life and death. If one set of criteria has been used to define death, could they also be used to define life? Death used to be defined by the cessation of heartbeat. A stopped heart was a clear sign of death. If the cessation of heartbeat could define death, could the onset of a heartbeat define life? The heart is formed by the eighteenth day in the womb. If heartbeat was used to define life, then nearly all abortions would be outlawed.

Physicians now use a more rigorous criterion for death: brain wave activity. A flat EEG (electroencephalograph) is one of the most important criteria used to determine death. If the cessation of brain wave activity can define death, could the onset of brain wave activity define life? Individual brain waves are detected in the fetus in about forty to forty-three days. Using brain wave activity to define life would outlaw at least a majority of abortions.

Opponents of abortion also raise the controversial issue of fetal pain. Does the fetus feel pain during abortion? The evidence seems fairly clear and consistent. Consider this statement made in a British medical journal: "Try sticking an infant with a pin and you know what happens. She opens her mouth to cry and also pulls away. Try sticking an 8-week-old human fetus in the palm of his hand. He opens his mouth and pulls his hand away. A more technical description would add that changes in heart rate and fetal movement also suggest that intrauterine manipulations are painful to the fetus."[12]

Obviously other medical criteria could be used. The point is simple. Medical science leads to a pro-life perspective rather than a pro-choice perspective. If medical science can be used at all to draw a line, the clearest line is at the moment of conception.

In addition to medical arguments, there are legal arguments against abortion. The case of *Roe v. Wade* violated standard legal reasoning. The Supreme Court decided not to decide when life begins and then turned around and overturned state laws against abortion. Most of the Court's decision rested on two sentences: "We need not resolve the difficult question of when life begins. When those trained in the respective disciplines of medicine, philosophy, and theology are unable to arrive at any consensus, the judiciary, at this point in the development of man's knowledge, is not in a position to speculate as to the answer."[13] Although these sentences sounded both innocuous and unpretentious, they were neither. The Court's nondecision was not innocuous. It overturned state laws that protected the unborn and has resulted in over 30 million abortions (roughly the population of Canada) in the United States.

The decision also seemed unpretentious by acknowledging that it did not know when life begins. But if the Court did not know, then it should have acted "as if" life was in the womb. A crucial role of government is to protect life. Government cannot remove a segment of the human population from its protection without adequate justification.

The burden of proof should lie with the life-taker, and the benefit of the doubt should be with the life-saver. Put another way: "When in doubt, don't." A hunter who hears rustling in the bushes should not fire until he knows what is in the bushes. Likewise, a Court that does not know when life begins should not declare open season on the unborn.

The burden of proof in law is on the prosecution. The benefit of doubt is with the defense. This is also known as a presumption of innocence. The defendant is assumed to be innocent unless proven guilty. Again the burden of proof is on the entity that would take away life or liberty. The benefit of the doubt lies with the defense.

The Supreme Court clearly stated that it did not know when life begins and then violated the very spirit of that legal principle by acting as if it just proved that no life existed in the womb. Even more curious was the fact that to do so, it had to ignore the religious community and international community on the subject of the unborn.

Had the religious community really failed to reach a consensus? Although some intramural disagreements existed, certainly the weight of evidence indicated that a Western culture founded on Judeo-Christian values held abortion to be morally wrong. People with widely divergent theological perspectives (Jewish, Catholic, evangelical and fundamental Protestants) shared a common agreement about the humanity of the unborn.

The same could be said about the international legal community. Physicians around the world subscribed to the Hippocratic Oath ("I will not give a woman a pessary to produce abortion"). The unborn were protected by various international documents like the Declaration of Geneva ("I will maintain the utmost respect for human life, from the moment of conception") and the U.N. Declaration of the Rights of the Child ("The child by reason of his physical and mental immaturity, needs special safeguards and care, including appropriate legal protection, before as well as after birth").[14]

One of the strongest legal arguments against abortion was that the Supreme Court decided not to decide when life begins. Then it violated one of standard legal principles that the burden of proof should lie with the life-taker. The Court did not prove its case and should not have overturned the laws of state laws governing abortion.

Philosophic arguments are a third set of arguments against abortion. A key philosophic question is, Where do you draw the line? Put another way, When does a human being become a person?

The Supreme Court's decision in *Roe v. Wade* separated personhood from humanity. In other words, the justices argued that a developing fetus was a human (i.e., a member of the species *Homo sapiens*) but not a person. Since only persons are given Fourteenth Amendment protection under the Constitution, the Court argued that abortion could be legal at certain times. The Court's position left to doctors, parents, or even judges the responsibility of arbitrarily deciding when personhood should be awarded to human beings.

The Court's cleavage of personhood and humanity made inevitable the ethical slide down society's slippery slope. Once the Court allowed people to start drawing lines, some drew them in unexpected ways and effectively opened the door for infanticide and euthanasia.

The Court, in the tradition of previous line-drawers, opted for biological criteria in their definition of a "person" in *Roe v. Wade*. In the past, such criteria as implantation or quickening had been suggested. The Court chose the idea of viability and allowed for the possibility that states could outlaw abortions performed after a child was viable. But viability was an arbitrary criterion, and there was no biological reason why the line had to be drawn near the early stages of development. The line, for example, could be drawn much later.

The ethicist Paul Ramsey frequently warned that any argument for abortion could logically be also used as an argument for infanticide.[15] As if to illustrate this point, Francis Crick demonstrated that he was unconcerned about the ethics of such logical extensions and proposed a more radical definition of personhood. He suggested in the British journal *Nature* that if "a child were considered to be legally born when two days old, it could be examined to see whether it was an 'acceptable member of human society.' "[16] Obviously this is not only an argument for abortion; it is an argument for infanticide.

Other line-drawers have suggested a cultural criterion for personhood. Ashley Montagu, for example, argued that "a newborn baby is not truly human until he or she is molded by cultural influences later."[17] Again, this is more than just an argument for abortion; it is also an argument for infanticide.

More recently some line-drawers have focused on a mental criterion for personhood. Joseph Fletcher argued in his book *Humanhood* that "humans without some minimum of intelligence or mental capacity are not persons, no matter how many of these organs are active, no matter how spontaneous their living processes are."[18] This is not only an argument for abortion and infanticide; it is also adequate justification for euthanasia and the potential elimination of those who do not possess a certain IQ. In other writings, Fletcher suggested that an "individual" was not truly a "person" unless he has an IQ of at least 40.[19]

By separating personhood from manhood, the Supreme Court opened the door for such bizarre line-drawing. The biblical perspective is clear that human beings are also persons created in the image of God. Those who promote abortion try to separate these two issues and thus open the door to dangerous line-drawing and such issues as infanticide and euthanasia.

ANSWERS TO PRO-ABORTION RHETORIC

The abortion debate has been full of rhetoric on both sides, but those supporting the right to abortion have been especially good at throwing out clichés in this debate. The pro-life movement needs to be able to respond to pro-abortion rhetoric in an effective way.

One of the most frequent clichés is this: "Every woman has a right to control her own body." We need to consider the four elements of this slogan. First are the words "every woman." Half of the aborted fetuses are female, so abortion is not exactly pro-woman. So the cliché only applies to grown women seeking abortion, not to females in the womb who would grow up to be women if they were not aborted. Second is the statement "has a right." Our legal system does not recognize an absolute right over one's body. We do not allow someone the "right" to get drunk and then drive a car. We do not give people an absolute right to use dangerous drugs, to commit suicide, or to walk around without clothes. Third is the verb "to control." If a woman wants to control her own body, she could have prevented the pregnancy before it happened. Abstinence is 100 percent effective. The final words are "her own body." As already discussed, pregnancy means there are *two* bodies. In a sense the baby controls the mother's body through various hormonal cues. The fetus would be rejected as foreign tissue if it were not for the placenta that creates an effective barrier between mother and child. The argument that a woman has a right to control her own body may sound good, but flaws emerge as we begin to analyze it.

Another cliché is, "Abortion should be every woman's legal right." As already noted, a woman does not have an absolute legal right over her own body. This is especially true when it comes to abortion that ends the life of the one in the womb. The Bible clearly shows that abortion is taking another human life. Even an injury to an unborn baby resulted in exacting a penalty (Ex. 21:22–25) just as if the child were already born. A woman may have many legal rights, but these must also be tempered by the right to life of the one in the womb.

A third cliché is, "The fetus is mere tissue and not a person." This slogan ignores the previous biblical arguments about the humanity of the fetus (Psalm 139) and the arguments that the unborn already posses the corrupted image of God (Ps. 51:5). God's care extended not merely to tissue that would become David, but to him (personal pronoun). God called many Old Testament prophets to their ministry while yet in their mother's womb (Samson, Isaiah, Jeremiah). These men were more than just pieces of protoplasm; they were prophets God called to ministry.

Pro-abortion advocates often argue, "Abortion is the best solution to a crisis pregnancy." Often an unplanned pregnancy seems like a crisis, but on further reflection it can become a wonderful blessing. But even if the child was conceived under stress or duress, two wrongs do not make a right. The Bible teaches that it is wrong to add sin to sin (Is. 30:1–2). If a mother cannot care for the child, she can give it to those who will care for him or her (Ps. 27:10). Adoption is a better option than abortion. The proliferation of crisis pregnancy centers around the country (there are now more crisis pregnancy centers in the United States than there are abortion clinics) provides an effective means for a woman to deal with her crisis pregnancy.

A corollary cliché is that "abortion is necessary because sometimes there is no other way out." A woman facing a crisis pregnancy often feels the only solution to her problem is abortion and so she fails to consider the potential implications, including infertility and emotional scars. In the Bible God says He will make a way when there seems to be no way out (Jer. 32:17; 1 Cor. 10:13; Heb. 4:15–16). We have the firm promise that if we call on Him, He will answer us (Jer. 33:3; James 1:5–7).

STEM CELL RESEARCH

An issue closely related to abortion is human stem cell research. The stem cell issue surfaced in November 1998 when scientists at the University of Wisconsin were successfully able to isolate and culture human embryonic stem cells.[20] The federal government provides funding for adult stem cell research and provides limited funding for embryonic stem cell research using the existing stem cell lines already developed.

Stem cells derive their name from their similarity to the stem of a plant that gives rise to branches, bark, and every other part of a plant. Embryonic stem cells are the cells from which all 210 different kinds of tissue in the human body originate. As an embryo develops into a blastocyst, a few layers of cells surround a mass of stem cells. If these stem cells are removed from the blastocyst, they cannot develop as an embryo, but they can be cultured and grown into these different tissues.

Stem cells are undifferentiated and self-replicating cells that have the potential to become the other differentiated cells in our body. And that is why there is so much scientific and political attention being paid to stem cells.

The potential for stem cell research is enormous and intoxicating. Nearly 100 million Americans have serious diseases that eventually may be treated or even cured by stem cell research. Many diseases (like Parkinson's, heart disease, diabetes) result from the death or dysfunction of a single cell type. Scientists believe that stem cells can be used to treat and even cure many of the most devastating human diseases.[21]

The moral problem with the research is that to obtain human embryonic stem cells, the embryo is destroyed. Embryos needed for human embryonic stem cell research can be obtained from three sources: (1) in vitro fertilization used to produce embryos, (2) frozen embryos that are spare embryos left over from in vitro fertilization, or (3) the human cloning of embryos.

In addition to the moral problem is the scientific reality that embryonic stem cell research has not been successful. Although human embryonic stem cells have the potential to become any type of human cell, no one has yet mastered the ability to direct these embryonic cells in a way that can provide possible therapy for humans afflicted with various diseases.

Numerous stories of the problems with human embryonic stem cells are surfacing. One of the more notable comes from China, where scientists implanted human embryonic stem cells into a patient suffering Parkinson's only to have them transform into a powerful tumor that eventually killed him.[22]

Lost in all of this discussion is the humanity of the unborn. Proponents of embryonic stem cell research argue that an embryo or fetus is a "potential" human life. Yet at every stage in human development (embryo, fetus, child, adult), we retain our identity as human beings. We are humans from the moment of conception. We do not have the right to dismember a human embryo because it is unwanted or located in a test tube in a fertility clinic.

Also lost in this discussion is the success of using stem cells from sources other than embryos. Successful clinical trials have shown that adult stem cells may provide cures for such diseases as multiple sclerosis, rheumatoid arthritis, and systematic lupus. Some studies seem to indicate that adult stem cells create "fewer biological problems" than embryonic ones.

No moral concerns surround the use of human adult stem cells since they can be obtained from the individual requiring therapy. Stem cells have also been found in tissues previously thought to be devoid of them (neural tissue). And human adult stem cells are also more malleable than previously thought. For example, bone marrow stem cells can produce skeletal muscle, neural, cardiac muscle, and liver cells. And they can be transplanted into a patient from whom they were obtained, thus avoiding problems with tissue rejection.[23] Bone marrow cells can even migrate to these tissues via the circulatory system in response to tissue damage and begin producing cells of the appropriate tissue type.[24]

Human adult stem cell research is already effective and raises none of the moral questions of human embryonic stem cell research. Even biotech industry proponents of embryonic stem cell research believe that we may be twenty years away from developing commercially available treatments using embryonic stem cells.[25]

HOW CAN THE CHURCH BE INVOLVED?

The church can be involved in the battle for life in many practical ways. First, individual Christians can become involved in the pro-life movement. Some may choose to join a pro-life organization and work to overturn abortion at the state or national level. Involvement can range from working full-time on the issue to lobbying legislators to writing an occasional letter about the issue of abortion.

Although it seems unlikely that abortion will be outlawed in the near future, individual Christians can do a number of things at the state and local level to limit the number of abortions that take place (legislation requiring parental consent or a specified waiting period).

One study found that restrictions on abortion do reduce the number of abortions.[26] The number of abortions in America declined from 1.03 million in 1992 to 854,000 in 2000. This correlated with changes in state laws. In 1992, no states were enforcing informed consent laws, while 27 states were doing so in 2000. And the number of states that adopted parental involvement statues rose from 20 states in 1992 to 32 states in 2000.

Another way the church can be involved is through prayer. The Bible admonishes Christians to be in prayer for their leaders (1 Tim. 2:1–2). The church and individual Christians should also be in prayer for various pro-life organizations (national, state, local). They should also pray for women facing abortion, as well as those who have been exploited by abortion.

A third area of involvement is financial, which can include financial gifts (one-time or monthly) to organizations fighting this issue. Also, gifts in kind (maternity clothes, baby clothes, baby items) given to crisis pregnancy centers are helpful. And when we give of our time and talents (as volunteers for pro-life groups or crisis pregnancy centers), we help reduce the financial needs of pro-life organizations.

Churches should consider providing finances for an ultrasound machine. Research indicates that 57 percent of women who visit a pregnancy center and report that they are considering abortion will decide to keep their baby after going through counseling. But that number increases to 79 percent when the women are able to see their unborn child through ultrasound images.[27]

Fourth, churches should also be centers of information. Christians should become informed through Christian media (TV, radio, newsmagazines) and organizational newsletters. They should also attend local rallies, debates, marches, and pickets. And Christians should disseminate this information through their churches and encourage action by the congregations.

Social action is a fifth area of involvement. Christians should find out if their local doctor and hospital perform abortions, and take necessary action. In some cases pro-life advocates may want to picket a local abortion clinic or hospital. Social action also includes voting intelligently about candidates and knowing where they stand on the issue of life.

Involvement in crisis pregnancy is another important action step. Christians should support or start a crisis pregnancy center in their community. They should also inform local churches of its existence and the extent of its services. Churches should consider funding a center as part of their local missions outreach and even provide counselor training not only for volunteers but also for members of the congregation.

Some churches have even developed a shepherding home within the congregation. This ministry provides temporary housing and care for unwed mothers with crisis pregnancy.

Sixth, pastors need to be informed about how to help women with crisis pregnancies. They should be willing to listen and have compassion. Pastors should be sensitive to the pressures on the woman from family, friends, and others. Pastors should involve another woman in the counseling or else refer the pregnant woman to a local center. In addition, pastors should be informed about how to minister to those exploited by abortion in their congregation.

7

EUTHANASIA

THE ETHICS OF DEATH and dying have always been troubling, but pastors and physicians today agonize even more as controversy intensifies over the ethics of euthanasia. Is it moral to withhold medical treatment from a terminally ill patient? Is it ever right to "pull the plug" on a patient? When euthanasia is done, is it mercy or murder? These are just a few of the difficult questions surrounding the issue of euthanasia.

The term *euthanasia* is derived from the Greek prefix *eu*, meaning "good" or "easy," and the Greek noun *thanatos*, meaning "death." Critics, however, have said that euthanasia is anything but easy and anything but good. Euthanasia means different things to different people: from keeping terminally ill patients free from pain to ending a life not deemed worthy of living. Most laypeople once assumed the focus was merely on what can properly be called "palliative care," which includes attempts by doctors and nurses to ease pain in terminal patients. Today, however, euthanasia means much more.

HISTORY OF EUTHANASIA

Debate over euthanasia is not a modern phenomenon. The Greeks carried on a robust debate on the subject. The Pythagoreans opposed euthanasia, while the Stoics favored it in the case of incurable disease. Plato approved of it in cases of terminal illness.[1] But these influences lost out to Christian principles as well as the spread of acceptance of the Hippocratic Oath: "I will neither give a deadly drug to anybody if asked for it, nor will I make a suggestion to that effect."

In 1935, the Euthanasia Society of England was formed to promote the notion of a painless death for patients with incurable diseases. A few years later the Euthanasia Society of America was formed with essentially the same goal. In the last few years debate about euthanasia has been advanced by two individuals: Derek Humphry and Jack Kervorkian.

Derek Humphry has used his prominence as head of the Hemlock Society to promote euthanasia in the United States. His book *Final Exit: The Practicalities of Self-Deliverance and Assisted Suicide for the Dying* became a bestseller and further influenced public opinion. A Gallup poll in 1975 found that 41 percent of the respondents said that they believed that someone in great pain with "no hope of improvement" had the moral right to commit suicide. By 1990 that figure had risen to 66 percent.[2]

Another influential figure is Jack Kervorkian, who has been instrumental in helping people commit suicide. His book *Prescription—Medicide: The Goodness of Planned Death* promotes his views of euthanasia and describes his patented suicide machine, which he calls "the Mercitron." He first gained national attention by enabling Janet Adkins of Portland, Oregon, to kill herself in 1990. They met for dinner and then drove to a Volkswagen van where the machine waited. He placed an intravenous tube into her arm and dripped a saline solution until she pushed a button that sent a drug causing unconsciousness and then a lethal drug that killed her. Since then Kervorkian has helped dozens of other people commit suicide.

Over the years the tragic cases of a number of women described as being in a "persistent vegetative state" have influenced public opinion. The first case involved Karen Ann Quinlan. Her parents, wanting to turn the respirator off, won approval in court. However, when it was turned off in 1976, Karen continued breathing and lived for another ten years. Another case involved Nancy Cruzan, who was hurt in an automobile accident in 1983. Her parents went to court in 1987 to receive approval to remove her feeding tube. Various court cases ensued in Missouri, including her parents' appeal that was heard by the Supreme Court in 1990. Eventually they won the right to pull the feeding tube, and Nancy Cruzan died shortly thereafter.

Seven years after the Cruzan case, the Supreme Court had occasion to rule again on the issue of euthanasia. On June 26, 1997, the Supreme Court rejected euthanasia by stating that state laws banning physician-assisted suicide were constitutional. Some feared that these cases (*Glucksburg v. Washington* and *Vacco v. Quill*) would become for euthanasia what *Roe v. Wade* became for abortion. Instead, the justices rejected the argument of a constitutional "right to die" and chose not to interrupt the political debate (as *Roe v. Wade* did). Instead, the Court urged that the debate on euthanasia continue "as it should in a democratic society."

Perhaps the best known case involved Terri Schiavo, who in 1990 suffered severe brain damage from cerebral hypoxia. A Florida circuit court ruled in 2000 that Schiavo was in a persistent vegetative state and authorized her husband to remove her gastric feeding tube. While the husband Michael Schiavo contended that he was carrying out his wife's wishes, her parents (Bob and Mary Schindler) and her brother and sister wanted to keep her alive. After major court battles in which the feeding tube was removed three times, Terri Schiavo died in 2005.

Crucial to any further debate on euthanasia is a proper definition of the various forms of euthanasia. Some forms of what is called euthanasia can be justified from a biblical perspective, while many others are clearly immoral and even criminal in nature.

FORMS OF EUTHANASIA

Ethical and medical discussions of euthanasia frequently include various forms of treatment or lack of treatment that fall under the general term *euthanasia*. Four categories of euthanasia are frequently discussed in medical literature.

1. *Voluntary, passive euthanasia.* This form of euthanasia assumes that medical personnel, at the patient's request, will merely allow nature to take its course. In the past, passive euthanasia meant that the physician did nothing to hasten death but did provide care, comfort, and counsel to dying patients.[3]

2. *Voluntary, active euthanasia.* Here, the physician, by request, hastens death by taking some active means (lethal injection). This form raises the controversial issue of whether nonmedical personnel such as a spouse or friend would be permitted to end the suffering of another.

3. *Involuntary, passive euthanasia.* This form assumes that the patient has not expressed a willingness to die or cannot do so. The medical personnel do not go to any extraordinary measures to save the patient, but they often withhold food (by removing nasogastric tubes), antibiotics, or life-support systems (respirator).

4. *Involuntary, active euthanasia.* This type of euthanasia begins to blur into genocide. In this case the physician does something active to hasten death, regardless of the patient's wishes, for humanitarian reasons, economic considerations, or genetic justifications.

In recent years these categories have been blurred by discussions of the right to die, death with dignity, patient autonomy, death selection, physician-assisted suicide, living wills, and a durable power of attorney. Nevertheless, these four categories provide the basis for an extended discussion of the various concepts surrounding the issue of euthanasia.

Voluntary, Passive Euthanasia

Voluntary, passive euthanasia is not truly euthanasia in the modern sense. In these situations death is assumed to be imminent and inevitable. At this point the medical personnel's attention turns from curing the disease to making the patient as comfortable as possible. Further medical treatment to prolong life becomes pointless, and an entirely different medical strategy is implemented. This medical strategy is frequently referred to as "palliative care." The prime focus is on alleviating pain, while not actually curing the patient.

One of the great fears of patients is the prospect of intractable pain in the dying process. But medical science has made great strides in treating pain. New ways of administering morphine, for example, can effectively manage pain and also lower the risk of respiratory complications. David Cundiff, a practicing oncologist and hospice care physician, said,

> It is a disgrace that the majority of our health care providers lack the knowledge and the skills to treat pain and other symptoms of terminal disease properly. The absence of palliative care training for medical professional results in sub-optimal care for almost all terminally ill patients and elicits the wish to hasten their own deaths in a few.[4]

Fear of pain is often unwarranted. Physicians can administer medications that deaden pain but do not dim consciousness, thus allowing patients to converse with their family and friends even in their last days.

Some patients can be released to hospices, where they can spend their last days with family and friends rather than in a clinical hospital setting. The hospice program provides a coordinated program of doctors, nurses, and special consultants who help dying patients and their families through their time of struggle.

But even voluntary, passive euthanasia is not without its controversy. Many physicians are reluctant to discontinue medical efforts to cure terminal patients. Their reluctance is not so much driven by a belief that they will be successful as it is by their concern about possible malpractice suits from the family. Patients who are ready "to go to be with the Lord" may find themselves at odds with doctors who are fearful that they may have to prove in a court of law that they did "all they could" for the patient.

Sometimes attempts to prolong life are futile and certainly not warranted from a biblical perspective. According to Job 14:5, "Man's days are determined; you have decreed the number of his months and have set limits he cannot exceed." Modern medicine sometimes tries to exceed those natural limits. Christians are not required to use extraordinary measures to keep a comatose person with an incurable disease alive by artificial means. In a sense using this technology would actually be working against God's appointed limits described in Job 14:5.

In certain medical situations, giving food or water can be futile and burdensome. Rita Marker of the Anti-Euthanasia Task Force wrote, "A patient who is very close to death may be in such a condition that fluids would cause a great deal of discomfort or may not be assimilated by his body. Food may not be digested as the body begins 'shutting down' during the dying process. There comes a time when a person is truly, imminently dying."[5]

In 1981, the President's Commission for the Study of Ethical Problems in Medicine provided guidelines for patients and also drafted a Uniform Determination of Death (to be discussed later). The commission came to the following conclusions concerning terminally ill patients.[6]

1. A terminally ill patient generally should have the right to choose to die without interference from lawyers, legislators, or bureaucrats.

2. Patients suffering loss of consciousness should have the type of care that is dictated largely by their families' wishes.

3. Resuscitation need not always be attempted on a hospitalized patient whose heart stops. Patients likely to suffer cardiac arrest should be informed before an operation and allowed to decide in advance for or against resuscitation.

4. Patients should have greater rights to give instructions in advance of becoming incapacitated. They should have the right to appoint a proxy to carry out their wishes.

These conclusions of the President's Commission have provided the basis for revision of state laws governing medical care of the terminally ill. In general they provide doctors with greater latitude in making decisions concerning dying patients. But they do raise significant questions for Christians.

First, is there such a thing as a "right to die"? From a Christian perspective this "right" is certainly questionable. But it also raises important legal questions never addressed by the founders of this country or by modern courts. While the Declaration of Independence does recognize a "right to life," it does not recognize (nor even assume) a "right to die."

Second, the conclusions suggest that a patient's decisions about life and death can be done by proxy. In most cases this has been done through what are known as advanced directives, which usually are found in one of three forms: (1) A living will outlines what medical treatment a patient might desire. A patient can specify what he or she wants and does not want. The legal limits vary from state to state. (2) Health-care proxy designates an agent (friend, family member) to act for the patient in health-care matters. This proxy is often included within a living will and may have limited powers. (3) A durable power of attorney is the most inclusive and comprehensive document, permitting the patient's agent to act for him or her in most health care matters.

Most states allow individuals to draw up an advanced directive like a living will or a Durable Power of Attorney (DPOA) in which they specify their desires regarding medical treatment if they become terminally ill and incompetent. A DPOA, in particular, gives a third party, or proxy, power to make decisions on behalf of the patient. In the past DPOAs covered only financial decisions, but court precedents have extended them to cover health-care decisions as well.

In 1991, the Patient Self-Determination Act became law. It requires medical facilities receiving federal reimbursements such as Medicaid and Medicare to inform patients of the right to some form of advance directives. Therefore, more and more patients are being confronted with questions and choices about their health care.

One problem with these directives is that they are often ignored. A study done by University of North Carolina at Chapel Hill researchers on the use of advanced directives found that treatment received was not in accord with the patients' instructions in 25 percent of the cases.[7] Similar findings have been reported in the *New England Journal of Medicine* and the AMA's *Archives of Internal Medicine*.

Critics of living wills say that signing a living will is like signing a blank check because it is too broad and cannot cover every contingency. The attending physician therefore must interpret a patient's wishes. A patient not wanting any heroic measures carried out may envision a heart/lung machine, whereas the attending physician may interpret such measures to mean something quite different.

Another problem with these proxy arrangements is that they are usually based on some "quality of life" standard and delegate the interpretation of those standards to someone else. A Christian perspective on human life sees all life as sacred and given by God. Decisions about life and death should be governed by a "sanctity of life" standard rather than by a "quality of life" standard.

Voluntary, Active Euthanasia

Voluntary, active euthanasia implies that something is done to hasten death, which raises both moral and legal questions. Does active euthanasia constitute an act of murder or assisted suicide? Or is it merely a compassionate act of mercy-killing?

It is helpful to distinguish between mercy-killing and what could be called mercy-dying. Taking a human life is not the same as allowing nature to take its course by allowing a terminal patient to die. The former is immoral (and perhaps even criminal), while the latter is not. However, drawing a sharp line between these two categories is not as easy as it used to be. Modern medical technology has significantly blurred the line between hastening death and allowing nature to take its course.

Certain analgesics, for example, ease pain, but they can also shorten a patient's life by affecting respiration. An artificial heart will continue to beat even after the patient has died and therefore must be turned off by the doctor. So the distinction between actively promoting death and passively allowing nature to take its course is sometimes difficult to determine in practice. But this fundamental distinction between life-taking and death-permitting is still an important philosophical distinction.

Another concern with active euthanasia is that it eliminates the possibility for recovery. While such an observation should be obvious, somehow this problem is frequently ignored in the euthanasia debate. Terminating a human life eliminates all possibility of recovery, while passively ceasing extraordinary means may not. Miraculous recovery from a bleak prognosis sometimes occurs. A doctor who prescribes active euthanasia for a patient may unwittingly prevent a possible recovery he did not anticipate.

A further concern with this so-called voluntary, active euthanasia is that these decisions might not always be freely made. The possibility for coercion is always present. Richard D. Lamm, the former governor of Colorado, said that elderly, terminally ill patients have "a duty to die and get out of the way."[8] Though those words were reported somewhat out of context, they nonetheless illustrate the pressure many elderly feel from hospital personnel.

The Dutch experience is instructive. In 1990, the Remmelink Committee surveyed Dutch physicians and found that 1,030 patients were killed without their consent. Of these, 140 were fully mentally competent and 110 were only slightly mentally impaired. The report also found that another 14,175 patients (1,701 of whom were mentally competent) were denied medical treatment without their consent and died.[9]

A more recent survey of Dutch physicians is even less encouraging. Doctors in the United States and the Netherlands found that though euthanasia in the Netherlands was originally intended for exceptional cases, it has become an accepted way of dealing with serious or terminal illness. The original guidelines established for Dutch doctors (that patients with a terminal illness make a voluntary, persistent request that their lives be ended) have been expanded to include chronic ailments and psychological distress. The surveyors also found that 60 percent of Dutch physicians do not report their cases of assisted suicide (even though reporting is required by law) and about 25 percent of the physicians admit to ending patients' lives without their consent.[10]

The former Surgeon General of the United States C. Everett Koop maintained that proponents of active euthanasia "have gotten across to a whole segment of the elderly population that somehow because they are living, they are depriving someone else of a prior right to resources. That is a most reprehensible thing." He added, "When I was doing research for *Whatever Happened to the Human Race?*, I went to nursing homes and talked to people who felt that pressure. Old people were apologizing to me for using a bed, for being alive, for taking medication, because they knew somebody else deserved it more. I think that's pitiful."[11]

Involuntary, Passive Euthanasia

In involuntary, passive euthanasia, which is an act of omission, medical personnel do not go to any extraordinary measures to save the patient. Not using extraordinary means can be morally acceptable when dealing with terminal patients.

Unfortunately this omission often includes actions that are more accurately described as active euthanasia. Withholding food (by removing nasogastric tubes), antibiotics, or life-support procedures (respirator) is much more than passive euthanasia. As already mentioned, candidates for euthanasia have been known to make miraculous recoveries, but such a possibility is eliminated when a patient is starved to death.

Sometimes, however, decisions must be made about "pulling the plug." A comatose patient without any brain wave activity, as indicated by a flat electroencephalogram, should be removed from life-support systems. But in other situations a comatose patient might recover. These difficult decisions should be left up to the neurophysiologist who can evaluate a patient's prognosis. But in general one may assume that the patient will recover and therefore life-support systems should be continued, thus placing the burden of proof on those who wish to "pull the plug."

Key to this discussion is an accurate definition of death. Prior to the 1960s, a terminally ill patient who stopped breathing and continued in that state was pronounced dead. With the advent of CPR and artificial respirators, that respiratory criterion for death had to be changed. In 1968, the Harvard Medical School developed more specific criteria for death: (1) lack of response to external stimuli, (2) absence of spontaneous muscular movements and spontaneous respiration, (3) no elicitable reflexes, and (4) a flat electroencephalogram (EEG).

In 1981, the President's Commission drafted a Uniform Determination of Death Act, which has been universally adopted. It defines death as irreversible cessation of circulatory and respiratory functions and irreversible cessation of all functions of the entire brain, including the brain stem. In other words brain death (a flat EEG) has become the established criterion for death and decisions about when to remove life-support systems.

Another concern about involuntary euthanasia is motive. Motives are frequently mixed. Are the medical personnel recommending euthanasia because of bed shortages or depleted medical facilities? Or are they suggesting euthanasia out of a compassionate concern for the patient? Is a son, for example, agreeing to euthanasia out of concern for his mother's well-being or out of a desire to gain her inheritance?

Koop said this about the importance of motive within the debate and discussion about euthanasia: "The whole thing about euthanasia comes down to one word: motive. If your motive is to alleviate suffering while a patient is going through the throes of dying, and you are using medication that alleviates suffering, even though it might shorten his life by a few hours, that is not euthanasia. But if you are giving him a drug intended to shorten his life, then your motivation is for euthanasia."[12]

The mixed motives behind these decisions are not easy to sort out, and they add further moral and legal questions to the medical landscape. Motives are clearer when nature is allowed to take its course and agonizing decisions are not thrust on the patient or family about when to terminate a patient's life.

Involuntary, Active Euthanasia

In involuntary, active euthanasia a second party makes decisions about whether active measures should be taken to end a life. Foundational to this discussion is an erosion of the doctrine of the sanctity of life. But ever since the Supreme Court ruled in *Roe v. Wade* that the life of unborn babies could be terminated for reasons of convenience, the slide down society's slippery slope has continued even though the Court has been reluctant to legalize euthanasia.

The progression was inevitable. Once society begins to devalue the life of an unborn child, it is but a small step to begin to do the same with a child who has been born. Abortion slides naturally into infanticide and eventually into euthanasia. In the past few years doctors have allowed a number of so-called "Baby Does" to die (either by failing to perform lifesaving operations or else by not feeding the infants).

The progression toward euthanasia is inevitable. Once society becomes conformed to a "quality of life" standard for infants, it will more willingly accept the same standard for the elderly. As Koop said, "Nothing surprises me anymore. My great concern is that there will be 10,000 Grandma Does for every Baby Doe."[13]

Again the Dutch experience is instructive. In the Netherlands, physicians have performed involuntary euthanasia because they thought that the family had suffered too much or were tired of taking care of patients. The American surgeon Robin Bernhoft related an incident in which a Dutch doctor euthanized a twenty-six-year-old ballerina with arthritis in her toes. Since she could no longer pursue her career as a dancer, she was depressed and requested to be put to death. The doctor complied with her request and merely noted that "one doesn't enjoy such things, but it was her choice."[14]

PHYSICIAN-ASSISTED SUICIDE

In recent years media and political attention has been given to the idea of physician-assisted suicide. Some states have even attempted to pass legislation that would allow physicians in this country the legal right to put terminally ill patients to death. While the Dutch experience should be enough to demonstrate the danger of granting such rights, other good reasons for rejecting this form of euthanasia exist as well.

First, physician-assisted suicide would change the nature of the medical profession itself. Physicians would be cast in the role of killers rather than healers. The Hippocratic Oath was written to place the medical profession on the foundation of healing not killing. For 2,400 years patients have had the assurance that doctors would follow an oath to heal them not kill them. The doctor-patient relationship would change with legalized euthanasia.

Second, medical care would be affected. Physicians would begin to ration health care so that elderly and severely disabled patients would not be receiving the same quality of care as everyone else. Legalizing euthanasia would result in less care for the dying rather than better care.

Third, legalizing euthanasia through physician-assisted suicide would effectively establish a right to die. The Constitution affirms that fundamental rights cannot be limited to one group (the terminally ill). They must apply to all. Legalizing physician-assisted suicide would open the door to anyone wanting the "right" to kill themselves. Soon this would apply not only to voluntary euthanasia but also to involuntary euthanasia as various court precedents begin to broaden the application of the right to die to other groups in society like the disabled or the clinically depressed.

BIBLICAL PERSPECTIVE

Foundational to a biblical perspective on euthanasia is a proper understanding of the sanctity of human life. For centuries Western culture in general and Christians in particular have believed in the sanctity of human life. Unfortunately this view is beginning to erode into a "quality of life" standard. The disabled, retarded, and infirm were seen as having a special place in God's world, but today medical personnel judge a person's fitness for life on the basis of a perceived quality of life or lack of such quality.

No longer is life seen as sacred and worthy of being saved. Now patients are evaluated, and life-saving treatment is frequently denied, based on a subjective and arbitrary standard for the supposed quality of life. If a life is not judged worthy to be lived any longer, people feel obliged to end that life.

The Bible teaches that human beings are created in the image of God (Gen. 1:26–27) and therefore have dignity and value. Human life is sacred and should not be terminated merely because life is difficult or inconvenient. Psalm 139 teaches that humans are fearfully and wonderfully made. Society must not place an arbitrary standard of quality above God's absolute standard of human value and worth. Believing in the sanctity of life does not mean that people will no longer need to make difficult decisions about treatment and care, but it does mean that these decisions will be guided by an objective, absolute standard of human worth.

The Bible also teaches that God is sovereign over life and death. Christians can agree with Job when he said, "The LORD gave and the LORD has taken away; may the name of the LORD be praised" (Job 1:21). The Lord said, "See now that I myself am He! There is no god besides me. I put to death and I bring to life, I have wounded and I will heal, and no one can deliver out of my hand" (Deut. 32:39). God has ordained our days (Ps. 139:16) and is in control of our lives.

Another foundational principle involves a biblical view of life-taking. The Bible specifically condemns murder (Ex. 20:13), and this would include active forms of euthanasia in which another person (doctor, nurse, or friend) hastens death in a patient. While there are situations described in Scripture in which life-taking may be permitted (self-defense or a just war), euthanasia should not be included with any of these established biblical categories. Active euthanasia, like murder, involves premeditated intent and therefore should be condemned as immoral and even criminal.

Although the Bible does not specifically speak to the issue of euthanasia, the story of the death of King Saul (2 Sam. 1:9–16) is instructive. Saul asked a soldier put him to death as he lay dying on the battlefield. When David heard of this act, he ordered the soldier put to death for destroying "the LORD's anointed." Though the context is not euthanasia per se, it does show the respect we must show for a human life even in such tragic circumstances.

Christians should also reject the attempt by the modern euthanasia movement to promote a so-called "right to die." Secular society's attempt to establish this "right" is wrong for two reasons. First, giving a person a right to die is tantamount to promoting suicide, and suicide is condemned in the Bible. Man is forbidden to murder and that includes the murder of oneself. Moreover, Christians are commanded to love others as they love themselves (Matt. 22:39; Eph. 5:29). Implicit in the command is an assumption of self-love as well as love for others.

Suicide, however, is hardly an example of self-love and is perhaps the clearest example of self-hate. Suicide is also usually a selfish act. People kill themselves to get away from pain and problems, often leaving those problems to friends and family members who must pick up the pieces when the one who committed suicide is gone.

Second, this so-called "right to die" denies God the opportunity to work sovereignly within a shattered life and bring glory to Himself. When Joni Eareckson Tada realized that she would be spending the rest of her life as a quadriplegic, she asked in despair, "Why can't they just let me die?" When her friend Diana, trying to provide comfort, said to her, "The past is dead, Joni; you're alive," Joni responded, "Am I? This isn't living."[15] But through God's grace Joni's despair gave way to her firm conviction that even her accident was within God's plan for her life. Now she shares with the world her firm conviction that "suffering gets us ready for heaven."[16]

The Bible teaches that God's purposes are beyond our understanding. Job's reply to the Lord shows his acknowledgment of God's purposes: "I know that you can do all things; no plan of yours can be thwarted. / You asked, 'Who is this that obscures my counsel without knowledge?' Surely I spoke of things I did not understand, things too wonderful for me to know" (Job 42:2–3). Isaiah 55:8–9 teaches, "For my thoughts are not your thoughts, neither are your ways my ways, declares the Lord. / As the heavens are higher than the earth, so are my ways higher than your ways and my thoughts than your thoughts."

Another foundational principle is a biblical view of death. Death is both unnatural and inevitable. It is an unnatural intrusion into our lives as a consequence of the Fall (Gen. 2:17). It is the last enemy to be destroyed (1 Cor. 15:26, 56). Therefore, Christians can reject humanistic ideas that assume death as nothing more than a natural transition. But the Bible also teaches that death (under the present conditions) is inevitable. There is "a time to be born and a time to die" (Eccl. 3:2). Death is a part of life and the doorway to another, better life.

When does death occur? Modern medicine defines death primarily as a biological event; yet Scripture defines death as a spiritual event that has biological consequences. Death, according to the Bible, occurs when the spirit leaves the body (Eccl. 12:7; James 2:26).

Unfortunately this does not offer much by way of clinical diagnosis for medical personnel. But it does suggest that a rigorous medical definition for death be used. A comatose patient may not be conscious, but from both a medical and biblical perspective he is very much alive and treatment should be continued unless crucial vital signs and brain activity have ceased.

On the other hand, Christians must also reject the notion that everything must be done to save life at all costs. Believers, knowing that to be at home in the body is to be away from the Lord long for the time when they will be absent from the body and at home with the Lord (2 Cor. 5:6, 8). Death is gain for Christians (Phil. 1:21). Therefore, they need not be so tied to this earth that they perform futile operations just to extend life a few more hours or days.

In a patient's last days everything possible should be done to alleviate physical and emotional pain. Giving drugs to a patient to relieve pain is morally justifiable. Proverbs 31:6 says, "Give strong drink to him who is perishing, and wine to him whose life is bitter." As previously mentioned, some analgesics have the secondary effect of shortening life. But these should be permitted since the primary purpose is to relieve pain, even though they may secondarily shorten life.

Moreover, believers should provide counsel and spiritual care to dying patients (Gal. 6:2). Frequently emotional needs can be met both in the patient and in the family. Such times of grief also provide opportunities for witnessing. Those suffering loss are often more open to the gospel than at any other time.

Difficult philosophical and biblical questions are certain to continue swirling around the issue of euthanasia. But in the midst of these confusing issues should be the objective, absolute standards of Scripture, which provide guidance for the hard choices of providing care to terminally ill patients.

8

GENETIC ENGINEERING

THE AGE OF GENETICS has arrived. Society is in the midst of a genetic revolution that some futurists predict will have a greater impact on American culture than the industrial revolution. Knowledge in genetics is doubling every few years. Genetic engineering is no longer science fiction; it is now scientific fact.

The future of genetics, like that of any other technology, offers great promise but also great peril. Nuclear technology has provided nuclear medicine and nuclear energy, yet it has also produced nuclear weapons. Genetic technology offers the promise of a diverse array of good, questionable, and bad technological applications. Christians, therefore, must help shape the ethical foundations of this technology and its future applications.

How powerful a technology is genetic engineering? For the first time in human history it is possible to completely redesign existing organisms, including man, and to direct the genetic and reproductive constitution of every living thing. Scientists are no longer limited to breeding and cross-pollination. Powerful genetic tools allow us to change genetic structure at the microscopic level and bypass the normal processes of reproduction.

For the first time in human history it is also possible to make multiple copies of any existing organism or of certain sections of its genetic structure. This ability to clone existing organisms or their genes gives scientists a powerful tool to reproduce helpful and useful genetic material within a population.

Scientists are also developing techniques to treat and cure genetic diseases through genetic surgery and genetic therapy. They can already identify genetic sequences that are defective, and soon scientists will be able to replace these defects with properly functioning genes.

GENETIC DISEASES

Genetic diseases arise from a number of causes. Single-gene defects are one cause. Some of these single-gene diseases are dominant and therefore cannot be masked by a second normal gene on the homologous chromosome (the other strand of a chromosome pair). An example is Huntington's chorea (a fatal disease that strikes later in life and leads to progressive physical and mental deterioration). Many other single-gene diseases are recessive and are expressed only when both chromosomes have a defect. Examples of these diseases are sickle-cell anemia, which leads to the production of malformed red blood cells, and cystic fibrosis, which leads to a malfunction of the respiratory and digestive systems.

Another group of single-gene diseases includes the sex-linked diseases. Because the Y chromosome in men is much shorter than the X chromosome it pairs with, many genes on the X chromosome are absent on the homologous Y chromosome. Therefore, men will show a higher incidence of genetic diseases such as hemophilia or color blindness. Even though these are recessive, males do not have a homologous gene on their Y chromosome that could contain a normal gene to mask it.

Another major cause of genetic disease is chromosomal abnormalities. Some diseases result from an additional chromosome. Down syndrome is caused by trisomy-21 (three chromosomes at chromosome twenty-one). Klinefelter's syndrome results from the addition of an extra X chromosome (these men have a chromosome pattern that is XXY). Other genetic defects result from the duplication, deletion, or rearrangement (called translocation) of a gene sequence.

GENETIC COUNSELING

As scientists have learned more about the genetic structure of human beings, they have been able to predict with greater certainty the likelihood of a couple bearing a child with a genetic disease. Each human being carries approximately three to eight genetic defects that might be passed on to their children. By checking family medical histories and taking blood samples (for chromosome counts and tests for recessive traits), a genetic counselor can make a fairly accurate prediction about the possibility of a couple having a child with a genetic disease.

Most couples, however, do not seek genetic counsel in order to decide if they should have a child, but instead seek counsel to decide if they should abort a child that is already conceived. In these cases where the mother is already pregnant, the focus is not whether to prevent a pregnancy but whether to abort the unborn child. These circumstances raise some of the same ethical concerns already discussed in the chapter on abortion.

Physicians also have powerful tools to discover major deformities as well as genetic defects within the womb. As recently as the 1950s, the genetic makeup of a child born in a delivery room was usually a surprise to both the doctor and the parents. A standard prenatal exam involved placing a stethoscope on the mother's stomach and listening for signs of life. The nature of prenatal exams began to change in the following decades.

Major deformities can be discovered through many advanced new techniques. One is ultrasound, which uses a type of sonar to determine the size, shape, and sex of the fetus. An ultrasound transducer is placed on the mother's abdomen and sound waves are sent through the amniotic sac. The sonar waves are then picked up and transmitted to a video screen that provides important information about the characteristics of the fetus.

Another important tool is laparoscopy. A doctor inserts a flexible fiber-optic scope through a small incision in the mother's abdomen, allowing the doctor to probe into the abdominal cavity. This procedure can also be used for microsurgery (to repair the fallopian tubes) or to take a blood sample from the fetus.

Various prenatal tests can also detect genetic defects. These tests can detect approximately two hundred genetic disorders.[1] In the mid-1960s, physicians began to use amniocentesis. A doctor inserts a four-inch needle into a pregnant woman's anesthetized abdomen in order to withdraw up to an ounce of amniotic fluid. As the fetus grows, its skin sheds cells that can be collected from the fluid and used to discover the sex and genetic make-up of the fetus.

For years, doctors used this procedure to identify congenital defects by the twentieth week of pregnancy. Now more doctors use another technique called chorionic villus sampling (CVS), which can produce the same information at ten weeks. Doctors also use a blood test known as maternal serum alfa-fetoprotein (MSAFP). This test, usually done between the fifteenth and twentieth week, can detect a neural tube defect of the spinal cord or brain, such as spina bifida or Down syndrome.

Using these techniques to give genetic information to couples is not wrong. But since most of these genetic diseases cannot be cured, the tacit assumption is that women will abort their defective fetuses. Many doctors and clinics will not do genetic tests unless a couple gives prior consent to abortion.

Preimplantation genetic diagnosis (PGD) raises even greater moral questions. This procedure provides prospective parents with the ability to check for both desirable and undesirable traits in a developing embryo. Since conception takes place outside the body in a petri dish, geneticists predict the genetic traits of an embryo before it is implanted in the womb.

Embryos with the desirable traits (or free of undesirable traits) are implanted. Embryos that do not meet the parent's selection criteria are destroyed or used for research. Therefore, the destruction of preborn children raises some of the same ethical questions as abortion.

Critics of PGD also believe that it fosters a eugenics mindset.[2] The latest ability to screen out undesirable genetic traits revives some of the attitudes that fostered the eugenics movement in the last century. We might be unwilling to welcome all human beings regardless of their genetic makeup. PGD allows us to screen out and eliminate undesirable people.

PGD also reduces children to their genetic makeup. A child is valuable or expendable because of his or her genetic material. Couples often select or reject a child based on his or her gender. Clinics providing PGD frequently advertise for "family balancing," thus allowing couples to choose the sex of the child.

In the future, genetic counseling will change because of advances in technology. Genetic engineering will allow doctors to treat genetic diseases as well as diagnose them. Genetic surgery and genetic therapy can already be used to replace or recondition existing genes. Gene splicing also known as recombinant DNA technology will help doctors diagnose and treat these genetic diseases.

GENE SPLICING

Recombinant DNA research (rDNA) began in the 1970s with new genetic techniques that allowed scientists to cut small pieces of DNA (known as plasmids) into small segments that could be inserted in host DNA. The new creatures that were designed have been called DNA chimeras because they are conceptually similar to the mythological Chimera (a creature with the head of a lion, the body of a goat, and the tail of a serpent)

Recombinant DNA technology is fundamentally different from other forms of genetic breeding used in the past. Breeding programs work on existing arrays of genetic variability in a species, isolating specific genetic traits through selective breeding. Scientists using rDNA technology can essentially "stack" the deck or even produce an entirely new deck of genetic "cards."

But this powerful ability to change the genetic deck of cards also raises substantial scientific concerns that some "sleight-of-hand" would produce dangerous consequences. Ethan Singer said, "Those who are powerful in society will do the shuffling; their genes will be shuffled in one direction, while the genes of the rest of us will get shuffled in another."[3] Another concern is that a reshuffled deck of genes might create an Andromeda strain similar to the one Michael Crichton envisioned in his book by the same title.[4] A microorganism might inadvertently be given the genetic structure for some pathogen for which there is no antidote or vaccine.

In the early days of rDNA research, scientists called for a moratorium until the risks of this new technology could be assessed. Even after the National Institute of Health issued guidelines, public fear was considerable. When Harvard University planned to construct a genetic facility for rDNA research, the mayor of Cambridge, Massachusetts, expressed his concern that "something could crawl out of the laboratory, such as a Frankenstein."[5]

The potential benefits of rDNA technology are significant. First, scientists can use the technology to produce medically important substances. The list of these substances is lengthy and would include insulin, interferon, and human growth hormone. The technology also has great application in the field of immunology. In order to protect organisms from viral disease, doctors must inject a killed or attenuated virus. Scientists can use rDNA to disable a toxin gene, thus producing a viral substance that triggers production of antibodies without the possibility of producing the disease.

A second benefit is in the field of agriculture. Recombinant DNA can improve the genetic fitness of various plant species. Basic research using this technology could increase the efficiency of photosynthesis, increase plant resistance (to salinity, to drought, to viruses), and reduce a plant's demand for nitrogen fertilizer.

Third, rDNA research can aid industrial and environmental processes. Industries that manufacture drugs, plastics, industrial chemicals, vitamins, and cheese will benefit from this technology. Also scientists have begun to develop organisms that can clean up oil spills or toxic wastes.

This last benefit, however, also raises one of the greatest scientific concerns over rDNA technology. The escape (or even intentional release) of a genetically engineered organism might wreak havoc on the environment. Scientists have created microorganisms that dissolve oil spills or reduce frost on plants. Critics of rDNA technology fear that radically altered organisms could occupy new ecological niches, destroy existing ecosystems, or drive certain species to extinction.

Legal concerns also surround this technology. The Supreme Court ruled that genetically engineered organisms as well as the genetic processes that created them can be patented. The original case involved an oil-slick eating microorganism patented by General Electric. Since 1981, the U.S. Patent and Trademark Office has approved nearly 12,000 patents for genetic products and processes.[6] Scientists have been concerned that the prospects of profit have decreased the relatively free flow of scientific information. Often scientists-turned-entrepreneurs refuse to share their findings for fear of commercial loss.

Even more significant is the question of whether life should even be patented at all. Most religious leaders say no. A 1995 gathering of 187 religious leaders representing virtually every major religious tradition spoke out against the patenting of genetically engineered substances. They argued that life is the creation of God, not humans, and should not be patented as human inventions.[7]

The broader theological question is *whether* genetic engineering should be used and, if permitted, *how* it should be used. The natural reaction for many in society is to reject new forms of technology because they are dangerous. Christians, however, should take into account God's command to humankind in the cultural mandate (Gen. 1:28). Christians should avoid the reflex reaction that scientists should not tinker with life; instead, Christians should consider how genetic technology should be used responsibly.

One key issue is the worldview behind most scientific research. Modern science rests on an evolutionary assumption. Many scientists assume that life on this planet is the result of millions of years of a chance evolutionary process. Therefore, they conclude that intelligent scientists can do a better job of directing the evolutionary process than nature can do by chance. Even evolutionary scientists warn of this potential danger. Ethan Singer believes that scientists will "verify a few predictions,

and then gradually forget that knowing something isn't the same as knowing everything. . . . At each stage we will get a little cockier, a little surer we know all the
possibilities."[8]

In essence rDNA technology gives scientists the tools they have always wanted
to drive the evolutionary spiral higher and higher. Julian Huxley looked forward to
the day in which scientists could fill the "position of business manager for the cos-
mic process of evolution."[9] Certainly rDNA enables scientists to create new forms
of life and alter existing forms in ways that have been impossible until now.

How should Christians respond? They should humbly acknowledge that God is
the sovereign Creator and that man has finite knowledge. Genetic engineering
gives scientists the technological ability to be gods, but they lack the wisdom,
knowledge, and moral capacity to act like God.

Even evolutionary scientists who deny the existence of God and believe that all
life is the result of an impersonal evolutionary process express concern about the
potential dangers of this technology. Erwin Chargaff asked, "Have we the right to
counteract, irreversibly, the evolutionary wisdom of millions of years, in order to
satisfy the ambition and curiosity of a few scientists?"[10] His answer is no. The
Christian's answer should also be the same when we realize that God is the Creator of life. We do not have the right to "rewrite the fifth day of creation."[11]

What is the place for genetic engineering within a biblical framework? The answer to that question can be found by distinguishing between two types of research.
The first could be called genetic repair. This research attempts to remove genetic
defects and develop techniques that will provide treatments for existing diseases.
Applications would include various forms of genetic therapy and genetic surgery as
well as modifications of existing microorganisms to produce beneficial results.

The Human Genome Project has been able to pinpoint the location and sequence of these human genes. Further advances in rDNA technology will allow
scientists to repair these defective sequences and eventually remove these genetic
diseases from our population.

Genetic disease is the result of the Fall (Genesis 3), not part of God's plan for
the world. Christians can apply technology to fight these evils without being accused of fighting against God's will.[12] Genetic engineering can and should be used
to treat and cure genetic diseases.

A second type of research is the creation of new forms of life. While minor
modifications of existing organisms may be permissible, Christians should be concerned about the large-scale production of novel life forms. That potential impact
on the environment and on mankind could be considerable. Science is replete with
examples of what can happen when an existing organism is introduced into a new
environment (the rabbit to Australia, the rat to Hawaii, or the gypsy moth in the
United States). One can only imagine the devastation that could occur when a
newly created organism is introduced into a new environment.

God created plants and animals as "kinds" (Gen. 1:24). While there is minor variability within these created kinds, built-in barriers exist between these created kinds. Redesigning creatures of any kind cannot be predicted the same way new elements on the periodic chart can be predicted for properties even before they are discovered. Recombinant DNA technology offers great promise in treating genetic disease, but Christians should also be vigilant. While this technology should be used to repair genetic defects, it should not be used to confer the role of creator on scientists.

CLONING

In 1970, Paul Ramsey devoted an entire chapter to human cloning in his book *Fabricated Man*.[13] And during much of the 1970s, ethicists debated the pros and cons of human cloning until scientists were able to convince nearly everyone that cloning a mammal (much less a human being) would be difficult to impossible.

All that changed when scientists in Scotland announced in 1997 that they had successfully cloned an adult sheep. Commentators were predicting that a "brave new world" was just around the corner, and ethicists began to dust off arguments that had been mothballed in the 1970s. The cloning of the sheep Dolly implied that it might eventually be possible to clone a human being.

A few years earlier, in 1993, two scientists from George Washington University announced the first artificial twinning of human embryos. The press erroneously announced that humans had been cloned. Actually this was not the case. What the scientists did was to begin with seventeen human embryos and multiply them like the Bible's loaves and fishes into forty-eight different embryos.

When an embryo grows, its cells begin to differentiate. Only that part of the genetic structure is utilized to form a skin cell or an eye cell. In a sense DNA is like a CD album that will only play a single track. The genetic melody for a skin cell is the only track of DNA that is actually played in a skin cell. The George Washington University scientists found a way to get adult cells to once again play each and every genetic note by putting them in a state of "quiescence." When the cell became dormant, all the genes once again had the potential of being played.

In their cloning of Dolly, the Scottish scientists took normal mammary cells from an adult ewe and starved them in order to allow the cells to reach a dormant stage which apparently allowed these cells to be deprogrammed. These were then fused with an egg cell that had its nucleus removed. The cell was then electrically stimulated so that it would begin cell division.

The successful cloning of a lamb raises the question: "Wherever the lamb went, was Mary sure to follow? In other words, how soon will scientists clone humans?"[14] Scientists point out that the procedure used to clone a sheep may not work for other mammals. Human beings use nuclear DNA differently from the way sheep embryos use DNA. And similar experiments, for example, have not worked in mice. Therefore, scientists may not be able to clone humans by this procedure.

Nevertheless, ethicists are once again considering the possibility that humans could be cloned.

The scientific concerns are significant. The procedure used to produce Dolly was extremely inefficient. Out of 277 cell fusions, researchers eventually produced only twenty-nine embryos that survived longer than six days. All twenty-nine embryos were implanted in ewes, thirteen became pregnant, and only one lamb was born as a result. These disastrous results alone should raise enough pro-life concerns considering the significant loss of human embryos that would be needed to produce one human clone.

Proponents of human cloning argue that it would be a worthwhile scientific endeavor for at least three reasons. First, cloning could be used to produce spare parts. The clone would be genetically identical to the original person so that a donated organ would not be rejected by the immune system. Second, they argue that cloning might be a way to replace a lost child. A dying infant or child could be cloned so that a couple would replace the child with a genetically identical child. Third, cloning could produce biological immortality. One woman approached scientists in order to clone her deceased father and offered to carry the cloned baby to term herself.[15]

While cloning of various organisms may be permissible, cloning a human being raises significant questions beginning with the issue of the sanctity of life. Human beings are created in the image of God (Gen. 1:26–27) and therefore differ from animals. Human cloning would certainly threaten the sanctity of human life at a number of levels. First, cloning is an inefficient process of procreation as shown in cloning of a sheep. Second, cloning would no doubt produce genetic accidents. Previous experiments with frogs produced numerous embryos that did not survive, and many of those that did survive developed into grotesque monsters. Third, researchers often clone human embryos for various experiments. Although the National Bioethics Advisory Commission did ban cloning of human beings, it permitted the cloning of human embryos for research. Since these embryos are ultimately destroyed, this research raises the same pro-life concerns discussed in the chapter on abortion.

Cloning (like artificial reproduction considered in the next chapter) represents a tampering with the reproductive process at the most basic level. Cloning a human being certainly strays substantially from God's intended procedure of a man and woman producing children within the bounds of matrimony (Gen. 2:24). All sorts of bizarre scenarios can be envisioned. Some homosexual advocates argue that cloning would be an ideal way for homosexual men to reproduce themselves.

Although cloning would be an alternative form of reproduction, it is reasonable to believe that human clones would still be fully human. For example, some people wonder if a clone would have a soul since this would be such a diversion from God's intended process of procreation. A traducian view of the origin of the soul (discussed in chapter 1) would imply that a cloned human being would have a soul. In a sense a clone would be no different from an identical twin.

Human cloning, like other forms of genetic engineering, could be used to usher in a "brave new world." James Bonner says that "there is nothing to prevent us from taking a thousand [cells]. We could grow any desired number of genetically identical people from individuals who have desirable characteristics."[16] Such a vision conjures up images of Alphas, Betas, Gammas, and Deltas from Aldous Huxley's book *Brave New World* and provides a dismal contrast to God's creation of each individual as unique.

Each person contributes to both the unity and diversity of humanity. Such a contribution is perhaps best expressed by the Jewish Midrash: "For a man stamps many coins in one mold and they are all alike; but the King who is king over all kings, the Holy One blessed be he, stamped every man in the mold of the first man, yet not one of them resembles his fellow."[17] Christians should reject future research plans to clone a human being and should reject using cloning as an alternative means of reproduction.

9

ARTIFICIAL REPRODUCTION

INFERTILITY has always been a devastating blow to any couple. In the past, little could be done. But recent advances in reproductive biology now provide millions of couples with the possibility of the wife becoming pregnant and their starting a family. While some reproductive technologies raise few moral concerns, many others are fraught with substantial ethical issues.

The demand for artificial reproduction has increased for two reasons: declining levels of fertility and legalized abortion. Male infertility has increased to a level estimated to be about one in ten. Various reasons have been suggested, including environmental factors such as pesticides, chemicals in food, and heightened levels of stress.[1] Female infertility may be due to congenital, environmental, and/or behavioral factors. The latter factor has become most significant because of increased sexual activity by young women who sustain low-level gynecological infections that may damage their reproductive system when left untreated.[2] Approximately one in every six couples of childbearing age has an infertility problem.[3]

Legalized abortion has also been a factor in the increased interest in artificial reproduction. Ready access to abortion has significantly reduced the number of children available for adoption. In the 1970s and 1980s, couples wanting a child began to seek medical solutions to infertility which were being developed, solutions that have fueled the revolution in reproductive technologies.

Artificial insemination is used as an alternative means of reproduction when male infertility is present. John Hunter, a London physician, was perhaps the first to use artificial insemination with humans in 1785. Today there are two types of artificial insemination: using the sperm of the husband (AIH: artificial insemination by the husband) and using the sperm of a donor (AID: artificial insemination by a donor). More recently artificial insemination has also been used for female infertility. Infertile women are impregnated with donor sperm from a husband or an outside donor so that couples can adopt children born to these surrogate mothers who carry the baby to term.

In vitro fertilization is also used for female infertility. Conception takes place outside the womb, which accounts for the popular term "test-tube-babies," even though conception occurs in a petri dish, not a test tube. The woman is treated with hormones to stimulate the maturation of eggs. The eggs are then removed by means of laparoscopy and placed in a petri dish and fertilized with sperm. After a period of time the developing embryos are surgically placed in the uterus.

Other forms of artificial reproduction include artificial sex selection, embryo transfer, and frozen embryos. Surrogate parenting is possible by using artificial insemination in which the husband's sperm is used to impregnate a donor mother.

ARTIFICIAL INSEMINATION BY THE HUSBAND

AIH consists of collecting the husband's sperm and injecting it into his wife. Couples often seek this procedure either because the husband is fertile but unable to participate in normal sexual relations or because the husband's sperm count is low. Periodically collecting sperm can increase the probability of pregnancy.

AIH is much less controversial than AID because it involves the husband. Although conception is not by means of the natural sex act, AIH does not destroy the personal and sexual aspects of the marriage bond and thus is open to less criticism. Few legal concerns surround this method since the child is genetically related to the parents. Questions of paternity and legal status are not a problem for a child conceived by AIH.

AIH raises few theological concerns as well. The only theological issue is the question of masturbation. The Roman Catholic Church has objected to AIH because it separates sex from the conjugal marital relationship. According to natural law theory, procreation through means other than those natural to the conjugal act is illicit and immoral.

To claim that masturbation in this case is sin is to remove it from its context. Although a couple does not experience the sex act together (though they can if they wish), the purpose is to provide a pregnancy and birth they will experience together. And if masturbation poses an ethical problem for the couple, the sperm can be collected from the vagina or a condom. Thus, AIH does not seem to inhibit sexual expression in the couple or to damage the marriage bond and is therefore an acceptable method of artificial reproduction.

ARTIFICIAL INSEMINATION BY A DONOR

AID is similar to AIH except that sperm from a donor is used instead of sperm from the husband. This singular exception leads to most of the questions surrounding this reproductive procedure. Most of those concerns are legal or ethical, but others are relevant as well.

More than twenty thousand children are born each year through AID. Sperm samples are usually obtained from undergraduate students or medical students who have had their genetic history checked thoroughly. Most doctors try to match the physical characteristics of the husband with those of the sperm donor.

Couples may seek AID for one of three reasons. First, the husband may be carrying a genetic disease he does not want to pass on to his child. Second, he may be sterile as a result of a disease or accident. Third, AID might be prescribed because of a concern over an antibody reaction from the mother (the husband may be Rh positive while she is Rh negative). In most cases injections of anti-Rh antibodies into the mother are sufficient to prevent damage to future Rh positive children.

The only major scientific concern with AID is the possibility of accidental incest. When the same sperm donor is used in many pregnancies, the potential for inbreeding increases. This is less of a concern in cities or larger communities, but looms larger in small communities, especially when the same sperm donor is used extensively. For example, researchers at the University of Wisconsin found that an average sperm donor is used for up to six pregnancies and some for as many as fifty pregnancies.[4]

Although AID has been practiced for many years, legal concerns can still surface. Most state laws concerning parent-child relations were not written with artificial insemination in mind. For that reason, sometimes the legal status of the child produced by AID can be uncertain. The major focus usually is on the legitimacy of the child. Since the child is not genetically related to the father, the potential exists that the child could be declared illegitimate by a court.[5]

The social concerns surrounding AID are significant. First, AID has increased the number of single-parent homes. Tens of thousands of single women each year use artificial insemination to bear a child. A survey of physicians that appeared in the *Journal of the American Medical Association* estimated that approximately 10 percent of the AID cases involved single women. Approximately half were heterosexuals without partners; the other half were lesbians using the procedure to produce a child for their "relationship."[6]

A second problem is that AID can adversely affect the marriage relationship. The psychological impact of AID can be quite profound in many marriages. Having to resort to AID is often a blow to the husband's masculinity.[7] His inability to produce children can develop into a deep feeling of failure or inferiority within a marriage relationship.

The secrecy surrounding the procedure often heightens the psychological trauma. The couple rarely know the identity of the donor and often do not make public the fact that they have used AID. The secret gives the procedure an illicit aura and can reinforce feelings of guilt.

A couple with an AID child may have difficulty explaining "who the child looks like," since they often want to keep the procedure secret. By contrast, a couple with an adopted child has less difficulty with these problems than a couple with an AID child. One psychotherapist found that AID mothers often struggled with guilt and fear that took on "undue proportion and power within the family."[8]

The major ethical and theological concern with AID is that it introduces a third party into the pregnancy, thereby weakening the marriage bond. This is especially true when artificial insemination is used by surrogate mothers. Surrogates are usually arranged through business associations that link women solicited through newspaper ads and chosen by couples according to their physical and mental characteristics as well as ethnic and religious backgrounds.

Whether donor sperm is used (normal AID) or a donor egg and a donor womb (surrogate mother) are used, both scenarios introduce a third party into the pregnancy. God's ideal for parenthood was for a man and woman to give birth to a child who is genetically related to them. While there are obvious exceptions to that ideal (adoptions), the divine ideal should be the standard used to judge AID.

Two Old Testament examples are often cited to support AID. The first is the story of Abraham and Sarah. When Sarah could not bear a child for Abraham, she said to him, "Go, sleep with my maidservant; perhaps I can build a family through her" (Gen. 16:2). The second is the provision of the levirate marriage of the kinsman-redeemer, who was to impregnate his deceased brother's wife if there was no heir (Deut. 25:5–10). Neither of these examples gives much support for AID. Nowhere does God approve Abraham and Sarah's act. If anything, Sarah's suggestion clouded God's lesson for them. Moreover, the application of either event to today is questionable. Abraham and Sarah's example took place within a polygamous relationship and levirate marriage was applicable only to the Old Testament theocracy. And in both examples the unitive and procreative aspects of marriage remained intact; these do not take place when AID is used.

Another theological question is whether AID is an act of adultery. Some similarities exist between the two. In normal AID, the wife becomes pregnant from someone else's sperm. In the case of surrogate parenting, the surrogate mother becomes pregnant from the husband's sperm. But the use of donor sperm is the only real similarity with adultery. Adultery involves sexual infidelity by a sexual relationship between a married person and someone not his or her spouse. AID involves the transfer of gametes between consenting adults. No sexual contact occurs, and there is mutual consent of the husband and wife.

The New Testament identifies two factors that constitute adultery: attitude and action. Jesus taught that "anyone who looks at a woman lustfully has already committed adultery with her in his heart" (Matt. 5:28). This attitude is not present in AID. Paul taught that a man becomes "one body" with a prostitute (1 Cor. 6:12–16). No such action is found in AID. Therefore, it is inappropriate to call AID a form of adultery.

Nevertheless, AID cannot be endorsed as a form of artificial reproduction. AID violates a biblical view of parenthood by introducing a third party into the pregnancy, and it also violates a biblical view of sexual relations by separating the unitive and procreative aspects of human sexuality within the bonds of marriage.

ARTIFICIAL SEX SELECTION

Artificial insemination has spawned a separate question: Should parents select the gender of their child? By using new sperm-separation techniques, couples can improve the probability of obtaining a child of the desired sex.

Until recently sex selection was nothing more than science fiction. Folklore contained many stories of how to predetermine the sex of a child. Aristotle and the Talmud recommended placing the bed on a north-south axis for those wanting boys. Anaxagoras believed that lying on the right side (considered the superior side) would produce a boy (considered the superior sex). One folk myth said a man should hang his pants on the right bedpost before sexual intercourse in order to have a son and on the left for a daughter. One German folk tradition recommended that a man take an ax along to bed in order to produce a son, and leave the ax in the woodshed to produce a daughter.

In 1970, David Rorvick wrote *Your Baby's Sex: Now You Can Choose,*[9] which focused on certain physical indications, such as those used in the rhythm method of birth control, to increase the likelihood of having a child of a particular gender. While somewhat more effective than chance, the techniques only slightly improved the odds over the 50:50 ratio.

New techniques have been developed based on reproductive physiology. The gender of a child is determined by the sperm of the male. Sperm with Y chromosomes will produce boys, while sperm with X chromosomes will produce girls. Researchers have found at least five methods by which to separate the two types of sperm, using such differences as sperm weight, sperm "swimming" speed, and electrical charge.

The most commonly used means is the Ericson method developed by the reproductive physiologist Ronald Ericson more than twenty years ago. Since Y sperm tend to swim faster and stronger under certain conditions, physicians can separate them from X sperm by having them swim through a series of viscous layers. Though not totally foolproof, the method has a published success rate of 75 percent for boys and 69 percent for girls.[10]

Future advances in the technology will no doubt improve the success rate. For example, scientists have observed slightly different charges on the two types of sperm. By using electrical charges, they can further separate Y sperm from X sperm and thereby make the procedure even more effective.

While sex selection may be very beneficial in agriculture and animal husbandry, its application to humans is more questionable. Some couples have used it to prevent a genetic disease that might be sex-linked. But most others use it to produce a child of the desired sex.

The social implications are significant. Research has shown that couples would choose the sex of their child if the procedure was relatively simple and inexpensive.[11] Of the couples who expressed a preference, about 90 percent wanted the firstborn to be a boy. If they could have only one child, 72 percent wanted a boy.

The actual impact on society would be difficult to determine. Surveys give only a rough guideline of actual preference. Sex selection may well be influenced by social pressure and personal taste. Also, only a fraction of couples are choosing artificial sex selection, and the technology is not 100 percent effective. But as more couples choose this procedure and as its effectiveness increases, the impact on society could be significant.

Widespread use of sex selection could dramatically increase the number of boys. And even if the procedure did not increase the number of boys, it could certainly transform society into a nation of older brothers and younger sisters, at least subtly implying that women are second-class citizens.

An important ethical question is whether parents have the right to determine the sex of their child. And a broader question is whether society at large has a right to decide the sex of children born into it.

At a time when more and more rights are being claimed, more parents will likely demand the right to determine the sex of their children. But will that right lead to demands for other rights? Is it not possible that the right of sex selection will eventually lead to the right of genetic specification? Selecting the gender of one's child is considered the most fundamental aspect of that child. Choosing hair color, eye color, stature, and other characteristics would be a logical next step.

Moreover, should we not be concerned about sexual stereotyping? The present chauvinistic condition in the world is troubling. Selecting the sex of a child is more than just picking out blue or pink baby outfits. And preferring boys over girls has led to disastrous consequences in other countries. Selective abortion and infanticide are routinely practiced in countries like India and China based on the assumption that boys have more value than girls.

The Bible teaches that children are a gift from God (Ps. 127:3) and are entrusted to parents for care and nurture. Parents who want control over the gender of their child should evaluate their motives and consider the possible implications of their decision, both to their family and to society.

IN VITRO FERTILIZATION

When Aldous Huxley wrote his famous book *Brave New World* in 1932, few thought what he predicted would take place in their lifetimes. When Louise Brown was born on July 25, 1978, as the first "test-tube" baby, many believed that a new era had arrived. In some ways the new reproductive technologies are a fulfillment of that vision, in most ways they are not.

In vitro fertilization (known as IVF) is a procedure that allows an egg to be fertilized and grown outside the womb for a short period of time. With the future development of an artificial placenta, this period could be extended to perhaps the entire gestational period.

Since the initial pioneering work on IVF, many other methods have been developed in an effort to treat millions of infertile couples in the U.S.[12] These include: Gamete Intrafallopian Transfer (GIFT), in which a physician using a laparoscope inserts eggs and sperm directly into a woman's fallopian tube so that fertilization can take place; Intrauterine Insemination (IUI), in which frozen sperm of the husband or a donor is inserted by a catheter into the uterus, bypassing the cervix and upper vagina; Zygote Intrafallopian Transfer (ZIFT), a two-step procedure whereby eggs are fertilized in the laboratory and any resulting zygotes are transferred to a fallopian tube; and Intracytoplasmic Sperm Injection (ICSI), in which a physician using a microscopic pipette injects a single sperm into an egg and the zygote is placed in the uterus.

Costs for these procedures vary dramatically since treatments can vary from fertility drugs to microsurgery to fairly exotic, high tech methods. The cost of an IVF treatment can range from $6,000 to more than $50,000 per live birth.[13] A national survey of all high-tech infertility treatments found an average cost of $7,000 with a range of prices from $4,000 to $11,000 per try.[14] Usually only the rich or the well-insured can afford these reproductive technologies.

How effective are these technologies? In 1993, the 267 clinics reporting to the American Society for Reproductive Medicine started 41,209 assisted-reproduction procedures and 8,741 resulted in live births, which is a "success rate" of 21.2 percent.[15]

Scientists have developed a test that appears to increase significantly the changes of a successful IVF treatment. At present only about 30 percent of women become pregnant after one round of IVF treatment. But a new test detects the presence of a genetic marker (called sHLA-G) can increase the chance of success to 60 percent.[16]

The major scientific concern with IVF was the limited amount of prior experimentation. Critics charged that experimentation should have been done before the technique was applied to human subjects. A moratorium had been proposed on IVF in 1972 in order to have time to determine the potential risk of abnormalities. One prominent scientist said, "It is my feeling that we must be very sure we are able to produce normal young by this method in monkeys before we have the temerity to move ahead in the human."[17] Nevertheless, concerns about potential abnormalities were quickly pushed aside as more and more test-tube babies were born.

A number of legal concerns have arisen from these reproductive procedures. The 1981 case of Mario and Elsa Rios demonstrates the legal tangle that can develop.

The Rioses wanted children and went to a clinic in Australia. Three of Mrs. Rios's eggs were fertilized in vitro with sperm from an anonymous sperm donor. One was implanted and the other two were frozen. Ten days later the implanted embryo spontaneously aborted. But before the clinic could implant the other two, the Rioses were killed in a plane crash in South America.

Two kinds of questions surfaced. First, did these frozen embryos have a right to inheritance and did they have a right to life? Mr. and Mrs. Rios were multimillionaires. Were those embryos potential millionaires? Did they have a right to inherit the Rios's fortune? Second, did those frozen embryos have a right to life? Was the IVF clinic obliged to protect embryos? Should the Australian clinic have implanted those embryos in a surrogate mother who would have had to carry them to term?

Other questions surfaced as well. For example, who were the legal father and mother? Were the legal parents Mr. Rios, Mrs. Rios, an anonymous sperm donor, a surrogate mother, and possibly an adoptive father and mother? The children that could have been born could have had as many as six "potential parents."

Questions of paternity especially loom large with surrogate parenting. The most famous case was the battle of custody over "Baby M." William and Elizabeth Stern entered into a contract with Mary Beth Whitehead to carry their child. As her pregnancy progressed, Whitehead began to have doubts and developed the inevitable maternal feelings a mother would expect to have for a child she is carrying. She decided to keep the child and forced a judge in New Jersey to resolve this modern-day "Solomon dilemma."

The reverse of the "Solomon dilemma" also occurred in a case in which neither the couple nor the surrogate mother wanted the child. Alexander Malahoff contracted with Judy Stiver to be a surrogate mother. Unfortunately young Christopher was born with an infection and microcephaly. Malahoff disavowed the child and threatened to sue. The issue was uncertain, and the child remained in a foster-care facility. Then during the airing of the Phil Donahue Show, blood and tissue tests were brought forward revealing that the child was Judy Stiver's and her husband's. They were required to raise the child.

A court has also ruled that a lesbian mother who gave birth to twin girls with eggs donated by her domestic partner is the sole legal parent of the children. The judge ruled that the donor relinquished her parental rights when she signed an egg donation consent form.[18]

The various legal issues surrounding IVF and related procedures merely underscore the proliferating nature of the technology. The reproductive endocrinologist Martin Quigley distinguished the "old fashioned IVF" from these newer forms. "The modern way," he noted, "mixes and matches donors and recipients."[19] A woman's egg could be fertilized by a donor's sperm, or a donor's egg might be fertilized by the husband's sperm. And any of these matches could then be placed in the wife or in a surrogate mother. The reproductive possibilities are staggering.

The surrogate mother could actually be a surrogate grandmother. In 1988, Pat

Anthony, a forty-nine-year-old grandmother in South Africa, gave birth to her own grandchildren. She was implanted with her daughter's eggs that had been fertilized in the laboratory and subsequently gave birth to triplets.[20]

As Anthony's example shows, age may no longer be a limitation for women wanting to become pregnant. Physicians have been able to take an egg from a younger woman and implant it in an older woman (one woman in her sixties gave birth in this way) even if she has been through menopause. Egg donation is also becoming more widely available and accepted as egg brokerage houses match recipients with donors.[21]

Some reproductive technologies open up the possibility of female reproduction without male involvement. Initial research on egg fusion at Vanderbilt University demonstrated the future possibility of taking an egg from one woman and fusing it with the egg of another woman.[22] The procedure has attracted the attention of lesbian groups because the procedure would produce a girl who is genetically related to each of the women who donated an egg.

A major ethical concern with IVF and other forms of reproductive technology is the status and loss of embryos. The low success rate of some of the procedures and the willingness of some clinics to fertilize many eggs and then choose a likely candidate raise moral questions about the status of the unborn being produced by artificial reproduction. Proponents argue that the loss is not excessive. Opponents argue that the loss is unacceptable or at least call for defining an acceptable level of success.

Another ethical concern is with the proliferating technologies. While IVF may be less ethically questionable, it has spawned a whole array of technologies that allow for mixing and matching genetic material and implanting in different women. The possible arrangements are nearly limitless, but the ethical consequences of many of these arrangements are questionable.

BIBLICAL PERSPECTIVE

Providing a comprehensive answer to IVF and the associated reproductive technologies is becoming more difficult because of the proliferation of such technologies. A better way to discern the ethics of these procedures is to consider each of them in light of the following biblical principles.

The first principle is the sanctity of human life. Human beings are created in the image of God (Gen. 1:26–27) and therefore have dignity and value. God's special care and protection extend even to unborn children (Ps. 139). Reproductive technologies that threaten the sanctity of human life come under the same criticism as abortion.

The sanctity of life may be threatened in at least three ways. First is the potential loss of fetal life. Some reproductive technologies are inefficient and therefore result in an unacceptable loss of life. Another threat is the practice of destroying fertilized ova if they appear abnormal. Finally, hyperfertilization is also problematic. Hyperfertilization is the process in which many eggs are fertilized simultaneously, one is selected for implantation, and the others are thrown away.

This is a concern not only for the clinical use of embryos; it also concerns the research use of embryos. In the past, the United States government placed a moratorium on research on embryo and fetal experimentation. The Clinton administration lifted the ban in the 1990s, and federal funding has been recommended on research on human embryos up to fourteen days after fertilization.[23] This research also violates the biblical principle of the sanctity of human life.

A second principle is a biblical view of sexual relations (Gen. 2:24). Many reproductive technologies separate the unitive from the procreative aspects of human reproduction. To use the vernacular phrases, "making love" and "making babies" are supposed to be associated in the same act. Sexual intimacy, the communication of love, and the desire for children are supposed to be unified within the bounds of matrimony. Artificial reproduction frequently separates these functions and thus poses a potential threat to the completeness God intended for marriage. While some ethicists believe that such an intervention is sufficient to reject all reproductive technologies, most others accept such an intervention as permissible if other ethical concerns are not present.

A third principle is a biblical view of parenthood (Genesis 1:28). God ordained marriage as the union of a man and a woman who would give birth to a child that is genetically related to them. While there are exceptions to this ideal, this standard should be used to judge reproductive technologies. As stated earlier, procedures such as surrogate parenting and embryo transfer clearly introduce a third party into the pregnancy and affect the marriage bond.

Motherhood may also be affected. Childbearing would no longer be a natural outcome of procreation. The proliferation of surrogate mothers blurs the true relationship between procreation and parenthood. God intends that the family thrive (Eph. 6:1–4; Col. 3:18–21), and some of these procedures pose a threat to the stability of the family.

By contrast, a family can survive without children. God determines birth (Genesis 4:1; 17:16; Ruth 4:13) and is in control over even barren wombs (Deut. 7:14). Childless women are not displeasing to God, as the testimonies of Sarah (Genesis 18), Rachel (Genesis 29—30), Hannah (1 Samuel 1), and Anna (Luke 2:36–38) attest. God is in control and can bring great blessing out of the heartbreak of infertility.

Couples considering artificial reproduction should also consider other less ethically questionable options. These options include medical options such as reconstructive surgery (tuboplasty) and drug treatments, adoption, foster care, or remaining childless and having more time for a church or community ministry.

Fundamental to all this should be an attitude of seeking the Lord's will. Abraham and Sarah asked the Lord for a child (Genesis 18). When He did not meet their timetable, they took matters in their own hands with disastrous results. By contrast Hannah (1 Samuel 1) sought the Lord and was patient for His provision. Before couples seek medical counsel, they should seek the Lord's will and then count the costs and consider the ethical issues involved.

10

SEXUAL ETHICS

APPROXIMATELY EIGHT THOUSANDS teenagers lose their virginity every day. In the process many will become pregnant and many more will contract a sexually transmitted disease (STD). Already one in four Americans has an STD, and this percentage is increasing each year.

The reason for the increase in sexual promiscuity is both philosophical and cultural. In the last few decades society has shifted from a Judeo-Christian foundation to a secular one. Two cultural forces have accelerated this philosophical shift. The first is the entertainment media (television, movies, rock music, MTV). The second is sex education (sex education classes, school-based clinics). These two forces have transformed the social landscape of America and made promiscuity a virtue and virginity a "problem" to be solved.

TEENAGE SEXUALITY

America faces a teenage sexuality crisis. A Lou Harris poll commissioned by Planned Parenthood discovered that 46 percent of sixteen-year-olds and 57 percent of seventeen-year-olds have had sexual intercourse.[1]

Moreover, these numbers are not skewed by impoverished, inner city youths from broken homes. One New York polling firm posed questions to 1,300 students in sixteen high schools in suburban areas in order to get a reading of "mainstream" adolescent attitudes. The firm discovered that 57 percent lost virginity in high school, and 79 percent lost virginity by the end of college. The average age of girls when they first had sex was 16.9. Thirty-three percent of the high school students had sex once a month to once a week, and 52 percent of the college students had sex once a month to once a week.[2]

In the 1960s, there were only 2 STDs and both were curable. At that time, 1 in every 32 teenagers had an STD. By 1983, the ratio was 1 in 18. Today the ratio is 1 in 4, and more than thirty STDs (nearly a third) are incurable.

Speaking to the National School Board Association, William Bennett, the secretary of education during the second Reagan Administration, warned that "the statistics by which we measure how our children—how our boys and girls—are treating one another sexually are little short of staggering."[3] Here are just a few of the heartbreaking statistics from his message:

- More than one-half of America's young people have had sexual intercourse by the time they are seventeen.

- More than one million teenage girls in the U.S. become pregnant each year. Of those who give birth, nearly half are not yet eighteen.

- Teen pregnancy rates are at an all-time high. A 25 percent decline in birth rates between 1970 and 1984 is due to a doubling of the abortion rate during that period. More than four hundred thousand teenage girls now have abortions each year.

- Unwed teenage births rose 200 percent between 1960 and 1980.

- Forty percent of fourteen-year-old girls will become pregnant by the time they are nineteen.

"These numbers," Bennett concluded, "are an irrefutable indictment of sex education's effectiveness in reducing teenage sexual activity and pregnancies."[4]

Kids are trying sex at an earlier age than ever before. More than a third of fifteen-year-old boys have had sexual intercourse as have 27 percent of the fifteen-year-old girls. Among sexually active teenage girls, 61 percent have had multiple partners.[5] The reasons for such early sexual experimentation are many.

Biology is one reason. Teenagers are maturing faster sexually because of better health and nutrition. Since the turn of the century, for example, the onset of menstruation in girls has dropped three months each decade. Consequently, urges that used to arise in the mid-teens now explode in the early teens. Meanwhile, the typical age of a person's first marriage has increased more than four years since the 1950s.

A sex-saturated society is another reason. Sex is used to sell everything from cars to toothpaste. Sexual innuendos clutter almost every TV program and movie. And explicit nudity and sensuality that used to be reserved for R-rated movies has found its way into homes through broadcast and cable television. Media researchers calculate that teenagers see approximately five hours of television each day, which means that they have seen nearly 14,000 sexual encounters within a year just on television.

Lack of parental supervision and direction is a third reason. Working parents and reductions in after-school programs have left teenagers with less supervision and a looser after-school life. In the inner city, the scarcity of jobs and parents, coupled with a cynical view of the future, invites teenage promiscuity and its inevitable consequences. Adolescent boys in the suburbs trying to prove their masculinity, herd into groups like the infamous score-keeping Spur Posse gang in California.

Even when teenagers want to sit out the sexual revolution, they often get little help from parents who may be too embarrassed or intimidated to talk to their children. Parents, in fact, often lag behind their kids in sexual information. At one sex-education workshop held by Girls Inc. (formerly Girls Club of America), nearly half of the mothers had never seen a condom. Other mothers did not want to talk about sex because they were molested as children and were fearful of talking about sex with their daughters.[6]

Teenagers are also getting mixed messages. In any given week they are likely to hear many of the following contradictory messages. "No sex unless you're married." "No sex unless you're older." "No sex unless you're protected." "No sex unless you're in love." No wonder adolescents are confused.

SEX EDUCATION

For more than thirty years proponents of comprehensive sex education have argued that giving sexual information to young children and adolescents will reduce the number of unplanned pregnancies and sexually transmitted diseases. In that effort nearly $3 billion has been spent on federal Title X family planning services, yet the number of teenage pregnancies and abortions rise.

Perhaps one of the most devastating popular critiques of comprehensive sex education came from Barbara Dafoe Whitehead. This journalist who said that Dan Quayle was right, also was willing to say that sex education was wrong. Her article "The Failure of Sex Education" demonstrated that sex education neither reduced pregnancy nor slowed the spread of STDs.[7]

Comprehensive sex education is mandated in at least seventeen states, so Whitehead chose one of those states and focused her analysis on the sex education experiment in New Jersey. Like other curricula the New Jersey sex education program rests on certain questionable assumptions.

The first assumption is that children are "sexual from birth." Sex educators reject the classic notion of a latency period until approximately age twelve. They argue that you are "being sexual when you throw your arms around your grandpa and give him a hug."[8]

Another assumption is that children are sexually miseducated. Parents, to put it simply, have not done their job, so we need "professionals" to do it right. Parents try to protect their children, fail to affirm their sexuality, and even discuss sexuality in a context of moralizing. The media, they say, is also guilty of providing sexual misinformation.

Finally, if miseducation is the problem, then sex education in the schools is the solution. Parents are failing miserably at the task, so "it is time to turn the job over to the schools. Schools occupy a safe middle ground between Mom and MTV."[9]

New Jersey uses the *Learning about Family Life* curriculum. While it discusses such things as sexual desire, AIDS, divorce, condoms, and masturbation, it nearly ignores such issues as abstinence, marriage, self-control, and virginity. One technique promoted to prevent pregnancy and STDs is noncoital sex, or what some sex educators call outercourse. Yet evidence exists to suggest that teaching teenagers to explore their sexuality through noncoital techniques will lead to coitus. Ultimately, outercourse will lead to intercourse.

Whitehead concluded that comprehensive sex education has been a failure. For example, the percentage of teenage births to unwed mothers rose from 67 percent in 1980 and to 84 percent in 1991. In the place of this failed curriculum, Whitehead described a better program. She found that "sex education works best when it combines clear messages about behavior with strong moral and logistical support for the behavior sought."[10] One example she cited was the Postponing Sexual Involvement program at Grady Memorial Hospital in Atlanta, Georgia, which offers more than a "Just say no" message. It reinforces the message by having adolescents practice the desired behavior and enlists the aid of older teenagers to teach younger teenagers how to resist sexual advances. Whitehead also found that "religiously observant teens" are less likely to experiment sexually, thus providing an opportunity for church-related programs to help stem the tide of teenage pregnancy.[11]

Contrast this, however, with what has been derisively called "the condom gospel." Sex educators today promote the dissemination of sex education information and the distribution of condoms to deal with the problems of teen pregnancy and STDs.

THE CASE AGAINST CONDOMS

At the 1987 World Congress of Sexologists, Theresa Crenshaw asked the audience, "If you had the available partner of your dreams and knew that person carried HIV, how many of you would have sex, depending on a condom for your protection?" None of the 800 members of the audience raised their hand.[12]

A workshop held in 2000 summarized "the scientific evidence of condom effectiveness for sexually transmitted diseases." The panel "found the published epidemiology literature to be inadequate" and could only conclude that condom use might be effective in reducing "the risk of HIV transmission in men and women and gonorrhea in men."[13]

Are condoms a safe and effective way to reduce pregnancy and STDs? Sex educators seem to think so. Every day sex education classes throughout this country promote condoms as a means of safe sex or at least safer sex. But the research on condoms provides no such guarantee.

For example, Susan Weller, writing in *Social Science Medicine*, evaluated all research published prior to July 1990 on condom effectiveness. She reported that condoms are only 87 percent effective in preventing pregnancy and 69 percent effective in reducing the risk of HIV infection.[14] This 69 percent effectiveness rate is also the same as a 31 percent failure rate in preventing AIDS transmission. And according to a study in the 1992 *Family Planning Perspectives*, 15 percent of married couples who use condoms for birth control end up with an unplanned pregnancy within the first year.[15]

So why has condom distribution become the centerpiece of the U.S. AIDS policy and the most frequently promoted aspect of comprehensive sex education? For many years the answer to that question was an a priori commitment to condoms and a safe sex message over an abstinence message. But in recent years sex educators and public health officials have been pointing to one study that seemed to vindicate the condom policy.

The study was presented at the Ninth International Conference on AIDS held in Berlin on June 9, 1993. The study involved 304 couples with one partner who was HIV positive. Of the 123 couples who used condoms with each act of sexual intercourse, not a single negative HIV partner became positive.[16] So proponents of condom distribution thought they had scientific vindication for their views.

Unfortunately that is not the whole story. Condoms do appear to be effective in stopping the spread of AIDS when used "correctly and consistently." Most individuals, however, do not use them "correctly and consistently." What happens to them? Well, it turns out that part of the study received much less attention. Of the 122 couples who could not be taught to use condoms properly, the non-HIV partner in 12 of those couples became HIV positive. Undoubtedly, over time even more partners will contract AIDS.

How well does this study apply to the general population? Not very well. This study group was quite dissimilar from the general population. For example, they knew the HIV status of their spouse and therefore had a vested interest in protecting themselves. They were responsible partners and in a committed monogamous relationship. In essence their actions and attitudes differed dramatically from teenagers and single adults who do not know the HIV status of their partners, are often reckless, and have multiple sexual partners.

The study did show that condoms will reduce the risk of STDs if they are used correctly and consistently. But what percentage of our population will use condoms in that way, especially when we begin to understand the strict requirements that must be met? Nicholas Fiumara, director of the Massachusetts Department of Public Health, explained the conditions necessary for condoms to work. For condoms to be effective, "there is no preliminary sex play, the condom is intact before use, the condom is put on correctly and taken off correctly. However, the male population has never been able to fulfill the very first requirement."[17]

Indeed, how many will fulfill that requirement each and every time? Contrary to claims by sex educators, condom education does not significantly change sexual behavior. The April 1988 issue of the *American Journal of Public Health* stated that a year-long effort at condom education in San Francisco schools resulted in only 8 percent of the boys and 2 percent of the girls using condoms every time they had sex.[18]

And even when sexual partners use condoms, sometimes condoms fail. Most consumers do not know that the Federal Drug Administration (FDA) quality-control standards allow for a maximum failure rate of 4 per 1,000 using a water fill test. Electron micrographs reveal voids five microns in size (about fifty times larger than the HIV virus) with some inherent flaws as large as fifty microns.

The Department of Health and Human Services reported that "one of every five batches of condoms tested in a government inspection program over the last four months failed to meet the minimum standards for leaks."[19] Present FDA standards allow up to four condoms per thousand to leak water in lots acceptable for sale to the public.[20] Many health professionals question the relevance of pouring ten ounces of water in a condom, especially when some data show that leakage in condoms is higher in biological situations.

And even if condoms are used correctly, do not break, and do not leak, they are still far from 100 percent effective. The Medical Institute for Sexual Health reported that "medical studies confirm that condoms do not offer much, if any, protection in the transmission of chlamydia and human papillomavirus, two serious STDs with prevalence as high as 40 percent among sexually active teenagers."[21]

Nevertheless, condoms have become the centerpiece of the U.S. AIDS policy and the major recommendation of most sex education classes in America. Many sex educators have stopped calling their curricula "safe sex" and have renamed them "safer sex," focusing instead on various risk reduction methods. But is this false sense of security and protection actually increasing the risks young people face? Victor Cline, professor of psychology at the University of Utah, thought so. He believed that the condoms-equal-safe-sex message offers kids a deadly false sense of security.

> If kids buy the notion that if they just use condoms they will be safe
> from AIDS or any other sexually transmitted disease whenever they
> have sex, they are being seriously misled. They should be correctly in-
> formed that having sex with any partner having the AIDS virus is
> life-threatening, condoms or no condoms. It would be analogous to
> playing Russian roulette with two bullets in your six chambers. Using
> condoms removes only one of the bullets. The gun still remains
> deadly with the potential of lethal outcome.[22]

SCHOOL-BASED HEALTH CLINICS

As comprehensive sex education curricula have been promoted in the schools, clinics have been established to provide teens greater access to birth control information and devices. Proponents cite studies that supposedly demonstrate the effectiveness of these clinics on teen sexual behavior. Yet a more careful evaluation of the statistics involved suggests that school-based health clinics do not lower the teen pregnancy rate.

A national study done by the Institute for Research and Evaluation showed that community-based clinics used by teenagers actually increased teen pregnancy. A two-year study by Joseph Olsen and Stan Weed found that teenage participation in these clinics lowered teen birth rates. But when pregnancies ending in miscarriage or abortion were factored in, the total teen pregnancy rates increased by as much as 120 pregnancies per 1,000 clients.[23] When their research was challenged because of their use of weighting techniques and reliance on statewide data, Olsen and Weed reworked the data to answer these objections for a second report and found that their conclusion was correct.

Douglas Kirby, the former director of the Center for Population Options, released the results of the Center's study of school-based health clinics. Even though committed to comprehensive sex education and school-based clinics, he had to admit the following: "We have been engaged in a research project for several years on the impact of school-based clinics. . . . We find basically that there is no measurable impact upon the use of birth control, not upon pregnancy rates or birthrates."[24]

The problem is simple, yet education is not the answer. Teaching comprehensive sex education, distributing condoms, and establishing school-based clinics are not effective. When your audience is impressionable teens entering puberty, explicit sex education does more to entice than to educate. Teaching them the "facts" about sex without providing any moral framework merely breaks down mental barriers of shame and innocence while encouraging teens to experiment sexually.

A Louis Harris poll conducted for Planned Parenthood found that the highest rates of teen sexual activity were among those who had comprehensive sex education, as opposed to those who had less.[25] In the 1980s, a Congressional study found that a decade-and-a-half of comprehensive, safe sex education resulted in a doubling in the number of sexually active teenage women.[26]

Perhaps the most disturbing statistic comes from Deborah Anne Dawson, a survey research consultant. Writing in Planned Parenthood's *Family Planning Perspectives*, she concluded that "prior contraceptive education increases the odds of starting intercourse [at the age of 14] by a factor of 1.5."[27] While a factor of 1.5 might not seem like much, it is a 50 percent increase. In other words comprehensive sex education increases a teenager's likelihood of sexual activity (thus increasing their changes of pregnancy and STDs) by 50 percent.

Sex education programs do not prevent pregnancy; they promote it. Education does not reduce the likelihood of getting pregnant and contracting disease; it increases it. Students' heads may be full of facts about sex, but such facts do not necessarily change their behavior. A *New York Times* writer vividly illustrated this point as she began her story about teenage pregnancy by relating a personal experience.

I was sitting at a table with half a dozen 16-year-old girls, listening with some amazement as they showed off their knowledge of human sexuality. They knew how long sperm lived inside the body and how many women out of 100 using a diaphragm were statistically likely to get pregnant. One girl recited the steps of the ovulation cycle from day one to day twenty-eight. There was just one problem with this performance. Every one of the girls was pregnant.[28]

Our society today is filled with teenagers and young adults who know a lot about human sexuality. They probably know more about sex than any generation that has preceded them, but education is not enough. Sex education can increase the knowledge students have about sexuality, but it does not necessarily affect their values or behavior. Since 1970, the federal government has spent nearly $3 billion on Title X sex education programs. During that period of time nonmarital teen births increased 61 percent and nonmarital pregnancy rates (fifteen-to-nineteen-year-olds) increased 87 percent.[29]

Douglas Kirby wrote these disturbing observations in the *Journal of School Health*:

> Past studies of sex education suggest several conclusions. They indicate that sex education programs can increase knowledge, but they also indicate that most programs have relatively little impact on values, particularly values regarding one's personal behavior. They also indicate that programs do not affect the incidence of sexual activity. According to one study, sex education programs may increase the use of birth control among some groups, but not among others. Results from another study indicate they have no measurable impact on the use of birth control. According to one study, they are associated with lower pregnancy rates, while another study indicates they are not. Programs certainly do not appear to have as dramatic an impact on behavior as professionals once has hoped.[30]

ABSTINENCE IS THE ANSWER

Less than a decade ago an abstinence-only program was rare in the public schools. Today directive abstinence programs can be found in many school districts while battles are fought in other school districts for their inclusion or removal. While proponents of abstinence programs run for school board or influence existing school board members, groups like Planned Parenthood bring lawsuits against districts that use abstinence-based curricula, arguing that such curricula are inaccurate or incomplete. At least a dozen abstinence-based curricula are on the market, with the largest being Sex Respect (Bradley, IL) and Teen-Aid (Spokane, WA).

Both popularity and politics caused the emergence of abstinence-only programs as an alternative to comprehensive sex education programs. Parents concerned about the ineffectiveness of the safe-sex message eagerly embraced the message of abstinence. And political funding helped spread the message and legitimize its educational value. The Adolescent Family Life Act, enacted in 1981 by the Reagan Administration, created Title XX and set aside $2 million a year for the development and implementation of abstinence-based programs. Although the Clinton Administration later cut funding for abstinence programs, the earlier funding in the 1980s helped groups like Sex Respect and Teen-Aid launch abstinence programs in the schools.

Parents and children have embraced the abstinence message in significant numbers. One national poll by the University of Chicago found that 68 percent of adults surveyed said premarital sex among teenagers is "always wrong."[31] A 1994 poll for *USA Weekend* asked more than 1,200 teens and adults what they thought of "several high profile athletes [who] are saying in public that they have abstained from sex before marriage and are telling teens to do the same." Seventy-two percent of the teens and 78 percent of the adults said they agree with the pro-abstinence message.[32]

A nationwide survey of parents with children age 17 or under living at home found that 68 percent want schools to teach teens that "individuals who are not sexually active until marriage have the best chances of marital stability and happiness." Ninety-one percent of parents "want teens to be taught to abstain from sexual activity during high school years."[33]

Parental and teen enthusiasm for abstinence-only education is well founded. Even though some opponents of have characterized the abstinence message as being naive or inadequate, good reasons exist for promoting abstinence in schools and society.

First, teenagers want to learn about abstinence. Contrary to the often-repeated teenage claim, not "everyone's doing it." More than half of teenagers are virgins until they are at least 17 years of age.[34] Data from the Centers for Disease Control and Prevention shows a reversal in teenage sexual behavior. The Center's 1990 report found that 54.3 percent of teens in grades 9–12 had had intercourse. But by 2001, 54.4 percent of high schoolers said that they had not had sexual relations.[35]

Not only is a majority of teenagers abstaining from sex; teens also want more help in staying sexually pure in a sex-saturated society. Emory University surveyed one thousand sexually experienced teen girls by asking them what they would like to learn to reduce teen pregnancy. Nearly 85 percent said, "How to say no without hurting the other person's feelings."[36]

While serving as the secretary of education, William Bennett delivered a speech to the National School Board Association and commented about the Emory University study.

A teen service program at Atlanta Grady Memorial Hospital, for example, found that of the girls under age sixteen surveyed, nine out of ten wanted to learn how to say "no." Let me underline this. This is not just Reagan and Bennett talking—it's girls under sixteen talking. Well, one way to help them to say "no" is for adults who care to teach them the reasons to say "no" and to give them the necessary moral support and encouragement to keep on saying it.[37]

Second, abstinence prevents pregnancy. Proponents of abstinence-only programs argue that abstinence will significantly lower the teenage pregnancy rate, and they cite numerous anecdotes and statistics to make their case. Consider the following examples:

- After the San Marcos Junior High in San Marcos, California, adopted the Teen-Aid abstinence-only program, the school's pregnancy rate dropped from 147 to 20 in a two-year period.[38]

- An abstinence-only program for girls in Washington, DC, has seen only one of four hundred girls become pregnant. Elayne Bennett, director of "Best Friends," says that between twenty and seventy pregnancies are common for this age-group in the District of Columbia.[39]

- Nathan Hale Middle School near Chicago adopted the abstinence-only program Project Taking Charge to combat its pregnancy rate among eighth-graders. Although adults were skeptical, the school graduated three pregnancy-free classes in a row.[40]

- Evaluations of the Sex Respect programs revealed a pregnancy rate of only 5 percent—far lower than a typical safe-sex program.[41]

Over a ten-year period (1991–2001) there was a rapid decline (a decrease of one-third) in teen pregnancies. Researchers found that more than half of this decline in teen pregnancies can be attributed to a reduction in teenage sexual activity.[42]

Critics of abstinence programs believe that teaching abstinence-only is unrealistic when young people are sexually active. These critics often question the statistics cited by proponents of abstinence. They often question the methodology of the studies and note that these studies are not subjected to peer-review journals. For example, the *San Diego Union* looked into the success story from San Marcos, California, where the pregnancy rate supposedly went from 147 to only 20. The reporter was not able to document the 20 figure.[43]

Sex Respect noted that Stan Weed was working on articles concerning the effectiveness of Sex Respect that will be submitted to peer-review journals.[44] Also Teen-Aid's response to the *San Diego Union* story was that the reporter did not talk to the right people and that the 147 figure and the 20 figure were the school district's figures.

A new study based on the data from the National Longitudinal Study of Adolescent Health showed that teens who make a virginity pledge have substantially lower levels of sexual activity and better life outcomes. In particular, adolescents who take a virginity pledge: (1) are less likely to experience a teen pregnancy, (2) are less likely to be sexually active while in high school, (3) are less like to give birth as teens or young adults, and (4) are less likely to give birth out of wedlock.[45]

Third, abstinence prevents STDs. After more than three decades the sexual revolution has taken many prisoners. Before 1960, doctors were concerned about only two STDs: syphilis and gonorrhea. Today there are more than twenty significant STDs ranging from the relatively harmless to the fatal. Twelve million Americans are newly infected each year, and 63 percent of these new infections are in people under twenty-five years of age. Astonishingly, 80 percent of those infected with an STD have absolutely no symptoms.[46]

Many Americans have not even heard of some of the newest STDs. Chlamydia first appeared in increasing numbers in the 1970s and is now the most common bacterial STD in the country. The human papillomavirus increased dramatically in the 1980s; it can cause venereal warts and can lead to deadly cancers. By the early 1990s, pelvic inflammatory disease (PIV) was affecting one million new women each year. The inevitable scarred fallopian tubes contributed to infertility and the shocking rise in tubal pregnancies. And of course there are the better known STDs such as AIDS, herpes, and resistant forms of venereal diseases that have brought so much fear and concern into our society.

Even less known to most Americans is the fact that teenagers face a greater risk from STDs than does the general population. For example, a teenage girl's cervix has a lining that produces mucus which provides a growth medium for viruses and bacteria. As a girl reaches her twenties or has a baby, this lining is replaced with a tougher, more resistant lining. This biological change puts teenage women at a greater risk for contracting an STD. A fifteen-year-old girl has a one-in-eight chance of developing PIV, while a twenty-four-year-old woman has a one-in-eighty chance under the same circumstances.

Doctors warn that if a person has sexual intercourse with another individual, he or she is not only having sexual intercourse with that individual but with every person with whom that individual might have had intercourse for the last ten years and all the people with whom *they* had intercourse. If that is true, then consider the case of one sixteen-year-old girl who was responsible for 218 cases of gonorrhea and more than 300 cases of syphilis. According to the reporter who documented that case, the girl's promiscuity illustrated the rampant transmission of STDs through multiple sex partners: "The girl had sex with sixteen men. Those men had sex with other people who had sex with other people. The number of contacts finally added up to 1,660." As one person interviewed in the story asked, "What if the girl had had AIDS instead of gonorrhea or syphilis? You probably would have had 1,000 dead people by now."[47]

Abstinence prevents the spread of STDs, whereas safe sex programs do not. Condoms are not always effective even when used correctly and consistently, and most sexually active people do not even use them correctly and consistently. Sex education programs have begun to promote "outercourse" instead of intercourse, but many STDs can be spread even through this method, and, as stated, outercourse almost always leads to intercourse. Abstinence is the only way to prevent the spread of a sexually transmitted disease.

Fourth, abstinence prevents emotional scars. Abstinence speakers relate numerous stories of young people who wish they had postponed sex until marriage. Sex is the most intimate form of bonding known to the human race, and it is a special gift to be given to one's spouse. Unfortunately too many young people throw it away and are filled with feelings of regret.

Sexually active girls age fourteen to seventeen have rates of depression that are three times higher than those who have not been sexually active. Sexually active boys are more than twice as likely to be depressed as those who are not sexually active.[48]

Surveys of young adults show that those who engaged in sexual activity regret their earlier promiscuity and wish that they had been virgins on their wedding night. Even secular agencies that promote a safe-sex approach acknowledge that premarital sex causes regrets. A Roper poll conducted in association with SIECUS (Sexuality Information and Education Council of the United States) of high schoolers found that 62 percent of the sexually experienced girls said that they "should have waited."[49]

Fifth, abstinence not only prevents pregnancy, STDs, and emotional scars; it also strengthens marriages. Premarital sex and cohabitation do not provide a strong foundation for marriage. One study published in the *Journal of Marriage and the Family* found that "cohabiting unions are much less stable than [unions] that begin as marriages." Specifically, 40 percent of cohabiting unions break up before marriage, and marriages that began as cohabiting unions have a 50 percent higher divorce rate than those that did not.[50]

Abstinence before marriage seems to lead to better sex within marriage. A 1992 University of Chicago survey of Americans between the ages of 18 and 59 found that monogamous married couples register the highest levels of sexual satisfaction. According to the survey 87 percent of all monogamous couples reported that they were "extremely" or "very" physically satisfied by their sexual relationship and 85 percent report that they are "extremely" or "very" emotionally satisfied. Those who were least satisfied sexually (both physically and emotionally) were those singles and couples who had multiple partners.[51]

Religious commitment also seems to be an important ingredient in a good marriage and a good sex life. A 1975 study of more than 100,000 women by *Redbook* magazine found that strongly-religious women were less likely to engage in sexual behavior before marriage and were more likely to describe their current sex lives as "good" or "very good" than moderately religious or nonreligious women. The study also found that strongly religious women were "more responsive" sexually than other women.[52]

Society is ready for the abstinence message, and it needs to be promoted widely. Anyone walking on the Washington Mall in July 1993 could not miss the acres of

"True Love Waits" pledge cards signed by over 200,000 teenagers. The campaign, begun by the Southern Baptist Convention, provided a brief but vivid display of the desire of teenagers to stand for purity and to promote abstinence. For every teenager who signed a card pledging abstinence, undoubtedly dozens of others plan to do the same.

Teenagers want and need to hear the message of abstinence. They want to promote the message of abstinence. Their health, and even their lives, are at stake.

11

PORNOGRAPHY

PORNOGRAPHY is tearing apart the very fabric of modern society. Yet Christians are often ignorant of its impact and apathetic about the need to control this menace.

Pornography is a ten-billion-dollar-a-year business.[1] The wages of sin are enormous when pornography is involved. Purveyors of pornography reap enormous profits through sales in so-called "adult bookstores" and the viewing of films and live acts at theaters.

Pornography involves books, magazines, videos, and devices, and has moved from the periphery of society into the mainstream through the renting of videocassettes, the sales of so-called "soft-porn" magazines, and the airing of sexually explicit movies on cable television. To some, pornography is nothing more than a few pictures of scantily-clad women in seductive poses. But pornography has become much more than just photographs of nude women.

DEFINITIONS

Pornography has been defined as material that "is predominantly sexually explicit and intended primarily for the purpose of sexual arousal." Hard-core pornography is "is sexually explicit in the extreme, and devoid of any other apparent content or purpose."[2]

Another important term is obscenity. In the 1973 Supreme Court case of *Miller v. California*, the justices set forth a three part test to define obscenity:[3]

(a) The average person, applying contemporary community standards would find the work, taken as a whole, appeals to the prurient interest.

(b) The work depicts or describes, in a patently offensive way, sexual conduct specifically defined by the applicable state law, and

(c) The work, taken as a whole, lacks serious literary, artistic, political, or scientific value.

TYPES OF PORNOGRAPHY

The first type of pornography is adult magazines, which are primarily (but not exclusively) directed toward adult male readers. The magazines with the widest distribution (*Playboy* and *Penthouse*) do not violate the *Miller* standards of obscenity and thus can be legally distributed. But other magazines which do violate these standards are still readily available in many adult bookstores.

The second type of pornography is video (videocassettes or DVDs). Videocassettes or DVDs are rented or sold in most adult bookstores and have become a growth industry for pornography. People who would never go into an adult bookstore or a theater to watch a pornographic movie can obtain these videocassettes through bookstores or in the mail and watch them in the privacy of their homes. Usually these videos display a high degree of hard-core pornography and illegal acts.

The third type of pornography is motion pictures. Ratings standards are being relaxed, and many pornographic movies are being shown and distributed carrying R and NC-17 ratings. Many of these so-called "hard R" rated films would have been considered obscene just a few decades ago.

A fourth type of pornography is television. As in motion pictures, standards for commercial television have been continuously lowered. But cable television poses an even greater threat. The Federal Communications Commission does not regulate cable in the same way it does public access stations. Thus, many pornographic movies are shown on cable television. Like videocassettes, cable television provides the average person with easy access to pornographic material. People who would never go to an adult bookstore can now view the same sexually explicit material in the privacy of their homes, making cable television "the ultimate brown wrapper."

A fifth type of pornography is audio porn, which includes "Dial-a-porn" telephone calls, the second fastest growth market of pornography. Although most of the messages are within the *Miller* definition of obscenity, these businesses continue to thrive and are often used by children.

A sixth type of pornography is "cyberporn," or pornography on computers and through modems. Virtually anyone can download and view hard-core pictures, movies, online chat, and even live sex acts through the Internet. Sexually explicit images can be found on web pages and in news groups, and are far too easy for anyone of any age to view.

The number of commercial pornography Internet sites in the N2H2 database (a software filter company) exceeds one million. Five years earlier the Internet contained approximately seventy thousand pornographic websites.[4] The allure of cyberporn is that "You can obtain it in the privacy of your home . . . and you can explore different aspects of your sexuality without exposing yourself to communicable diseases or public ridicule."[5]

Robert Weiss of the Sexual Recovery Institute found that cyberporn quickly leads to sexual addiction because "it works so quickly and it's so instantly intense." He observed "a whole population of clients who have never had a history with the problem, but for the first time, they're beginning one particular activity and getting hooked."[6]

Pornography is not only a problem outside the church. It is also a problem inside the church. According to a 2000 survey by *Christianity Today*, 40 percent of clergy have acknowledged visiting sexually explicit websites.[7]

Attempts at legislating Internet pornography issue have not been very successful. Congress has passed the Communications Decency Act (1996), the Child Online Protection Act (1998), and the Children's Internet Protection Act (2000). Each of these pieces of legislation were challenged under the First Amendment.

THE DOCUMENTED EFFECTS OF PORNOGRAPHY

Defenders of pornography argue that it is not harmful, and thus should not be regulated or banned. In 1970, the Presidential Commission on Obscenity and Pornography concluded that no relationship existed between exposure to erotic material and subsequent behavior. But more than a decade of research, as well as the production of more explicit and violent forms of pornography, has shown that pornography can have profound effects on human behavior.

The 1986 *Final Report of the Attorney General's Commission on Pornography* examined five classes of material: sexually violent material; nonviolent materials depicting degradation, domination, subordination, or humiliation; nonviolent and nondegrading materials; nudity; and child pornography. The first two categories demonstrated negative effects; the third showed mixed results; the fourth was not found harmful, but commissioners agreed it was morally objectionable; and the fifth involves sexual exploitation and is already outlawed.

Psychological Effects

Edward Donnerstein, psychologist at the University of Wisconsin, found that brief exposure to violent forms of pornography can lead to antisocial attitudes and behavior. Male viewers tended to be more aggressive toward women, less responsive to the pain and suffering of rape victims, and more willing to accept various myths about rape.[8]

Other researchers also found that exposure to pornography (especially violent pornography) can produce an array of undesirable effects, including rape and sexual coercion[9] increased fantasies about rape,[10] and desensitization to sexual violence and the trivialization of rape.[11]

In an attempt to isolate the role of violence from sex in pornography-induced situations, James Check, of the York University in Canada, conducted an experiment in which men were exposed to different degrees of pornography, some violent, some not. All groups exhibited the same shift in attitude, namely, a higher inclination to use force as part of sex.[12]

In one study the researchers Dolf Zillman and Jennings Bryant investigated the effects of nonviolent pornography on sexual callousness and the trivialization of rape. They demonstrated that continued exposure to pornography had serious adverse effects on beliefs about sexuality in general and on attitudes toward women in particular. They also found that pornography desensitizes people to rape as a criminal offense.[13] In a previous study, Zillman, Bryant, and R.H. Carveth also confirmed that massive exposure to pornography encourages a desire for increasingly deviant materials that encourage violence (such as sadomasochism and rape).[14]

In another study, Zillman measured the impact of viewing pornography on the subjects' views as to what constitutes normal sexual practice. The group that saw the largest amount of pornography gave far higher estimates of the incidence of oral sex, anal sex, group sex, sadomasochism, and bestiality than did the other two groups.[15]

A 1995 meta-analysis of many studies found that violent pornography might reinforce aggressive behavior and negative attitudes toward women.[16] One study demonstrated that pornography can diminish a person's sexual happiness.[17] The researchers found that people exposed to nonviolent pornography reported diminished satisfaction with their sexual partner's physical appearance, affection, curiosity, and sexual performance. They were also more inclined to put more importance on sex without emotional involvement.

In a nationwide study the University of New Hampshire researchers Larry Baron and Murray Strauss discovered a strong statistical correlation between circulation rates of pornographic magazines and rape rates.[18] They found that in states with high circulation rates of pornographic literature, rape rates were also high, but in states with low circulation rates, rape rates also tended to be low.

Of course, a statistical correlation does not prove that pornography causes rape. Certainly not everyone who uses pornography becomes a rapist. And it is possible that rape and pornographic consumption are only indirectly related through other factors, like social permissiveness and "macho" attitudes among men. In fact, Baron and Strauss did examine some of these factors in their study and did not find any significant correlation.

Subsequent studies have had similar results. The Ohio State University researchers Joseph Scott (who testifies frequently for pornographers in court) and Loretta Schwalm examined even more factors than Baron and Strauss (including the circulation of nonsexual magazines) and could not eliminate the correlation between pornography and rape.[19]

Darrell Pope, a Michigan state police detective, found that in 41 percent of the 38,000 sexual assault cases in Michigan (between 1956 and 1979), the perpetrators viewed pornographic material just before or during the crime. Pope's statistics corroborates the research done by the psychotherapist David Scott, who found that "half the rapists studied used pornography to arouse themselves immediately prior to seeking out a victim."[20]

Addiction to Pornography

Victor Cline, a psychologist, documented how men become addicted to pornographic materials, then begin to desire more explicit or deviant material, and finally act out what they have seen.[21] He maintained "that memories of experiences that occurred at times of emotional arousal (which could include sexual arousal) are imprinted on the brain by epinephrine, an adrenal gland hormone, and are difficult to erase. This may partly explain pornography's addicting effect."[22]

Other research showed that biochemical and neurological responses in individuals who are aroused release the adrenal hormone epinephrine in the brain, which is why one can remember pornographic images seen years before. In response to pleasure, nerve endings release chemicals called opioids that reinforce the body's own desire to repeat the process.[23] Kimberly Young, an authority on Internet addiction, found that 90 percent of those who became addicted to cyberporn became addicted to the two-way communication functions: chat rooms, newsgroups, and e-mail.[24]

Psychologists identified a five-step pattern in pornographic addiction. The first step is exposure. Addicts have been exposed to pornography in many ways, ranging from sexual abuse as children to looking at widely available pornographic magazines.

The second step is addiction. People who continually expose themselves to pornography "keep coming back for more and more" in order to get new sexual highs. James L. McCough of the University of California at Irvine said that "experiences at times of emotional or sexual arousal get locked in the brain by the chemical epinephrine and become virtually impossible to erase."[25]

A third step is escalation. Previous sexual highs become more difficult to attain; therefore users of pornography begin to look for more exotic forms of sexual behavior to bring them stimulation.

A fourth step is desensitization. What was initially shocking becomes routine. Shocking and disgusting sexual behavior is no longer avoided but is sought out for more intense stimulation. Concern about pain and degradation get lost in the pursuit of the next sexual experience.

A fifth step is acting out fantasies. People do what they have seen and find pleasurable. Not every pornography addict will become a serial murderer or a rapist. But many do look for ways to act out their sexual fantasies

Gary R. Brooks, in his book *The Centerfold Syndrome: How Men Can Overcome Objectification and Achieve Intimacy with Women*, identified four symptoms of steady consumption of soft-core pornography: (1) *voyeurism*—an obsession with visual stimulation that trivializes all other features of a healthy relationship; (2) *objectification*—obsessive fetishes over body parts and the rating of women by size and shape; (3) *trophyism*—treatment of women as collectibles and property; and (4) *fear of intimacy*—inability to get beyond glossy, centerfold images of women to have a real relationship.[26]

Social Effects

Defining the social effects of pornography has been difficult because of some of the prevailing theories of its impact. One theory was that pornography actually performs a positive function in society by acting like a "safety valve" for potential sexual offenders. The most famous proponent of this theory was Berl Kutchinsky, a criminologist at the University of Copenhagen. His famous study on pornography found that when the Danish government lifted restrictions on pornography, the number of sex crimes decreased.[27] Therefore, he concluded that the availability of pornography siphons off dangerous sexual impulses. But when the data for his "safety-valve" theory was further evaluated, many of his research flaws began to show.

For example, Kutchinsky failed to distinguish between different kinds of sex crimes (such as rape and indecent exposure) and instead merely lumped them together, effectively masking an increase in rape statistics. He also failed to consider that increased tolerance for certain crimes (public nudity and sex with a minor) may have contributed to a drop in the reported crimes.

Proving cause and effect in pornography is virtually impossible because, ethically, researchers cannot do certain kinds of research. As Zillman said, "Men cannot be placed at risk of developing sexually violent inclinations by extensive exposure to violent or nonviolent pornography, and women cannot be placed at risk of becoming victims of such inclinations."[28]

Deborah Baker, a legal assistant and executive director of an anti-obscenity group, agreed that conclusively proving a connection between pornography and crime would be very difficult.

> The argument that there are no established studies showing a connection between pornography and violent crime is merely a smokescreen. Those who promote this stance well know that such research will never be done. It would require a sampling of much more than a thousand males, exposed to pornography through puberty and adolescence, while the other group is totally isolated from its influence in all

its forms and varying degrees. Each group would then have to be monitored through the commission of violent crimes or not. In spite of the lack of formal research, though, the FBI's own statistics show that pornography is found at 80 percent of the scenes of violent sex crimes, or in the homes of the perpetrators.[29]

Nevertheless, a number of compelling statistics suggest that pornography does have profound social consequences. For example, of the 1,400 child sexual molestation cases in Louisville, Kentucky, between July 1980 and February 1984, adult pornography was connected with each incident and child pornography with the majority of them.[30] Extensive interviews with sex offenders (rapists, incest offenders, and child molesters) have uncovered a sizable percentage of offenders who use pornography to arouse themselves before and during their assaults.[31] Police officers have seen the impact pornography has had on serial murders. In fact, pornography consumption is one of the most common profile characteristics of serial murders and rapists.[32]

Professor Cass Sunstein, writing in the *Duke Law Journal*, said that some sexual violence against women "would not have occurred but for the massive circulation of pornography." Citing cross-cultural data, he concluded, "The liberalization of pornography laws in the United States, Britain, Australia, and the Scandinavian countries has been accompanied by a rise in reported rape rates. In countries where pornography laws have not been liberalized, there has been a less steep rise in reported rapes. And in countries where restrictions have been adopted, reported rapes have decreased."[33]

CENSORSHIP AND FREEDOM OF SPEECH

Attempts to regulate and outlaw pornography within a community are frequently criticized as censorship and a violation of the First Amendment. But the Supreme Court clearly stated in *Roth v. United States* (1957) that obscenity was not protected by the First Amendment. Federal, state, and local laws apply to the sale, display, distribution, and broadcast of pornography. Pornographic material, therefore, can be prohibited if it meets the legal definition of obscenity.

As previously discussed, the Court ruled in the case of *Miller v. California* (1973) that a legal definition of obscenity must meet a three-part test. If material appeals to the prurient interest, is patently offensive, and lacks serious value (artistically, politically, or scientifically), then that material is considered obscene and is illegal.

The Court further ruled in *Paris Adult Theatre v. Slaton* (1973) that material legally defined as obscene is not accorded the same protection as free speech in the First Amendment. The court concluded that even if obscene films are shown only to "consenting adults," that fact did not grant them immunity from the law.

In *New York v. Ferber* (1982) the Court declared that child pornography was not protected under the First Amendment even if it was not legally defined as obscene under their three-part test. Since children cannot legally consent to sexual relations, child pornography constitutes sexual abuse. Congress also passed the Child Protection Act in 1984, which provided tougher restrictions on child pornography.

Cable television is presently unregulated since it is not technically "broadcasting" as defined in the Federal Communications Act. Thus, cable television is able to show pornographic movies with virtual impunity. The Federal Communications Act needs to be amended so that the Federal Communications Commission can regulate cable television.

BIBLICAL PERSPECTIVE

God created men and women in His image (Gen. 1:27) as sexual beings. But because of sin in the world (Rom. 3:23), sex has been misused and abused (Rom. 1:24–25).

Pornography attacks the dignity of men and women created in the image of God. Pornography also distorts God's gift of sex, which should be shared only within the bounds of marriage (1 Cor. 7:2–3). When the Bible refers to human sexual organs, it often employs euphemisms and indirect language. Although there are some exceptions (a woman's breasts and womb are sometimes mentioned), generally Scripture maintains a basic modesty toward a man's or woman's sexual organs.

Moreover, Scripture specifically condemns the practices that result from pornography such as sexual exposure (Gen. 9:21–23), adultery (Lev. 18:20), bestiality (Lev. 18:23), homosexuality (Lev. 18:22; 20:13), incest (18:6–18), and prostitution (Deut. 23:17–18).

A biblical perspective of human sexuality must recognize that sexual intercourse is exclusively reserved for marriage for the following purposes. First, it establishes the one-flesh union (Gen. 2:24–25; Matt. 19:4–6). Second, it provides for sexual intimacy within the marriage bond. The word "know" indicates a profound sense of sexual intimacy (Gen. 4:1). Third, sexual intercourse is for the mutual pleasure of husband and wife (Prov. 5:18–19). Fourth, sexual intercourse is for procreation (Gen. 1:28).

The Bible also warns against the misuse of sex. Premarital and extramarital sex is condemned (1 Cor. 6:13–18; 1 Thess. 4:3). Even thoughts of sexual immorality (often fed by pornographic material) are condemned (Matt. 5:27–28).

Moreover, Christians must realize that pornography can have significant harmful effects on the user. These effects include a comparison mentality, a performance-based sexuality, a feeling that only forbidden things are sexually satisfying, increased guilt, decreased self-concept, and obsessive thinking.

Christians, therefore, must do two things. First, they must work to keep themselves pure by fleeing immorality (1 Cor. 6:18) and thinking on things that are pure (Phil. 4:8). As a man thinks in his heart, so he is (Prov. 23:7). Christians must make no provision for the flesh (Rom. 13:14). Pornography will fuel the sexual desire in abnormal ways and can eventually lead to even more debase perversion. Therefore, we must abstain from fleshly lusts that war against the soul (1 Pet. 2:11). Second, Christians must work to remove this sexual perversion of pornography from society.

STEPS TO COMBAT PORNOGRAPHY

First, parents must teach a wholesome, biblical view of sex to their children. Second, we must evaluate our exposure to media (magazines, television shows, rock music) with inappropriate sexual themes. Parents, for example, should set a positive example for their children, and take time to discuss these stories, programs, and songs with them.

Third, pastors should warn their congregations about the dangers of pornography and instruct them in a proper view of sexuality. Like Joseph in the Old Testament, we should flee immorality, which can entice us into sin. Sermons should also be preached to build strong Christian homes.

Fourth, parents should block cyberporn with software. Many commercial services as well as special software can screen and block areas children may try to investigate. These programs will block out sexual hot spots on the Internet and can detect an offending phrase that might be used in an online chat room.

Unfortunately, Internet filters also do not provide a complete answer. Groups like Consumer Reports tested various filtering system on sites with sexually explicit, violent, or otherwise inappropriate content. The best blocked eighty-six percent. The worst only blocked ten percent of the sites.[34]

Parents should also evaluate the location of the family computer and try to be around their children when they are online and ask them things about online computing. Extensive late night use may be an indication of a problem.

Fifth, individual Christians should get involved with national (National Coalition Against Pornography, Enough is Enough) or local decency groups organized to fight pornography . These groups have been effective in many localities in ridding their communities of the porno plague.

Sixth, we should express our concern to local officials (through letters and petitions) about adult movie houses and bookstores in our communities. Seventh, if we receive pornographic material in the mail, we should report the sender to the local postmaster with the request that federal agents take action. Eighth, Christians should not patronize stores that sell pornographic materials. Boycotts and pickets can be organized to get community attention focused on the problem.

Christians can make a difference. Following these common-sense procedures can begin to rid a community of the porno plague and return a standard of decency to the community.

12

HOMOSEXUALITY

WITHIN THE PAST thirty years homosexuality has moved from the margins of society to the mainstream. Though many homosexuals may not be "out of the closet," homosexuality is. In the years following the beginning of the gay rights movement in 1969, homosexuality has been publicly debated and promoted in almost every arena.

Homosexuality has become an issue of public policy and morality. Homosexuals march for equal treatment under the law, comparing their plight to disadvantaged minorities. They call for total acceptance of the gay lifestyle free from criticism and condemnation.

Against these claims the Bible provides signposts that warn people away from the dangers of sexual relations outside of God's ordained plan. All sexual sins (fornication, adultery, homosexuality) represent an attempt by mankind to deviate from God's best and trespass into dangerous areas. Unfortunately many in the homosexual community have tried to alter the biblical teaching on homosexuality. They argue that the Bible does not condemn homosexuality at all.

OLD TESTAMENT PASSAGES

Genesis and the Sin of Sodom

Foundational to a Christian understanding of sexuality is God's plan in creation found in Genesis 1 and 2. God created humans as male and female in His image and likeness (1:27). Human sexuality is manifested in two genders, not three, four, or five.[1] The Bible teaches that it was not good that man was alone (2:18), so God created woman to be man's counterpart and colaborer.

Homosexuality cannot fulfill the unitive and the procreative aspects of human sexuality as ordained by God, which is precisely why the Bible refers to homosexual relations in various passages as unnatural. Homosexuality is a violation of the natural process God intended for human sexuality.

The first reference to homosexuality in the Bible is in Genesis 19. Lot entertained two angels who came to the city to investigate its sins. In the evening all the men from every part of the city of Sodom surrounded Lot's house and ordered him to bring out the visitors so that "we may know them" (19:5, NKJV). The men of Sodom did not know that the visitors were angels. The Hebrew word for "know" (*yadah*) means that the men of the city wanted to have sex with the visitors, which is why the New International Version renders the clause, "so that we can have sex with them."

Proponents of homosexuality have argued that biblical commentators misunderstand the story of Sodom.[2] They maintain that the men of the city merely wanted to meet these visitors. Either the men were anxious to extend Middle Eastern hospitality, or they wanted to interrogate the visitors and make sure that they were not spies. In either case, homosexuals argue, the passage has nothing to do with homosexuality. They say that the sin of Sodom was inhospitality, not homosexuality.

Pro-homosexual commentators point out that *yadah* can mean "to get acquainted with" as well as "to have intercourse with." In fact, the word appears over nine hundred times in the Old Testament, and only twelve times does it mean "to have sex with" someone. Therefore, they conclude that the sin of Sodom had nothing to do with homosexuality.

The problem with this argument is the context. Statistics is not the same as exegesis. Word count alone is not the sole criterion for determining meaning of words. And even if a statistical count should be used, the argument backfires. Of the twelve times *yadah* is used in the Book of Genesis, it does mean "to have intercourse with" in ten of those occurrences.

Second, the context does not warrant the interpretation that the men of Sodom only wanted to get acquainted with the strangers. Consider Lot's reply: "So Lot went out to them through the doorway, shut the door behind him, and said, 'Please my brethren, do not so wickedly! See now, I have two daughters who have not known a man; please let me bring them out to you, and you may do to them as you wish; only do nothing to these men, since this is the reason they have come'" (Gen. 19:6–8, NKJV). One can sense Lot's panic as he foolishly offered his virgin daughters to the crowd instead of the foreigners. His reaction was not the action of a man merely responding to the crowd's request "to become acquainted with" the men.

Lot described his daughters as women who "have not known a man." Clearly this statement implies sexual intercourse and does not mean "to be acquainted with." It is unlikely that the first use of *yadah* (v. 5) differs from its second use (v. 8). Both times *yadah* means "to have intercourse with" or "to have sex with." This is the only consistent translation for the passage.

Third, Jude 7 provides a fitting commentary on Genesis 19. This New Testament reference clearly states that the sin of Sodom involved "gross immorality and perversion." The word "perversion" (rendered "strange flesh" in the NKJV) could imply homosexuality or even bestiality,[3] and provides further evidence that the sin of Sodom was homosexuality, not inhospitality.

The Mosaic Law

The Mosaic Law condemns homosexual practices. Two passages in Leviticus call it detestable (or "an abomination," NKJV): "Do not lie with a man as one lies with a woman; it is detestable" (18:22), and "If a man lies with a man as one lies with a woman, both of them have done what is detestable" (20:13). The word for "detestable" or "abomination," used several times in Leviticus 18, is a strong term of disapproval, implying that something is abhorrent to God.

Commentators see these verses as an expansion of the Seventh Commandment. Though not an exhaustive list, the sexual sins listed in Leviticus are representative of the common, sinful practices of nations surrounding Israel.

Pro-homosexual commentators have more difficulty dealing with these clear passages, but they usually offer one of two responses. Some argue that because these verses appear in the "holiness code" of Leviticus, they apply only to the priests and ritual purity.[4] Therefore, according to this perspective, the holiness code contains only religious prohibitions, not moral ones. Others argue that these prohibitions were merely for the Old Testament theocracy and are not relevant today. They suggest that if Christians wanted to be consistent with the Old Testament law code in Leviticus, they should avoid eating rare steak, wearing mixed fabrics, and having marital intercourse during the wife's menstrual period.[5]

Do these passages apply merely to ritual purity rather than moral purity? Part of the problem comes from making the two issues distinct. The priests were to model moral behavior within their ceremonial rituals. Moral purity and ritual purity cannot be separated, especially when discussing the issue of human sexuality. To hold to this rigid distinction would imply that such sins as adultery were not immoral (see Lev. 18:20) or that bestiality was morally acceptable (see Lev. 18:23).

The second argument concerns the relevance of the Mosaic Law today. Few Christians today keep kosher kitchens or balk at wearing clothes interwoven with more than one fabric. The logical extension of the argument that the Old Testament admonition against homosexuality is irrelevant today would be that bestiality and incest are also morally acceptable since prohibitions against these two sins surround the prohibition against homosexuality. If the Mosaic Law is irrelevant to homosexuality, then it is also irrelevant to having sex with animals (Lev. 18:23) or having illicit sex with someone's daughter (Lev. 18:17).

More to the point, to say that the Mosaic Law has ended is not to say that God has no laws or moral codes for mankind. Even though the ceremonial law has passed, the moral law remains. The New Testament speaks of the "law of the

Spirit" (Rom. 8:2) and the "law of Christ" (Gal. 6:2). One cannot say that something that was sin under the Law is not sin under grace. Ceremonial laws concerning diet or wearing mixed fabrics no longer apply, but moral laws (especially those rooted in God's creation order for human sexuality) continue. Moreover, these prohibitions against homosexuality can also be found in the New Testament.

NEW TESTAMENT PASSAGES

Three key New Testament passages concerning homosexuality are Romans 1:26–27; 1 Corinthians 6:9–10; and 1 Timothy 1:10. Of the three, the most significant is the Romans passage because it deals with homosexuality within the larger cultural context.

> Because of this, God gave them over to shameful lusts. Even their women exchanged natural relations for unnatural ones. In the same way the men also abandoned natural relations with women and were inflamed with lust for one another. Men committed indecent acts with other men, and received in themselves the due penalty for their perversion.

Here the apostle Paul set forth the Gentile world's guilt before a holy God and focused on the arrogance and lust of the Hellenistic world. Gentiles turned away from the true worship of God so that "God gave them over to shameful lusts." Rather than follow God's instruction in their lives, they suppressed "the truth by their wickedness" (Rom. 1:18), following passions that dishonor God.

Another New Testament passage dealing with homosexuality is 1 Corinthians 6:9–10: "Do you not know that the wicked will not inherit the kingdom of God? Do not be deceived: Neither the sexually immoral nor idolaters nor adulterers nor male prostitutes nor homosexual offenders nor thieves nor the greedy not drunkards nor slanderers nor swindlers will inherit the kingdom of God." Making use of the "abuse" argument, pro-homosexual commentators point out that Paul was only singling out homosexual offenders. In other words, they argue that Paul was condemning homosexual abuse rather than responsible homosexual behavior.

In essence, these commentators suggest that Paul was calling for temperance rather than abstinence. But this approach could not be applied to other sins listed in 1 Corinthians 6 or 1 Timothy 1. Was Paul calling for responsible adultery or responsible prostitution? Is there such a thing as moral theft and swindling? Obviously the argument breaks down. Scripture never condones sex outside of marriage (including premarital sex, extramarital sex, and homosexual sex). God created man and woman for the institution of marriage (Gen. 2:24).

BIOLOGICAL CAUSES OF HOMOSEXUALITY

Is there a biological cause or causes for homosexuality? The answer is not as simple as homosexual activists would have us believe. A complex set of factors influence human sexuality. Therefore, providing a single cause for homosexuality is impossible. No "typical homosexual" exists, and it is doubtful that we would ever find a single causal factor for homosexuality. Physiological, psychological, and spiritual factors all play a part.

For years scientists have been looking for biological causes for homosexuality. Finding such a factor (hormones or a gay gene) would give support to the frequently heard homosexual cliché that "I was born this way." It would give credence to the concept that homosexuality is not a sin but a biological condition entitled to legal and social recognition.[6]

Some researchers have published different studies to show a correlation between sexual orientation and brain structure, genetic structure, finger length, eye blinking, and hormonal differentiation. The three most prominent studies have been a brain study by Simon LeVay, a twins study by Michael Bailey and Richard Pillard, and a genetic study by Dean Hamer.

Simon LeVay, a neuroscientist at the Salk Institute, argued that homosexuals and heterosexuals have notable differences in the structure of their brains. In 1991, he studied forty-one cadavers (nineteen homosexual men, sixteen heterosexual men, six heterosexual women). He found that a specific portion of the hypothalamus, the area of the brain that governs sexual activity, was consistently smaller in homosexuals than in heterosexuals.[7] Therefore, he argued that there is a distinct physiological component to sexual orientation. In other words "biology is destiny."

Numerous problems exist with this study, however. First, there was considerable range in the size of the hypothalamic region. In a few homosexual men this region was the same size as that of the heterosexuals, and in a few heterosexuals this region was as small as that of a homosexual. So the statistical correlation is not as strong as news reports of the initial study might lead one to believe.

Second is the chicken-and-egg problem. When there is a difference in brain structure, is the difference the cause of sexual orientation or is it the result of sexual orientation? Researchers, for example, have found that when people who become blind begin to learn Braille, the area of the brain controlling the reading finger actual grows larger. Could this be a possible explanation for the size difference between the hypothalami of homosexuals and heterosexuals?

Third, LeVay later had to admit that he did not know the sexual orientation of some of the cadavers in the study. He acknowledged that he was not sure if the heterosexual males in the study were actually heterosexual. Since some of those he identified as "heterosexual" died of AIDS, critics have raised doubts about the accuracy of his study.

Fourth, there was the potential for bias in the study. LeVay has said he was

driven to study the potential physiological roots of homosexuality after his homosexual lover died of AIDS. He even admitted that if he failed to find a genetic cause
for homosexuality that he might walk away from science altogether.[8] Later he did
just that by moving to West Hollywood to open up a small, unaccredited "study
center" focusing on homosexuality.

In December 1991, Michael Bailey of Northwestern University joined Richard
Pillard of the Boston University School of Medicine in publishing a study of homosexuality in twins.[9] They surveyed homosexual men about their brothers and
discovered what they believe proved that sexual orientation is biological. Of the homosexuals who had identical twin brothers, 52 percent of those twins were also homosexual, 22 percent of those who had fraternal twins said that their twin was gay,
and only 11 percent of those who had adopted siblings said that their adopted
brothers were also homosexual. Bailey and Pillard attributed the differences in
those percentages to the differences in genetic material shared.

Though it has also been touted as proving a genetic basis to homosexuality, the
study contained significant flaws. First, Bailey and Pillard's theory is not new. It
was first proposed in 1952. Since that time three other separate research studies
have come to different conclusions.[10] Therefore, the conclusions of the Bailey-
Pillard study should be considered in the light of other contradictory studies.

Second, most published reports did not mention that only 9 percent of the non-
twin brothers of homosexuals were homosexuals. Fraternal twins share no more genetic material than non-twin brothers, yet homosexuals are more than twice as
likely to share their sexual orientation with a fraternal twin than with a non-twin
brother. Whatever the reason, the answer cannot be genetic.

Third, why are not nearly all identical twin brothers of homosexuals also homosexual? In other words if biology is determinative, why are nearly half the identical
twins not homosexual? Bailey admitted that "there must be something in the environment to yield the discordant twins."[11] And that is precisely the point; there is
something (perhaps everything) in the environment to explain sexual orientation.

Fraternal incest, for example, has been statistically shown to be much higher for
twins than non-twins.[12] Could the social and emotional closeness of twins explain
similar sexual orientation? An identical twin of a homosexual who sleeps in the
same bed or bedroom is more apt to be physically closer to his twin. As one biologist put it, "In order for such a study to be at all meaningful, you'd have to look at
twins raised apart. It's such badly interpreted genetics."[13]

Fourth, there was potential for bias in the twins study. Bailey is a homosexual
and has been an outspoken proponent of a pro-gay agenda in science. While the
study should be evaluated on its merits, it is important to be aware of potential bias
in any scientific study.

The third major study usually cited as providing a biological cause for homosexuality is the so-called "gay gene" study. In 1993, a team of researchers led by Dean Hamer
of the National Cancer Institute announced "preliminary" findings from research

into the connection between homosexuality and genetic inheritance.[14] In a sample of seventy-six homosexual males, the researchers found a statistically higher incidence of homosexuality in their male relatives (brothers, uncles) on their mother's side of the family, which suggested a possible inherited link through the X chromosome. A follow-up study of forty pairs of homosexual brothers found that thirty-three shared a variation in a small section of the chromosome region known as Xq28.

Although the press promoted this study as evidence of the discovery of a gay gene, some of the same concerns raised with the previous two studies apply here. First, the findings involve a limited sample size and are therefore sketchy. Even the researchers acknowledged that these were "preliminary" findings. In addition to the sample size being small, the researchers did no control testing for heterosexual brothers. Critics also raised questions about the insufficient research done on the social histories of the homosexuals' families.

Second, similarity does not prove cause. Just because thirty-three pairs of homosexual brothers share a genetic variation does not mean that variation causes homosexuality. And what about the other seven pairs that did not show the variation but were homosexuals? Some of the same concerns raised about the Bailey-Pillard study are relevant here.

Third, research bias may again be an issue. Hamer and at least one of his other team members is homosexual, which apparently was deliberately kept from the press and was only revealed later. Hamer, it turns out, is not merely an objective observer. He has presented himself as an expert witness on homosexuality and has stated that he hopes that his research would give comfort to men feeling guilty about their homosexuality.[15]

Each of these three studies looking for a biological cause for homosexuality has its flaws. Does that mean there is no physiological component to homosexuality? Not at all. Actually it is probably too early to say conclusively. Scientists may indeed discover a clear biological predisposition to sexual orientation. But a predisposition is not the same as a determination. Maintaining this difference leads to some key distinctions, according to Sherwood Cole.

> Assuming that biological influences on homosexuality are "predisposing" rather than "determining" also allows one to make some additional important distinctions. For example, "predisposing" influences are much more likely to influence one's orientation (desires, attitudes, preferences, attractions, and fantasies) than one's behavior. While these influences are not to be treated lightly, it may or may not result in the overt expression of homosexual behavior. Since the Bible's condemnation and prohibition of homosexuality (Lev. 18:22; 20:13; Rom. 1:26–27; 1 Cor. 6:9; 1 Tim. 1:10) address behavioral practices, not orientation, this distinction is important to the debate. The individual who, in spite of a homosexual orientation, refrains from the practice of this lifestyle is to be commended, not condemned.[16]

The social and moral implications of this distinction are also relevant. Some people may inherit a predisposition for anger, depression, or alcoholism, yet society does not condone these behaviors. And even if violence, depression, or alcoholism were proven to be inborn (determined by genetic material), would we accept them as normal and refuse to treat them? Of course not. The Bible has clear statements about such things as anger and alcoholism. Likewise the Bible has clear statements about homosexuality.

PSYCHOLOGICAL CAUSES OF HOMOSEXUALITY

Because human sexuality is so complex, finding a single cause for homosexuality is unlikely. There is, however, growing evidence that a number of environmental factors in a family or an individual's experience seems to influence one's sexual orientation.

Since the time of Sigmund Freud, counselors have noticed a pattern of family relationships that frequently appears in a homosexual's family of origin: a domineering mother and a passive or absent father. Though this is a stereotype with obvious exceptions, the pattern still manifests itself in the lives of many homosexual men. One counselor summarized the various research findings in this way: "In his book *Male Homosexuality* . . . Dr. Richard Friedman cites 13 independent studies from 1959 to 1981 on the early family lives of homosexuals. Out of these 13, all but one concluded that, in the parent-child interactions of adult homosexuals, the subject's relationship with the parent of the same sex was unsatisfactory, ranging from a distant, nonintimate relationship to an outright hostile one."[17]

Another factor is early sexual experience. Many homosexuals cite backgrounds of being sexually molested or having had sexual experiences early in their childhood. These experiences may range from sexual abuse (from another homosexual and/or a family member) to an early childhood sexual experience that could be described as pleasurable. In an attempt to rationalize the feelings that surface from this experience, the child often begins to act on those feelings and pursue similar sexual experimentation.

Much less research has been done on lesbians, but sexual abuse does seem to be a frequent pattern in the history of women with homosexual tendencies. This abuse may be physical, sexual, and/or emotional. When the abuse comes from a man, she may view men as tyrants and avoid them. When the abuse comes from a woman, she may grow up longing for womanly love and protection she did not receive.

Psychologists have identified certain emotional needs everyone has. Homosexuals report that one or more of these emotional needs are unmet.[18] Is it possible that homosexuals attempt to meet these legitimate needs in relating to the same sex in illegitimate ways that manifest themselves in their sexual patterns? Three emotional needs are relevant to this discussion.

The first is the need for gender identity. In other words, what does it mean to be male or female? Boys with gender identity problems do not feel masculine. Showing "effeminate" behavior is not femininity; it is a lack of confidence of someone's ability to be masculine. Often this behavior derives from a lack of bonding with the same-sex parent ("I'm unacceptable to my father, so I must be unacceptable to other males"). For lesbians, the trigger will be the opposite of the homosexual. In other words, while the trigger for the male can be a weak father, the trigger for a female may be a distant mother.

The second need is for a healthy role model. How does an emotionally healthy man or woman act? Children learn what masculinity and femininity are by watching how proper sexuality is modeled in the lives of those close to them. When the role models are missing, the cues and influences may be missing or mixed, thereby leading to a different sense of identity and sexual orientation.

The third need is for same-sex bonding. Bonding with members of one's own sex is a basic psychological need, which would include bonding with a nurturer (usually a parent), a mentor (a coach, a teacher, a discipler), and comrades (peers and friends of the same sex). Research shows that only after bonding with the same sex has been fulfilled can relationships move on to the opposite sex. Often, however, bonding with others of the same sex does not happen. A boy, for example, may bond with the women in his life, or with no one at all. Some counselors suggest that people struggling with homosexual feelings are not so much having a sexual problem as much as they are having a relational problem. This same sex "deficit" may be an explanation for homosexual behavior.

SPIRITUAL CAUSES OF HOMOSEXUALITY

Ultimately homosexuality is a manifestation of the sin nature that strikes us all (Rom. 3:23). Because of the Fall (Genesis 3), God's creation was spoiled and human behavior has fallen into degrading passions (Rom. 1:24). Sin has spoiled every aspect of our being (spiritual, intellectual, emotional, physical, sexual). Therefore, we should not be surprised that anyone (heterosexual or homosexual) could have sexual fantasies and temptations in this area. Those who choose to act on those feelings and temptations are acting outside God's plan for human sexuality.

A society that turns from God's plan accelerates sexual irresponsibility. Homosexuals are told they "were born that way" and should celebrate their sexuality. Heterosexuals are encouraged to experiment and expand their sexual choices. People with guilt feelings over their sexual experiences and temptations are encouraged to accept their feelings with the cliché "once gay, always gay." The ultimate problem is not physiological or even psychological, but an unwillingness to deal with the spiritual problem of sin. Psychological and spiritual counsel, therefore, is the answer to homosexuality.

ONCE GAY, ALWAYS GAY?

One of the most frequent clichés heard in homosexual circles is, "once gay, always gay." In a sense it is a corollary cliché to the slogan "you are born gay." Secular counselors routinely tell patients struggling with homosexual feelings that they were born that way, that they cannot change, and that they should simply learn to affirm their feelings.

Despite such clichés and counseling there is hope for the person struggling with homosexual feelings. Groups like Exodus International provide a network of ninety organizations that specialize in helping homosexuals leave their lifestyle and change their sexual orientation. Consider this sampling of quotations from experts in the sexual counseling field:

- "Some people do change their sexual orientation."[19]

- "Despite the rhetoric of homosexual activists, all studies which have attempted conversion from homosexuality to heterosexuality have had significant success,"[20]

- "I have recently had occasion to review the result of psychotherapy with homosexuals and have been surprised by the findings—a considerable percentage of overt homosexuals became heterosexual."[21]

Perhaps one of the most definitive statements came from an unlikely source. Robert Switzer, professor of psychiatry at Columbia University, was instrumental in removing homosexuality in 1973 from the American Psychiatric Association's list of mental disorders. He wrote a study published in the October 2003 *Archives of Sexual Behavior* contending that people can change their "sexual orientation" from homosexual to heterosexual.[22]

Recent press reports, as well as academic studies, suggest that sexual preference among young teen women is much more fluid and influenced by choice and cultural circumstances. According to Laura Sessions Stepp, "Recent studies among women suggest that female homosexuality may be grounded more in social interaction, may present itself as an emotional attraction in addition to or in place of a physical one, and may change over time."[23]

Lisa Diamond of the University of Utah conducted a longitudinal study of women (ages 16 to 23) who were attracted to other women. She found that nearly two-thirds changed their sexual labels during the period of study.[24]

The success rate for homosexual counseling varies, given the different approaches and circumstances. William Masters and Virginia Johnson reported successful results in 71.6 percent of all cases after a six-year follow-up period.[25] Others have reported similar success rates in that range.

Ultimately it is Christ's loving act of redemption that can free someone bound by the ropes of sexual addiction (heterosexual or homosexual). Some people experience no further homosexual temptations, but most struggle with their sexual temptations in the process of sanctification. Individual Christians and churches must find creative ways to reach out to those caught in the bondage of homosexuality by learning to love the sinner while hating the sin.

13

COHABITATION

"COHABITATION is replacing marriage as the first living together experience for young men and women," and couples who live together before they get married are putting their future marriage in danger. These are some of the conclusions of the sociologists David Popenoe and Barbara Dafoe Whitehead in their study for the National Marriage Project.[1]

Cohabitation used to be called "living in sin" or "shacking up." Today, it has been replaced by more neutral terms like "living together" or cohabitation. Cohabitation is currently the generally accepted term in society and law, and has been defined as "two unrelated persons of the opposite sex who share common living arrangements in a sexually intimate relationship without legal or religious sanction."[2]

Cohabitation, as a lifestyle, is on the rise. Consider the significant growth in cohabitation rates in the last few decades. In 1960 and 1970, about a half million couples were living together. But by 1980, that number was 1.5 million. By 1990, the number was nearly three million. And by 2000, the number was almost five million.[3]

Researchers estimate that today as many as 50 percent of Americans cohabit at one time or another prior to marriage.[4] And the stereotype of two young, childless people living together is not completely accurate. Currently, 40 percent of cohabiting relationships involve children.[5]

America also appears to be changing its attitude toward cohabitation. George Barna reported that 60 percent of Americans believed that the best way to establish a successful marriage is to cohabit prior to marriage.[6] Another survey found that two thirds (66 percent) of high school senior boys agreed or mostly agreed with the statement, "it is usually a good idea for a couple to live together before getting married in order to find out whether they really get along."[7]

Cohabitation is not the same as marriage, nor is it recognized as marriage by the state. And the participants are living together because it is their intent *not* to be married, at least for the time being.

Although some people will say that a cohabiting couple is "married in the eyes of God," that is not true. They are not married in God's eyes because they are living contrary to biblical statements about marriage. And they are not married in their own eyes because they have specifically decided *not* to marry.

Cohabitation is without a doubt changing the cultural landscape of our society. The proportion of first marriages preceded by cohabitation has increased ten-fold in the last few decades. And the increasing number of cohabiting couples sends a mixed message to our children. On the one hand, they hear parents and pastors proclaim the value of marriage. But on the other hand, they see a culture condoning cohabitation.

COHABITATION AND TEST-DRIVE RELATIONSHIPS

"I think we should live together before we get married to see if we are compatible." How many times have we heard that line? But many of the current assumptions about living together are incorrect.

Linda Waite and Maggie Gallagher wrote *The Case for Marriage: Why Married People Are Happier, Healthier and Better Off Financially.*[8] It not only makes the case for marriage; it also challenges contemporary assumptions about cohabitation. The thesis of the book is simple. In the 1950s, the rules were clear: first love, next marriage, and only then the baby carriage. But the social tsunami that struck in the 1960s, changed everything. The Pill, the sexual revolution, gay pride, feminism, mothers in the workplace, no-fault divorce, and the rise of illegitimate births changed our views of marriage and family. The authors marshal the evidence to show that marriage is a good thing. As the subtitle says, married people are happier, healthier, and better off financially.

Nevertheless, the conventional wisdom is that you should "try before you buy." In fact, one of the oft-repeated questions justifying living together is: "You wouldn't buy a car without a test drive would you?" The problem with such questions and slogans is they dehumanize the other person. If I decide not to buy a car (or a pair of shoes or whatever the inanimate object), the car does not feel rejected. When you test-drive your car, you do not pack your personal luggage in the trunk. And rejecting a car model does not bring emotional baggage into the next test-driving experience. The car does not need psychological counseling so that it can trust the next car buyer. Frankly, test-driving a relationship is only positive if you are the driver.

Research demonstrated that those who cohabited tended to view marriage negatively because marriage involved the assumption of new responsibilities that contrasted with their former freedoms. On the other hand, those marrying through the conventional route of dating and courtship did not feel constrained by marriage, but liberated by marriage.[9]

Consider the contrast. A couple living together has nearly everything marriage has to offer (including sex) but few commitments or responsibilities. So cohabiting people feel trapped when they enter marriage. They must assume new responsibilities while getting nothing they did not already have.

Couples entering marriage through dating and courtship experience just the opposite, especially if they maintain their sexual purity. Marriage is the culmination of their relationship and provides the full depth of a relationship they have long anticipated.

However, cohabitation does not guarantee marital failure, nor does marriage through the conventional route guarantee marital success. There are exceptions to this rule, but people who live together before marriage stack the odds against them and their future marriage.

COHABITATION AND PERCEPTIONS

One report on cohabitation concluded that if couples live together before they get married, they are putting their future marriage in danger. The sociologists David Popenoe and Barbara Dafoe Whitehead released their conclusions through the National Marriage Project at Rutgers University. Their study confirmed earlier studies about the danger of cohabiting and added additional detail.[10]

They found that cohabiting appears to be so counterproductive to long-lasting marriage that unmarried couples should avoid living together, especially if it involves children. They argued that living together is "a fragile family form" that poses increased risk to women and children.

Part of the reason for the danger is the difference in perception. Men often enter the relationship with less intention to marry than do women. They may regard it more as a sexual opportunity without the ties of long-term commitment. Women, however, often see the living arrangement as a step toward eventual marriage. So while the women may believe that they are headed for marriage, the man has other ideas. Some men actually resent the women they live with and view them as easy. Such a woman is not his idea of a faithful marriage partner.

People who live together in uncommitted relationships may be unwilling to work out problems. Since there is no long-term commitment, often it is easy to leave the current living arrangement and seek less fractious relationships with a new partner.

The ten-fold increase in cohabitation in the last few decades is staggering. The reasons for the growth are many: fewer taboos against premarital sex, earlier sexual maturity, later marriage, and adequate income to live apart from their families.

Whatever the reasons for cohabiting, the Popenoe-Whitehead study documented the dangers. Couples who live together are more likely to divorce than those who do not. They are less happy and score lower on well-being indices, including sexual satisfaction. And cohabiting couples are often poorer than married couples.

Even if millions are doing it, living together is a bad idea. As we will see later, the Bible clearly prohibits premarital sex. But apart from these biblical prohibitions are the ominous sociological predictions of failure when a couple considers cohabitation rather than marriage. The latest research supports what the Bible has said for millennia.

THE CONSEQUENCES OF COHABITATION

Contrary to conventional wisdom, cohabitation can be harmful to marriages as well as to the couples and their children. One study based on the National Survey of Families and Households found that marriages that had prior cohabitants were 46% more likely to divorce than marriages of non-cohabitants. The authors concluded from their study and a review of previous studies that the risk of marital disruption following cohabitation "is beginning to take on the status of an empirical generalization."[11]

Some have tried to argue that the correlation between cohabitation and divorce is artificial since people willing to cohabit are more unconventional and less committed to marriage. In other words, cohabitation does not cause divorce but is merely associated with it because the same type of people are involved in both phenomena. Yet, even when this "selection effect" is carefully controlled statistically, a "cohabitation effect" remains.

Marriages are held together by a common commitment that is absent in most, if not all, cohabiting relationships. Partners who live together value autonomy over commitment and tend not to be as committed as married couples in their dedication to the continuation of the relationship.[12]

Cohabitation affects individuals as well as the marriage relationship. According to Michael D. Newcomb and P. M. Bentler, "Cohabiters experienced significantly more difficulty in their marriages with adultery, alcohol, drugs, and independence than couples who had not cohabited."[13] Research also showed that cohabiting couples (when compared to married couples) have "lower relationship quality, lower stability, and a higher level of disagreements."[14]

One study found that "living with a romantic partner prior to marriage was associated with more negative and less positive problem solving support and behavior during marriage." The reason is simple. Since there is less certainty of a long-term commitment, "there may be less motivation for cohabiting partners to develop their conflict resolution and support skills."[15]

Couples living together, however, miss out on more than just the benefits of marriage. Annual rates of depression among cohabiting couples are more than three times higher than they are among married couples.[16] Those who cohabit are much more likely to be unhappy in marriage and much more likely to think about divorce.[17]

Women in cohabiting relationships are more than twice as likely than married women to suffer physical and sexual abuse.[18] And women in cohabiting relationships are nine times more likely to be killed by their partner than are women in marital relationships.[19]

Cohabitation is especially harmful to children. Several studies have found that children currently living with a mother and her unmarried partner have significantly more behavior problems and lower academic performance than children in intact families.[20] Second, there is the risk that the couple will break up creating even more social and personal difficulties for children. Third, many of these children were not born in the present union but in a previous union of one of the adult partners (usually the mother). Living in a house with a mother and an unmarried boyfriend is tenuous at best. Legal claims to child support and other sources of family income are absent.

COHABITATION AND THE BIBLE

The Bible teaches that the act of sexual intercourse can have a strong bonding effect on two people. When done within the bounds of marriage, the man and the woman become one flesh (Eph. 5:31). But sexual intercourse outside of marriage also has consequences. When the apostle Paul wrote to the church in Corinth, he said that when a man joins himself to a prostitute, he becomes one body with her (1 Cor. 6:16). The context of this teaching arose from a problem within the church. A man in the church was having sexual relations with his father's wife (1 Cor. 5:1–3). Paul called this relationship sinful. First, it was incestuous, which is condemned in the Old Testament (Lev. 18:8; Deut. 22:30). Second, there was no marital union but instead an example of cohabitation. Paul's admonition to us is to flee sexual immorality (1 Cor. 6:18).

The New Testament contains about twenty-five passages condemning sexual immorality. The Greek word for sexual immorality is *porneia*, which includes all forms of illicit sexual intercourse. Jesus taught, "For from within, out of men's hearts, come evil thoughts, sexual immorality, theft, murder, adultery, greed, malice, deceit, lewdness, envy, slander, arrogance and folly. All these evils come from inside and make a man unclean" (Mark 7:21–23). Paul said, "It is God's will that you should be sanctified: that you should avoid sexual immorality; that each of you should learn to control his own body in a way that is holy and honorable, not in passionate lust like the heathen, who do not know God" (1 Thess. 4:3–5).

Marriage is God's plan. Marriage provides intimate companionship for life (Gen. 2:18). Marriage provides a context for the procreation and nurture of children (Eph. 6:1–2). And finally, marriage provides a godly outlet for sexual desire (1 Cor. 7:2).

In the New Testament, believers are warned against persistent sin, including sexual sin (1 Cor. 5:1–5). The church is to keep believers accountable for their behavior. Believers are to judge themselves, lest they fall into God's hands (1 Cor 11:31–32). Sexual sin should not even be named among believers (Eph. 5:3).

Living together outside of marriage not only violates biblical commands but it puts a couple and their future marriage at risk. If you want a good marriage, do not do what society says; do what the Bible teaches you to do.

14

ADULTERY

ADULTERY has been committed throughout history, though today it seems more rampant than ever. Tabloid stories report the affairs of politicians, millionaires, and movie stars. Television and films feature and even promote adultery.

How prevalent is adultery? Two of the most reliable studies of adultery came to similar conclusions. The *Janus Report on Sexual Behavior* estimated that "More than one-third of men and one-quarter of women admit having had at least one extramarital sexual experience."[1] A survey by the National Opinion Research Center (University of Chicago) found lower percentages: 25 percent of men had been unfaithful and 17 percent of women. Even when these lower ratios are applied to the current adult population, that means that 19 million husbands and 12 million wives have had an affair.[2]

Whatever the actual numbers, the point is that adultery is much more common than we would like to admit. Frank Pittman, a family therapist and psychiatrist, contended that "There may be as many acts of infidelity in our society as there are traffic accidents."[3] He further argued that the proliferation of adultery has altered society's perception of it. He said, "We won't go back to the times when adulterers were put in the stocks and publicly humiliated, or become one of those societies— and there are many—in which adultery is punishable by death. Society in any case is unable to enforce a rule that the majority of people break, and infidelity is so common it is no longer deviant."[4]

Men and women have affairs for different reasons. Research reveals that women seek affairs in order to be loved, have a friend, and feel needed. Men seek affairs for sexual fulfillment, friendship, and fun.[5]

It appears the percentage of female infidelity is increasing. In 1991, the National Opinion Center asked married women if they had ever had sex outside their marriage, and 10 percent said yes. When the same pollsters asked the same question in 2002, the percentage had increased to 15 percent.[6] During this same period the percentage for married men stayed the same.

It also appears that women who are employed full-time outside of the home are more likely to have an affair than full-time homemakers. Several studies came to this same conclusion. One study found that 47 percent of wives who were employed full-time and 27 percent of full-time homemakers had been involved in an affair before they were 40 years old.[7] And *New Woman* magazine found that 57 percent of employed wives who had an affair met their lover at work.[8]

One conclusion is that adultery is becoming more common, and researchers are finding that women are as likely as men to have an affair. A 1983 study found that 29 percent of married people under 25 had had an affair, with no statistical difference between the number of men and women who chose to be unfaithful to their spouses early in life.[9] By comparison, only 9 percent of spouses in the 1950s under the age of 25 had been involved in extramarital sex. Another study concluded that by age 40 about 50 to 65 percent of husbands and 45 to 55 percent of wives become involved in an extramarital affair.[10]

Affairs are usually more than a one-time event. A 1987 study surveyed 200 men and women and found that their affairs lasted an average of two years.[11] In fact, affairs go through transitions over time. They may begin as romantic, sexual, or emotional relationships and may become intimate friendships. Affairs that become friendships can last decades or a lifetime.

Is this just a problem with non-Christians in society, or is it also a problem in the church? There is growing evidence that adultery is also a problem in Christian circles. *Newsweek* magazine noted that various surveys suggest that as many as 30 percent of male Protestant ministers have had sexual relationships with women other than their wives.[12]

The Journal of Pastoral Care reported a survey of Southern Baptist pastors in which 14 percent acknowledged that they had engaged in "sexual behavior inappropriate to a minister." The survey also reported that 70 percent of the pastors had counseled at least one woman who had had intercourse with another minister.[13]

A survey of nearly 1,000 Protestant clergy by *Leadership* magazine found that 12 percent admitted to sexual intercourse outside of marriage, and that 23 percent had done something sexually inappropriate with someone other than their spouse. The researchers also interviewed nearly 1,000 subscribers to *Christianity Today* who were not pastors. They found that the numbers were nearly double: 45 percent indicated having done something sexually inappropriate, and 23 percent revealed having extramarital intercourse.[14]

MYTHS ABOUT ADULTERY

Marital infidelity destroys marriages and families, and often leads to divorce. Public sentiment against adultery is actually strong, as approximately 80 percent of Americans disapprove of adultery.[15]

Yet, even though most people consider adultery to be wrong and know that it can be devastating, our society still perpetuates a number of untruths about adultery through a popular mythology about extramarital affairs. At this point we want to examine some of the myths about adultery.

Myth #1: "Adultery is about sex." Often just the opposite seems the case. When a sexual affair is uncovered, observers often say, "What did he see in her?" or "What did she see in him?" Frequently the sex is better at home, and the marriage partner is at least as attractive as the adulterous partner.

Being pretty, handsome, or sensual is usually not the major issue. Partners in affairs are not usually chosen because they are prettier, more handsome, or sexier. They are chosen for various sorts of strange and nonsexual reasons. Usually the other woman or the other man in an adulterous relationship meets needs the spouse does not meet in the marriage. Willard Harley listed five primary needs for a man and five primary needs for a women in his book *His Needs, Her Needs: Building an Affair-Proof Marriage*.[16] He stated that unmet needs, by either partner, are a primary cause of extramarital affairs. He has also found that people wander into these affairs with astonishing regularity, in spite of whatever strong moral or religious convictions they may hold. A lack of fulfillment in one of these basic emotional areas creates a dangerous vacuum in a person's life. And, unfortunately, many will eventually fill that need outside of marriage.

Frank Pittman, author of the book *Private Lies: Infidelity and the Betrayal of Intimacy*, found in his own personal study of people who committed adultery that many of his patients who had affairs had a good sex life, but came from marriages with little or no intimacy. He concluded that "Affairs were thus three times more likely to be the pursuit of a buddy than the pursuit of a better orgasm."[17]

Sex may not even be involved in some affairs. The relationship may be merely an emotional liaison. Counselor Bonnie Weil warned that these so-called "affairs of the heart can be even more treacherous than the purely physical kind. Women, particularly, are inclined to leave their husbands when they feel a strong emotional bond with another man."[18]

Myth #2: "Adultery is about character." In the past, society looked down on alcoholics as having weak character because of their problem. Now we see it as an addiction or even a disease. While that does not excuse the behavior, we can see that alcoholism cannot be merely labeled as bad character.

There is growing psychological evidence that adulterous behavior in parents dramatically affects children when they reach adulthood. Just as divorce in a family influences the likelihood of the adult children to consider divorce, so adulterous behavior by parents seems to beget similar behavior by their offspring. Is this not one more example of the biblical teaching that the sins of one generation being visited upon the next?

Myth #3: "Adultery is therapeutic." Some of the psychology books and women's magazines in our culture promote extramarital affairs as positive. The myth that an affair can revive a dull marriage is a devastating lie. Depending on which source you are reading, an affair will make you a better lover, help you with your mid-life crisis, bring joy into your life, or even bring excitement back into your marriage. Nothing could be further from the truth. An affair might give you more sex, but it could also give you a sexually transmitted disease. It might bring your marriage more excitement, if you consider divorce court exciting. Remember that adultery results in divorce 65 percent of the time. As Pittman observed, "For most people and most marriages, infidelity is dangerous."[19]

Myth #4: "Adultery is harmless." Movies are just one venue in which adultery has been promoted positively. *The English Patient*, ranked as 1996's best film by *Time* magazine and the *Los Angeles Times*, received twelve Oscar nominations including best picture of the year for its depiction of an adulterous relationship between a handsome count and the English-born wife of his colleague. *The Bridges of Madison County* related the story of an Iowa farmer's wife who has a brief extramarital affair with a *National Geographic* photographer that supposedly helped re-energize her marriage. *The Prince of Tides* received seven Oscar nominations in 1991 and portrayed a married therapist committing adultery with one of her married patients.

Notice the euphemisms society has developed over the years to excuse or soften the perception of adultery. Many are not repeatable, but ones that are include: fooling around, sleeping around, flings, affairs, and dalliances. These and many other phrases perpetuate the notion the adultery is guilt-free and hurts no one.

Forbidden sex is an addiction that can have devastating consequences to an individual and a family. Adultery shatters trust, intimacy, and self-esteem. It breaks up families, ruins careers, and leaves a trail of pain and destruction in its path. This potential legacy of emotional pain for one's children should be enough to make a person stop and count the costs before it is too late.

Even when affairs are never exposed, emotional costs are involved. For example, adulterous mates deprive their spouses of energy and intimacy that should go into the marriage. They deceive their marriage partners and become dishonest about their feelings and actions. As Pittman observed, "The infidelity is not in the sex, necessarily, but in the secrecy. It isn't whom you lie with. It's whom you lie to."[20]

Myth #5: "Adultery has to end in divorce." Only about 35 percent of couples remain together after the discovery of an adulterous affair; the other 65 percent divorce. Perhaps nothing can destroy a marriage faster than marital infidelity.

The good news is that it does not have to be that way. One counselor claimed that 98 percent of the couples she treats remain together after counseling.[21] Granted, this success rate is not easy to achieve and requires immediate moral choices and forgiveness, but it does demonstrate that adultery does not have to end in divorce.

ONLINE AFFAIRS

The Internet is becoming a breeding ground for adultery. Peggy Vaughn is the author of *The Monogamy Myth* and also serves as an expert for America Online on problems caused by infidelity. She predicted that one "role of the Internet in the future will be as a source of affairs."[22] When she was writing a second book on the subject of adultery, she said she could base half of it just on the letters she receives from people who started an affair online.

An online affair (or cyberaffair) is an intimate or sexually explicit communication between a married person and someone other than their spouse that takes place on the Internet. Usually this communication takes place through an online service. Participants usually visit a chat room to begin a group conversation and then often move into a one-to-one mode of communication. Chat room categories range from "single and liking it" to "married and flirting" to "naked on the keyboard."

Women in a chat room are often surprised at what develops in a fairly short period of time. At first the conversation is stimulating, though flirtatious. Quickly, however, women are often confronted with increasingly sexual questions and comments. Even if the comments do not turn personal, women find themselves quickly sharing intimate information about themselves and their relationships that they would never share with someone in person. Vaughn said, "Stay-at-home moms in chat rooms are sharing all this personal stuff they are hiding from their partners." She found that the intensity of women's online relationships can "quickly escalate into thinking they have found a soulmate."[23]

The Internet has become a new source for adultery just as it has become a new source of pornography for many people. Online relationships frequently go over the line leaving pain, heartbreak, and even divorce in their wake. Even though these online affairs do not involve sex, they can be intense and threaten a marriage just the same.

Even though online affairs do not involve a physical component, the emotional attachment is still there. Online affairs develop because of the dual attraction of attention and anonymity. Someone who has been ignored by a spouse (or at least perceives that he or she is ignored) suddenly becomes the center of attention in a chat room or a one-on-one e-mail exchange. A woman finds it exciting, even intoxicating, that all these men want to talk to her. And they are eager to hear what she says and needs.

Online affairs are seductive. An Internet addict who wants to remain online calls out "one more minute" just as an alcoholic justifies "one more drink." Cyberaffairs provide an opportunity to become another person and chat with distant and invisible neighbors in the high-tech limbo of cyberspace. Social and emotional needs are met, flirting is allowed and even encouraged, and an illusion of intimacy feeds the addiction that has caught so many unsuspecting Internet surfers.

In 1975, Linda Wolfe published *Playing Around* after she studied twenty-one women who were having affairs to keep their marriages intact.[24] The reasoning for many of these women was that if they could meet their own needs, their marriages would be more successful. Many said that they were desperately lonely. Others were afraid, believing their husbands did not love them or were not committed to their marriage. Five years after the initial study, only three of the twenty-one women were still married.

PREVENTING ADULTERY

The general outline for some of following ideas comes from Pittman's *Private Lies*, although I have added additional material. He has counseled 10,000 couples over the last forty years, and about 7,000 have experienced infidelity. He developed nineteen specific suggestions for couples on how to avoid affairs, eight of which are discussed below.[25]

First, accept the possibility of being sexually attracted to another person and of having sexual fantasies. Frank Pittman advised that you should acknowledge that such thoughts can develop so that you will not suppress them. But he also warned that you should not act on them.

Second, you should associate with monogamous people. He said, "They make a good support system." To state it negatively, "Do not be deceived: 'Bad company corrupts good character.' " (1 Cor. 15:33).

Third, work on your marriage. He advised keeping your marriage sexy and working to be intimate with your spouse. He also said to make marriage an important part of your identity. In other words, "Carry your marriage with you wherever you go."

Fourth, be realistic about your marriage. Pittman cautioned, "Don't expect your marriage to make you happy. See your partner as a source of comfort rather than a cause of unhappiness." Accept the reality of marriage; it is not always beautiful. Also accept that you are both imperfect.

Fifth, keep the marriage equal. Share parenting duties because if you do not share, "one partner will become the full-time parent, and the other will become a full-time child" who seeks to be taken care of. And keep your relationship equal. Pittman observed, "The more equal it is, the more both partners will respect and value it."

Sixth, if you are not already married, be careful in your choice of a spouse. For example, marry someone who believes in, and has a family history of, monogamy. Pittman warned, "It is a bad idea to become the fifth husband of a woman who has been unfaithful to her previous four." Also, marry someone who respects and likes your gender because "they will get over the specialness of you yourself and eventually consider you as part of a gender they dislike."

Seventh, call home every day you travel; "otherwise, you begin to have a separate life." Also stay faithful: "If you want your partner to (stay faithful), it is a good idea to stay faithful yourself." And make sure you are open, honest, and authentic. Lies and deception create a secret life that can allow an affair to occur.

Finally, do not overreact or exaggerate the consequences of an affair if it occurs. Pittman said, "It doesn't mean there will be a divorce, murder or suicide. Catch yourself and work your way back into the marriage."

Affairs can destroy a marriage. Take the time to affair-proof your marriage so that you avoid the pain, guilt, and regret that inevitably results. And if you have fallen into an affair, work your way back and rebuild your marriage.

THE CONSEQUENCES OF ADULTERY

When God commands, "You shall not commit adultery" (Ex. 20:14), He did so for our own good. There are significant social, psychological, and spiritual consequences to adultery.

A major social consequence is divorce. An affair that is discovered does not have to lead to divorce, but often it does. About one third of couples remain together after the discovery of an adulterous affair, while the other two thirds usually divorce.

Not surprisingly, the divorce rate is higher among people who have affairs. Annette Lawson, the author of *Adultery: An Analysis of Love and Betrayal*, found that spouses who did not have affairs had the lowest rate of divorce. Women who had multiple affairs (especially if they started early in the marriage) had the highest rate of divorce.[26]

A lesser known fact is that those who divorce rarely marry the person with whom they are having the affair. For example, Jan Halper's study of successful men (executives, entrepreneurs, professionals) found that few men who have affairs divorce their wife and marry their lovers. Only 3 percent of the 4,100 successful men surveyed eventually married their lovers.[27]

Frank Pittman found that the divorce rate among those who married their lovers was 75 percent.[28] The reasons for the high divorce rate include the intervention of reality, guilt, expectations, a general distrust of marriage, and a distrust of the guilty spouse.

The psychological consequences are also significant, even if they are sometimes more difficult to discern. People who pursue an affair often do so for self-esteem needs, yet they often further erode those feelings by violating trust, intimacy, and stability in a marriage relationship. Affairs do not stabilize a marriage; they upset it.

Affairs destroy trust. It is not surprising that marriages formed after an affair and a divorce have such a high divorce rate. If your new spouse cheated before, what guarantee do you have that this person will not begin to cheat on you? Distrust of marriage and distrust of the guilty spouse are significant issues.

Adultery can have long-term consequences. For example, it can lead to unwanted pregnancies. According to one report, "Studies of blood typing show that as many as 1 out of every 10 babies born in North America is not the offspring of the mother's husband."[29] Affairs can also result in sexually transmitted diseases like syphilis, chlamydia, herpes, or even AIDS. Many of these diseases are not curable and will last for a lifetime.

Finally, affairs have spiritual consequences. We grieve the Lord by our actions. We disgrace the Lord as we become one more statistic of moral failure within the body of Christ. We threaten the sacred marriage bond between us and our spouse. We bring guilt into our lives and shame into our marriage and family. Affairs extract a tremendous price in our lives and the lives of those we love and hold dear.

15

DIVORCE

MARRIAGES AND FAMILIES are falling apart in record numbers, and divorce is usually the reason. But often the impact of divorce is overlooked because of its subtle yet insidious erosion of the family structure. When the divorce rate increased in the 1960s, few would have predicted its dire consequences decades later. Divorce quickly moved from the margins of society to the mainstream and changed both the structure of the family.

The preceding conclusions are not just those of Christians; they are also the conclusions of researchers working in the social science field. For example, Diane Medved, a clinical psychologist, set out to write a book to help couples facing transitions due to divorce. She began her book with this startling statement:

> I have to start with a confession: This isn't the book I set out to write.
> I planned to write something consistent with my previous professional
> experience—helping people with decision making. . . . For example, I
> started this project believing that people who suffer over an extended
> period in unhappy marriages ought to get out. . . . I thought that
> striking down taboos about divorce was another part of the ongoing
> enlightenment of the women's, civil-rights, and human potential
> movements of the last twenty-five years. . . . To my utter befuddle-
> ment, the extensive research I conducted for this book brought me to
> one inescapable and irrefutable conclusion: I had been wrong.[1]

She titled her book, *The Case against Divorce.*

Until recently, divorce has been a relatively rare phenomenon. Certainly there have always been some couples who have considered divorce an option. But fundamental changes in our society in the last few decades have changed divorce from being rare to routine.

The number of divorces tripled from 400,000 in 1962 to 1.2 million in 1981, and during the 1970s the divorce rate doubled.[2] To put these statistics in perspective, compare the two most recent generations of women. Just 14 percent of white women who married in the 1940s eventually divorced. A single generation later, almost 50 percent of those married in the late sixties and early seventies have already divorced.[3] Essentially the increase in the divorce rate came not from older couples but from the baby boomer generation. One Stanford University sociologist calculated that while men and women in their twenties comprised only about 20 percent of the population, they contributed 60 percent of the growth in the divorce rate in the 1960s and early 1970s.[4]

This increase was due to at least two major factors: attitude and opportunity. The baby boomers' attitude toward such issues as fidelity, chastity, and commitment were strikingly different from that of their parents. Their parents would stay in a marriage in order to make it work. Baby boomers, however, were less committed to the ideal of marriage and were quite willing to end what they felt was a bad marriage and move on with their lives. While their parents might keep a marriage going "for the sake of the kids," the baby-boom generation as a whole was much less concerned about such issues.

Economic opportunities also seem to be a significant factor in divorce. The rise in divorce closely parallels the increase in the number of women working. Women with a paycheck are less likely to stay in a marriage that was not fulfilling to them. Armed with a measure of economic power, many women have less incentive to stay in a marriage and work out their differences with their husbands. The sociologist David Popenoe surveyed a number of studies on divorce and concluded that "nearly all have reached the same general conclusion. It has typically been found that the probability of divorce goes up the higher the wife's income and the closer that income is to her husband's."[5]

Age, religious faith, and family background also affect the divorce rate. Divorce rates are highest among those who marry young, and those rates are three times greater for people who never attend religious services.[6] Marital failure often breeds marital failure. One study showed that adult children of divorced parents are four times more likely to get divorced than adult children of intact couples.[7]

DIVORCE MYTHS

Two statistical myths surrounding divorce need to be discussed. First, the divorce rate is *not* 50 percent. That percentage comes from comparing two fairly reliable social statistics: the number of marriage licenses issued and the number of divorce decrees issued. The problem arises from comparing the two numbers inappropriately.

In any given year there are approximately two million marriages and one million divorces. Comparing these two numbers produces the frequently-cited 50 percent figure. But only a very small percentage of the people divorced in any given year were also married in that year. Comparing divorces to marriages in this way is a case of statistically mixing apples and oranges.

A better way to estimate the divorce rate is to take the percentage of the total adult population that is currently or has never been married (72 percent) and to compare that number to the number of people who are currently divorced (9 percent). This calculation produces a 13 percent current divorce rate.

The second myth is related to the first: most marriages *do not* end in divorce. While there has been much concern and hand-wringing over the rising divorce rate, we should not lose sight of the fact that a majority of marriages do not end in divorce court. Substantial media attention on divorce overlooks the fact that approximately 50 million established marriages are "flowing along like Ol' Man River."[8] These marriages may run into white water and the ride may be bumpy at times, but they continue to flow along the channel of marital stability and fidelity.

DIVORCE AND FAMILIES

Although the divorce rate is not as bad as advertised, it is still having a devastating impact on both adults and children. Every year, parents of over one million children divorce. These divorces effectively cut one generation off from another. Children are reared without the presence of their father or mother. Children are often forced to take sides in the conflict. And children often carry the scars of the conflict and frequently blame themselves for the divorce.

One demographer looking at this ominous trend of divorce and reflecting on its impact acknowledged, "No one knows what effect divorce and remarriage will have on the children of the baby boom. A few decades ago, children of divorced parents were an oddity. Today they are the majority. The fact that divorce is the norm may make it easier for children to accept their parents' divorce. But what will it do to their marriages in the decades ahead? No one will know until it's too late to do anything about it."[9]

What little is known about the long-term impact of divorce is disturbing. In 1971, Judith Wallerstein began a study of sixty middle-class families in the midst of divorce. Her ongoing research has provided a longitudinal study of the long-term effects of divorce on parents and children. Like Diane Medved, Wallerstein had to revise her previous assumptions. According to the prevailing view in 1971, divorce was seen as a brief crisis that would resolve itself. Wallerstein and Sandra Blakeslee's *Second Chances: Men, Women and Children a Decade after Divorce* vividly illustrated the long-term psychological devastation wrought not only on the children but also on the adults.[10] Here are just a few of their findings of the aftershocks of divorce:

- Three out of five children felt rejected by at least one parent.

- Five years after their parents' divorce, more than one-third of the children were doing markedly worse than they had been before the divorce.

- Half of the children grew up in settings in which the parents were warring with each other even after the divorce.

- One-third of the women and one-fourth of the men felt that life had been unfair, disappointing, and lonely.

Some have criticized the Wallerstein-Blakeslee study because it was not a representative study. For example, more than three-fourths of both mothers and fathers in their study had at least some college training, many with advanced degrees. But the fact that the study was unrepresentative made their conclusions all the more shocking. White, educated, upper-middle-class children whose lives before divorce were relatively untroubled economically and emotionally should (at least theoretically) have the least problems with divorce. Their long-term conflicts clearly demonstrated that the emotional tremors register on the psychological Richter scale many years after the divorce.

The researcher Robert Coombs came to similar conclusions about the impact of divorce on adults. He found that:

- Divorced men and women experience far greater health problems than their married or never-married counterparts.

- A greater number of divorced men and women are admitted for psychiatric care than married or single people, and their treatments are less successful.[11]

One review of thirty-two studies on the long-term effects of divorce concluded, "Adults of divorced parents have more problems and lower levels of well-being than adults whose parents stay married. They are depressed more frequently, feel less satisfied with life, get less education, and have less prestigious jobs. Even their physical health is poorer."[12]

For children the emotional impact also has a detrimental educational impact. Two researchers came to the following conclusions about the impact of divorce on children:

- Children of divorce do poorer in school, exhibit greater behavioral problems at home and in school, and engage in sexual activity and criminal behavior earlier in life than children whose parents remain married.[13]

- Compared with those from intact families, adults who experienced divorce as children have poorer psychological adjustment, lower socioeconomic attainment, and greater marital instability.[14]

One national study found an overall average of one lost year of education for children in single-parent families.[15]

Divorce also significantly affects fragmented families. Family rules, relationships, and traditions suffer. By their own reports, divorced mothers are less likely to read to their children, share meals with them, and supervise school activities than married mothers. Compared with married mothers, single mothers exercise less control and have fewer rules about bedtimes, television watching, homework, and household chores.[16]

These fragmented families are also affected economically. After divorce the income of households with children declines and a sizable percentage of divorce and separated women with kids live in poverty. In fact, the middle class in the United States has been rocked by the one-two punch of divorce and illegitimacy, creating what has been called the "feminization of poverty." Census Bureau statistics show that single moms are five times more likely to be poor than are their married sisters.[17]

Remarriage after divorce adds another additional twist to modern relationships. Nearly half of all marriages in 1990 involved at least one person who had been down the aisle before, up from 31 percent in 1970.[18]

These changing family structures complicate relationships. Divorce and remarriage shuffle family members together in foreign and awkward ways. Clear lines of authority and communication get blurred and confused in these newly revised families. One commentator trying to get a linguistic handle on these arrangements called them "neo-nuclear" families.[19] The rules for these neo-nukes are complex and ever-changing. Children looking for stability are often insecure and frustrated. One futuristic commentator imagined this possible scenario:

> On a spring afternoon, half a century from today, the Joneses are gathered to sing "Happy Birthday" to Junior. There's Dad and his third wife, Mom and her second husband, Junior's two half-brothers from his father's first marriage, his six stepsisters from his mother's spouse's previous unions, 100-year-old Great Grandpa, all eight of Junior's current "grandparents," assorted aunts, uncles-in-law and stepcousins. While one robot scoops up the gift wrappings and another blows out the candles, Junior makes a wish . . . that he didn't have so many relatives.[20]

The stress on remarried couples is difficult enough, but it intensifies when stepchildren are involved. Conflict between a stepparent and stepchild is inevitable and can often threaten the stability of a remarriage. According to one study remarriages that involve stepchildren are more likely to end in divorce than those that do not.[21] Seventeen percent of marriages that are remarriages for both husband and wife and that involve stepchildren break up within three years.[22]

NO-FAULT DIVORCE

Historically the laws of the United States governing marriage were based on the traditional Judeo-Christian belief that marriage was intended to be a permanent institution. Thus, the desire for divorce was not held to be self-justifying. Legally the grounds for divorce had to be circumstances that justified making an exemption to the assumption of marital permanence. The spouse seeking a divorce had to *prove* that the other spouse had committed one of the "faults" recognized as justifying the dissolution of the marriage. In most states the classic grounds for divorce were cruelty, desertion, and adultery.

This legal foundation changed when California enacted a statute in 1969 that allowed for no-fault divorce. Before 1969, society erected a formidable barrier to prevent (or at least hinder) the dissolution of marriage. The legal change to no-fault divorce effectively led to what could now be called "divorce-on-demand." One by one, various state legislatures enacted no-fault divorce laws so that today, this concept has become the de facto legal principle in every state.

Although marriage was to be "for better or worse, for richer or poorer," no ethic of self-sacrifice was likely to endure the self-indulgent 1960s. Perhaps the rise in divorce was inevitable, but the changes in the divorce law made it more certain. Obviously the increase in the divorce rate could not be solely explained by the implementation of no-fault divorce laws. The divorce rate was already going up when many states passed no-fault provisions. But these laws no doubt contributed to the increase. A University of Oklahoma study found that in the three years after no-fault divorce, the divorce rates in 44 of 50 states rose.[23]

Arguments for no-fault divorce seemed compelling at the time. The changes in the divorce laws were hailed as an overdue reform of a hypocritical system rife with conflict and lurid accusations. Legislators were promised that no longer would partners have to prove fault with clandestine photographs and private investigators. Proponents of no-fault divorce promised that marital separation would be more amicable.

The fault-based system of divorce law had its roots in the understanding that marriage was a sacrament and indissoluble. The current no-fault provisions changed this perception. Marriage is no longer viewed as a covenant; it is seen instead as a contract. But it is an even less reliable contract than a standard business contract.

Classic contract law holds that a specific promise is binding and cannot be broken merely because the promisor changes his or her mind. In fact, the concept of "fault" in divorce proceedings is more like tort law than contract law in that it implies a binding obligation between two parties which has been breached, thus leading to a divorce. When state legislatures implemented no-fault divorce provisions, they could have replaced the fault-based protections with contract-like protections. Unfortunately they did not. In just a few decades we have moved from a position where divorce was permitted for a few reasons to a position in which divorce is permitted for *any* reason, or no reason at all.

Robert Plunkett, vice-dean of the Southern California Institute of Law, described the case against no-fault divorce in this way: "The wedding vow has devolved from being the most serious and solemn oath a typical person ever made into being less than a contract. An oral contract made with a two-year-old is more binding than the contract of marriage; it at least binds one party, the adult. A marriage contract is binding on no one."[24]

The impact on the institution of marriage has been devastating. Marginal marriages are much easier to dissolve, and couples who may have tried to stick it out and work out their problems instead opt for a no-fault divorce.

But all marriages (not just marginal marriages) are at risk. After all, marriages do not start out marginal. Most marriages start out on a solid footing. But after the honeymoon comes the more difficult process of learning to live together harmoniously. The success of the process is affected by both internal factors (such as willingness to meet each other's needs) and external factors (such as the availability of divorce). But even these factors are interrelated. If the law gives more protection to the marriage contract, a partner may be more likely to love sacrificially and invest effort in the marriage. If the law gives less protection, a partner may be more likely to adopt a "looking-out-for-number-one" attitude.

The breakdown of marriage and family through divorce has eroded the social significance of the institution of marriage. Pitrim Sorokin, a Russian sociologist, predicted decades ago that "divorces and separations will increase until any profound difference between socially sanctioned marriages and illicit sex-relationships will disappear."[25]

With millions of people divorced and millions more unwed couples living together, social acceptance for nontraditional lifestyles and relationships rises. Just as bad money drives out good money, so do these relationships cheapen the sacred institution of marriage.

In her book *The Abolition of Marriage*, Maggie Gallagher wrote:

> The law now forbids private individuals from distinguishing between married and unmarried couples in many cases. For example, many landlords and home mortgage companies, for a host of sound business as well as social reasons, once showed a certain favoritism for married couples and intact families. But with the rise in divorce rates, legislatures and courts established laws forbidding discrimination in housing or credit on the basis of marital status.[26]

Under the current laws and the current social climate, marriage is but one of many social lifestyles and options.

Various divorce reform bills have been proposed to rectify the current legal situation regarding divorce. Here are a few of the provisions found in many of these bills:

1. *Proving fault:* When one spouse opposes the divorce, the other spouse must prove fault.

2. *Family counseling:* All parties in uncontested divorces must seek therapy and counseling. In contested cases, therapy would be a court's discretion.

3. *Family plan:* Divorcing parents must establish a plan for their children's physical care and financial future.

4. *Prenuptial counseling:* Premarital counseling would be required for couples.

Before no-fault divorce was instituted, women held a potent weapon. If a man wanted his freedom, he would have to pay for it. Usually she gained a measure of economic security through bargaining. Currently under no-fault divorce laws, one spouse (even over the objections of the other) can obtain a divorce for essentially any reason at any time. By giving all the legal clout to the party that wants to break the marriage (and virtually none to the party that wants to preserve it), less culpable parties are forced to seek concessions from their estranged spouses. Often these concessions take the form of women being forced to accept insufficient child support payments.

Returning to a fault basis for marriage would level the playing field and reduce the number of divorces. Currently 80 percent of divorces in the United States are unilateral rather than truly mutual decisions.[27] Putting couples through the bother of offering proof of fault is also a good way of separating the cases where both mutually desire to divorce from other cases where the non-initiating party has merely given up.

BIBLICAL PERSPECTIVE

The Bible speaks to the issue of divorce in both the Old and New Testaments. The most important Old Testament passage on divorce is Deuteronomy 24:1–4:

> If a man marries a woman who becomes displeasing to him because he finds something indecent about her, and he writes her a certificate of divorce, gives it to her and sends her from his house, and if after she leaves his house she becomes the wife of another man, and her second husband dislikes her and writes her a certificate of divorce, gives it to her and sends her from his house, or if he dies, then her first husband, who divorced her, is not allowed to marry her again after she has been defiled. That would be detestable in the eyes of the Lord. Do not bring sin upon the land the Lord your God is giving you as an inheritance.

These verses were not intended to endorse divorce. The intention was to regulate the existing custom of divorce, not to put forth God's ideal for marriage. Jesus taught that this was a concession to human sinfulness and to those whose "hearts were hard" (Matt. 19:8).

Divorce was widespread in the ancient Near East. The certificate of divorce apparently was intended to protect the reputation of the woman and to give her the right to remarry. This public declaration also protected her from charges of adultery. The Mishnah, for example, stated that a divorce certificate was not valid unless the husband explicitly said, "You are free to marry any man."[28]

Key to understanding Deuteronomy 24:1–4 is the definition of "something indecent." It probably did not mean adultery, since that was subject to the penalty of death (Deut. 22:22), or premarital intercourse with another man (Deut. 22:20–21), since that carried the same penalty. The precise meaning of the phrase is unknown and was subject to some debate even during the time of Christ. The conservative rabbinical school of Shammai understood "something indecent" to mean a major sexual offense. The liberal rabbinical school of Hillel taught that it referred to anything displeasing to the husband, including something as trivial as spoiling his food. The apparent purpose of this law was to prevent frivolous divorce and to protect a woman who was divorced by her husband. The passage in no way encourages divorce; instead, it regulates the consequences of divorce.

Another significant Old Testament passage is Malachi 2:10–16:

> Have we not all one Father? Did not one God create us? Why do we
> profane the covenant of our fathers by breaking faith with one an-
> other? . . . Has not the LORD made them one? In flesh and spirit
> they are his. And why one? Because he was seeking godly offspring.
> So guard yourself in your spirit, and do not break faith with the wife
> of your youth. "I hate divorce," says the LORD God of Israel.

This passage deals with breaking a prior agreement or covenant. It specifically addresses the issue of illegal intermarriage and the issue of divorce. Malachi taught that husbands and wives are to be faithful to each other because they have God as their Father. Their marriage relationship is built on a solemn covenant. While God may tolerate divorce under some of the circumstances described in Deuteronomy 24, the instructions were given to protect the woman if a divorce should occur. This passage in Malachi reminds us that God hates divorce.

The Gospel of Matthew provides the clearest teachings by Jesus on the subject of divorce: "It has been said 'Anyone who divorces his wife must give her a certificate of divorce.' But I tell you that anyone who divorces his wife, except for marital unfaithfulness, causes her to commit adultery, and anyone who marries a woman so divorced commits adultery" (5:31–32). "I tell you that anyone who divorces his wife, except for marital unfaithfulness, and marries another woman commits adultery" (19:9).

In these passages Jesus challenged the views of the two schools of Jewish thought (Shammai and Hillel), teaching that marriage is for life and should not be dissolved by divorce. Defining the word *porneia* (translated "marital unfaithfulness" in Matt. 5:32) is a key element in trying to understanding the passages. While some commentators teach that this word refers to incestuous relationships or sexual promiscuity during the betrothal period, most scholars believe the word applies to relentless, persistent, and unrepentant adultery. Among those holding to this "exception clause" for adultery, some believe remarriage is possible, while others do not.

The other significant section of teaching on divorce in the New Testament is Paul's teaching on divorce in 1 Corinthians 7:10–15:

To the married I give this command (not I, but the Lord): A wife must not separate from her husband. But if she does, she must remain unmarried or else be reconciled to her husband. And a husband must not divorce his wife. To the rest I say this (I, not the Lord): If any brother has a wife who is not a believer and she is willing to live with him, he must not divorce her. And if a woman has a husband who is not a believer and he is willing to live with her, she must not divorce him. For the unbelieving husband has been sanctified through his wife, and the unbelieving wife has been sanctified through her believing husband. Otherwise your children would be unclean, but as it is, they are holy. But if the unbeliever leaves, let him do so. A believing man or woman is not bound in such circumstances; God has called us to live in peace.

In the first section, Paul addressed Christians married to one another. Paul was obviously aware of the prevalence of divorce in the Greek world and of the legal right that a wife had to initiate a divorce. He gave the command for believers to stay married.

In the next section Paul addressed the issue of mixed marriages. He said that even though the couples in such marriages are religiously incompatible, the believing spouse is not to seek divorce. Some divorces may have been initiated because of the command of Ezra to the Israelites in Jerusalem after the exile to divorce themselves from pagan spouses (Ezra 10:11). Paul affirmed the same biblical principle: do not seek divorce. However, if the unbelieving spouse insists on divorce, the believer may have to concede to those proceedings and is not bound in such circumstances.

Based on the preceding verses we can conclude that a Christian can acquiesce to divorce in cases of marital infidelity by the other spouse or in cases of desertion by an unbelieving spouse. Yet even in these cases the church should not encourage divorce. Certainly in troubling cases that involve mental, sexual, or physical abuse, legal separation is available as a remedy to protect the abused spouse. God hates divorce; therefore, Christians should never be in the position of encouraging or promoting divorce. Instead, they should be encouraging reconciliation.

One final question is whether a divorced person is eligible for a leadership position within the church. First Timothy 3:12 calls for a church leader to be above reproach and "the husband of one wife." Rather than prohibiting a divorced person from serving in leadership, the language of this verse actually focuses on practicing polygamists. Polygamy was practiced in the first century and was even found among Jewish and Christian groups. The phrase is literally "a one-woman man," that is, a man who is faithful to and focused on his wife. If Paul intended to prohibit a divorced person from leadership, he could have used a much less ambiguous term.

As Christians in a society where divorce is rampant, we must come back to these important biblical principles concerning marriage. Christians should work to build strong marriages. Pastors must frequently preach and teach about the importance of marriage. Christians should encourage others to attend various marriage enrichment seminars and ministries in their communities.

Christians should also reach out to those who have been divorced and communicate Christ's forgiveness to them in the midst of their shattered lives. They need counseling and support groups. Many times they also need financial help and direction as they begin to put together the shattered pieces of their lives.

Churches must be careful that their ministry to divorced people does not compromise their theology. Christians must reach out with both biblical convictions and biblical compassion. Marriage for life is God's ideal (Genesis 2); nevertheless, millions of people have been devastated by divorce and need to feel the compassionate outreach from Christians.

Churches have unfortunately erred on one side or another. Most churches have maintained a strong stand on marriage and divorce. While this strong biblical stand is admirable, it should also be balanced with compassion toward those caught in the throes of divorce. Strong convictions without compassionate outreach often seems to communicate that divorce is the unforgivable sin.

On the other hand, some churches in their desire to minister to divorced people have compromised their theological convictions. By starting without biblically based convictions about marriage and divorce, they have let their congregation's circumstances influence their theology.

Christians must simultaneously reach out with conviction and compassion. Marriage for life is God's ideal, but divorce is a reality in our society. Christians should reach out with Christ's forgiveness to those whose lives have been shattered by divorce.

16

CRIME AND CAPITAL
PUNISHMENT

CRIME, and its appropriate punishments, is a fundamental issue in society and certainly one that Christians must address. How do we deal with crime? What punishments are acceptable? Is capital punishment justifiable from a biblical perspective?

Crime in America is certainly a concern. Listen to the ticks of the crime clock: one murder every twenty-two minutes, one rape every five minutes, one robbery every forty-nine seconds, and one burglary every ten seconds.[1] And the cost of crime continues to mount: $78 billion for the criminal justice system, $64 billion for private protection, $202 billion in loss of life and work, $120 billion in crimes against business, $60 billion in stolen goods and fraud, $40 billion from drug abuse, and $110 billion from drunk driving. When all the costs are added, crime costs Americans a stunning $675 billion each year.[2]

CRIME MYTHS

The amount of information and misinformation about crime is staggering. Hardly any other issue is more fraught with myths, lies, and distortions than the issue of crime. Moreover, most citizens have become almost numb to the impact of crime

In his famous 1992 essay "Defining Deviancy Down," Daniel Patrick Moynihan described how society was willing to redefine deviant behavior as normal. He noted, "In 1929 in Chicago during Prohibition, four gangsters killed seven gangsters on February 14. The nation was shocked. The event became legend. It merits not one but two entries in the *World Book Encyclopedia*. I leave it to others to judge, but it would appear that the society in the 1920s was simply not willing to put up with this degree of deviancy."[3]

In contrast, Americans today have "normalized" street crime. They avoid bad neighborhoods and public parks. They lock their doors and windows, install burglar alarms, and live in gated communities. And they try not to think of crime, accepting assurances from politicians the problem is getting better. In essence people are willing to "define deviancy down."

Christians who want to make their faith relevant to the public arena—especially the criminal justice system—must overcome both ignorance and apathy. It is essential that Christians learn to navigate the maze of misinformation and get to the facts about crime. To make our homes and neighborhoods safe, Christians should first understand why crime has become such a problem. Here are a few keys facts and statistics about crime.

First, the crime rate has been increasing for decades. The recent string of heinous crimes does not represent a sudden wave of crime in America. Nor does the gradual drop in crimes signal an end to the long-term crime wave in this country.

Since the 1960s, the crime rate has risen steadily. While the population has increased only 41 percent since 1960, crime has increased over 300 percent. Moreover, the violent crime rate has increased more than 550 percent.[4] In fact, the rate of violent crime in the United States is worse than in any other industrialized country.

Second, teenagers are responsible for a disproportionate share of violent crime. The violent-crime rate seems to rise and fall in tandem with the number of teens in the population. But recently teen violence has exploded. Teen arrests for all violent crimes have doubled within the last few decades, and murder arrests of teens have also doubled even though the teen population remained relatively steady during that period. Also disturbing has been the fact that as the arrest rate for white teen males has doubled, the arrest rate for blacks has multiplied three and a half times.[5]

Third, the median age of criminals is dropping. The perception that criminals are getting younger and younger is backed up by statistics. Kids barely entering puberty are just as likely as twenty-year-old thugs to pull a gun and use it. In 1982, 390 teens between the ages of thirteen and fifteen were arrested for murder. A decade later this total jumped to 740.[6]

Why the increase? Hopelessness is one reason. More than one in five American children already live below the poverty line, and the percentage of illegitimate births is increasing. Single-parent families is another reason. Teen boys without a strong male role model often pick up the values of the street. Kids from broken and dysfunctional homes find acceptance in gangs and relief from their emotional pain in drugs and alcohol. Already more than 30 percent of all births are out of wedlock, and some social commentators predict that the percentage could swell to 40 percent.

Drugs and the growing "gun culture" among urban youth are another reason for increasing juvenile violence. Battles between gangs over turf and drugs are dangerous enough. But the proliferation of automatic weapons and other lethal firearms in the hands of young criminals further fuels the fire of violent juvenile crime.

Fourth, habitual criminals commit the majority of crimes. The criminologist Marvin Wolfgang compiled arrest records for males born and raised in Philadelphia (in 1945 and in 1958). He found that just 7 percent in each age-group committed two-thirds of all violent crime. This percentage included three-fourths of the rapes and robberies, and nearly all the murders. The 7 percent had five or more arrests before the age of eighteen (and this did not include getting away with dozens of additional crimes). One article using Wolfgang's statistic concluded that about 75,000 new, young, habitual criminal predators are added to our population each year.[7]

Later studies found that a minority of this minority is extremely violent and persistent. A Rand study of these so-called "super predators" found that even among prison populations, they were responsible for a disproportionate number of burglaries and drug deals.[8]

Another point: crime does (unfortunately) pay. Most criminals are not caught or convicted. Recent statistics show that nearly three of every four convicted criminals are not incarcerated and fewer than one in ten serious crimes results in imprisonment.[9]

Contrary to popular belief, crime is not an irrational act. Some crimes are irrational, such as crimes of passion and drug-induced crimes, but not all. Many crimes are actually calculated decisions based on cost/benefit. If the expected punishment is low, potential criminals commit a crime. If the expected punishment is high, many potential criminals are deterred. Expected punishment can be calculated by multiplying four probabilities: the probability of being arrested for a crime, the probability of being prosecuted, the probability of being convicted, and the probability of going to prison.

Morgan Reynolds of Texas A&M University compiled interesting facts regarding expected punishment for burglary. Each month 500,000 burglaries occur; 250,000 of these are reported to the police; 35,000 arrests are made; 30,450 prosecutions take place; 24,060 are convicted; and 6,010 are sent to prison (the rest are paroled). Thus, of the 500,0000 burglaries each month, only 6,000 burglars went to jail. Stated another way, essentially 98 percent of all burglaries never result in a prison sentence! And if this 2 percent effectiveness ratio is not disturbing enough, Reynolds found that the average time served was only thirteen months.[10]

Since more than 98 percent of the burglaries never result in a prison sentence and since the average burglary sentence is thirteen months, if we multiply 98 percent times 13 months, we get an expected punishment for burglary of 4.8 days.[11] On the average a potential criminal can expect to spend only 4.8 days in prison for each act of burglary. Put another way, stealing is profitable as long as the object stolen is worth more than five days behind bars. No wonder crime has increased in this country.

Finally, prison rehabilitation programs do not reduce crime. The United States has one of the highest incarceration rates in the world. Putting violent criminals behind bars may make the world a safer place by keeping them from committing crimes. But when these criminals return to society, usually their attitude and behavior have not changed. They are likely to end up in jail again. Currently the recidivism rate—the percentage of released criminals who committee crimes again—hovers at about 70 percent.

HOW TO FIGHT CRIME

First, place more police on the streets. The statistics from Reynolds cited earlier illustrate why America has a problem with burglary. Less than 2 percent of all burglaries result in a prison sentence. Similar statistics exist for other major crimes including murder. Twenty-five years ago, there were three police officers for every crime committed. Today 3.3 times as many violent crimes are committed as there are police officers [12] It is not surprising that we have an epidemic of crime in this country when the chances of being caught, prosecuted, and convicted are so low. The average criminal has no reason to fear law enforcement. The obvious solution is to increase the deterrent through more police and through swift and sure punishments.

Second, put violent criminals in prison. The premise is simple: a criminal in prison cannot shoot your family. While the idea of incarceration is not new, some of the recent findings are. The Justice Department's "The Case for More Incarceration" showed the following:[13]

- Incarceration is cheaper than letting a criminal out on the streets.

- Although the crime rate is high, the rate of increase has been going down since we started putting more people in prison.

- Blacks and whites are treated equally and the vast majority of law-abiding African-Americans would gain most from more incarceration of criminals because African-Americans are more likely to be victims of violent crime.

Putting criminals behind bars keeps them off the streets and is less expensive to society than letting them back out on the streets.

But is it really less expensive to keep criminals in prison? What about the expense of building new prisons? While the cost of building prisons is high, a study by the National Institute of Justice suggested that the cost of *not* building prisons is even higher. Their study demonstrated that a typical career offender turned loose in society will engage in a personal crime wave that is seventeen times more costly than incarceration.[14]

The cost of sending someone to prison for one year is about $25,000. A Rand

Corporation survey of professional criminals estimated that an average criminal commits 187 to 287 crimes a year each, costing society an average of $2,300.[15] Therefore, releasing a career criminal would cost $430,000 a year—compared to $25,000 for the cost of imprisonment.

Third, focus on habitual criminals. One publication by the Justice Department stated that most violent crimes are committed by people who have already been in the criminal justice system. This statistic included those who have been arrested, convicted, or imprisoned, or who are on probation or parole. The chronic offender has had five or more arrests by the age of eighteen and has gotten away with dozens of other crimes.

Police departments that target "serious habitual offenders" and put them behind bars have found that the number of violent crimes as well as property crimes drop significantly. Arresting, prosecuting, convicting, and incarcerating this small percentage of criminals will make communities safer.

Fourth, keep violent criminals in prison longer. Contrary to the popular assumption that judges "lock 'em up and throw away the keys," most criminals serve much less time than their sentences. Most citizens are shocked to learn that violent criminals serve only five and a half years for murder, three years for rape, two and a fourth years for robbery, and one and a fourth years for assault. Those are the sobering facts wrought from lenient early-release practices and prison overcrowding.

Government statistics (for thirty-six states and the District of Columbia) show that although violent offenders received an average sentence of seven years and eleven months imprisonment, they actually served an average of only two years and eleven months in prison—or only 37 percent of their imposed sentences. The statistics also show that, typically, 51 percent of violent criminals were discharged from prison in two years or less, and 76 percent were back on the streets in four years or less.[16]

Incarceration incapacitates violent criminals and keeps them off the streets. Incarceration also deters would-be criminals. Criminologists have shown that an increase in arrest rates reduces the crime rate, and they have also demonstrated that an increase in sentence length also decreases crime rates. Catching more criminals, convicting more criminals, and keeping more criminals behind bars will reduce the crime rate.

Finally, provide alternative sentencing for nonviolent offenders. Criminals who are not a physical threat to society should not be locked up with violent criminals but should be sentenced to projects that will pay back the community. Check forgers and petty thieves should not be thrown in prison alongside murderers and rapists. This involves paying the cost of incarcerating someone who should work off his or her debt to society and provide restitution for the victim. All criminals should pay restitution to their victims, but nonviolent criminals can do so without being sent to prison.

Two key biblical principles concerning crime and punishment are retribution and restitution. Retribution is the act of punishing a criminal. This concept can be seen in the *lex talionis* principle found in such passages as Exodus 21:23–25 and Leviticus 24:17–21, and in other regulations in the Mosaic Law (Deut. 19:16–21; 22:24; 25:11–12). Another key principle is restitution, repaying to the victim what was lost or stolen. The numerous fines described in Exodus 21:18—22:17 were not paid to the government; they were paid to the victim by the offender.

Locking up violent criminals makes sense; locking up nonviolent criminals does not. Currently it costs more to warehouse a criminal for one year than it does to send the brightest student to Harvard University. Alternative sentencing for non-violent offenders will reduce taxpayer cost and generate funds that can provide restitution for the crime committed.

Most crimes are not committed against the state; they are committed against people. These victims will benefit more if a criminal is paying them restitution, and the taxpayers will benefit by not having to warehouse criminals who pose little danger to society.

A key to fighting crime is to transform the lives of criminals. The crime roblem will not go away merely by locking up criminals. As stated previously, they will eventually return to society and commit more crimes if they do not change their attitudes and behaviors. Texas, for example, has one of the largest prison systems in the world, with more than 145,000 inmates behind bars in 1995. But these prisoners will not stay behind bars indefinitely. Penologists estimate that 95 percent of these inmates will be returned to society within five years. They also estimate that 43 percent of those released will be back in prison within three years of their release date.[17]

Government prison rehabilitation programs are a dismal failure. More than 70 percent of all prisoners will return to prison. Prison does not transform lives. Often it perpetuates criminal behavior.

Prison ministries can and do make a difference. Convicts involved with Christian organizations that minister to prisoners have a recidivism rate in the single digits.[18] Government should encourage more groups like these to continue and to expand their ministries in prison. Churches should encourage their members to work with these ministries and consider developing their own outreach to those in prison.

Government programs can also make a difference. Boot camps for young offenders and drug treatment for drug offenders can change behavior. The criminal justice system should also require inmates to attend school, undergo drug testing and treatment, and work in prison-based industries. The importance of work, education, and drug-free living will greatly increase a released prisoner's chance to return to a productive life when he or she returns to society.

Community programs also deter crime. Many cities have introduced curfews prohibiting minors from being on the streets from 10 p.m. to 6 a.m. Exceptions are made for those passing through town or on their way to or from a political or religious event.

Other neighborhoods have erected roadblocks. Drug dealing drops dramatically when police check for driver's licenses and when local citizens write down license plate numbers or when they film such activities with hand-held video cameras. Setting up a neighborhood crime watch program has also been a major deterrent to crime in many communities.

Citizens and legislators need to take back the streets. Implementing these commonsense measures in the legislature and in our communities will help make our streets safe again. But crime is also fed by the explosion of the drug culture. The problem of drugs in our society must also be addressed.

Christians need to see their responsibility in this area of social service. Most citizens only think about crime when they have been affected by it. Christians need to be salt and light in society and use the government to reduce crime and use the church to be a positive influence on those caught up in criminal activity.

What about capital punishment? Should Christians support the death penalty? The answer to that question is controversial, and Christians are somewhat divided on the issue. Many feel that the Bible has spoken to the issue, but others believe that the New Testament ethic of love replaces the Old Testament law.

CAPITAL PUNISHMENT AND THE OLD TESTAMENT

The Old Testament records a number of cases in which God commanded the use of capital punishment. The Old Testament is replete with references and examples of God taking life. In a sense God used capital punishment to deal with Israel's sins and the sins of nations surrounding Israel.

One example was the flood in Noah's day (Genesis 6—8). God destroyed all human life and animal life except what was in the ark. Another example is God's destruction of Sodom and Gomorrah (Genesis 18—19) because of their heinous sin. In the time of Moses, God took the lives of the Egyptian firstborn (Exodus 11) and destroyed the Egyptian army in the Red Sea (Exodus 14). When the Israelites were wandering in the wilderness God punished people at Kadesh Barnea (Numbers 13—14) and caused 14,700 to die of a plague because of Korah's sin (Numbers 16:49).

The Old Testament also teaches that God instituted capital punishment in the Mosaic Law, although the principle of capital punishment preceded the Old Testament law code. According to Genesis 9:6, capital punishment is based on the sanctity of life: "Whoever sheds man's blood by man his blood shall be shed; for in the image of God, has God made man." This verse clearly established the principle of capital punishment: murder is to be punished by death because of the sanctity of human life. Humans are created in the image of God, and murder is an offense against man and an outrage against God.

Some scholars have pointed to the style in that which pronouncement is given. The verse displays chiastic parallelism, in that every word of the first section is repeated in reverse order in the second section. Apparently this reflects the principle of measure for measure in God's system of justice.[19]

The Mosaic Law set forth numerous offenses punishable by death. The first is murder (Exodus 21). Premeditated murder (or what the King James Version refers to as "lying in wait") was punishable by death. A second offense punishable by death was involvement in the occult (Exodus 22; Lev. 20:6; Deuteronomy 18—19). This included sorcery, divination, or being a medium. Third, capital punishment was also to be used against perpetrators of certain sexual sins such as rape, incest, or homosexuality (Lev. 20:11–13).

Within the Old Testament theocracy capital punishment was extended to various offenses beyond murder. While the death penalty for these offenses is limited to that particular dispensation of revelation, the principle in Genesis 9:6, as noted, preceded the theocracy. The principle of *lex talionis* (a life for a life, an eye for an eye) is tied to the creation order. Capital punishment is implemented because of the sanctity of life.

CAPITAL PUNISHMENT AND THE NEW TESTAMENT

Some Christians believe that capital punishment does not apply to the the church age. However, as already discussed, capital punishment was established long before the New Testament era. Even so, some Christians argue that in the Sermon on the Mount, Jesus seemed to be arguing against capital punishment. However, He was speaking against the personal desire for vengeance. He was not denying the power and responsibility of the government; instead, He was telling believers that they should not try to replace government. They should love their enemies and turn the other cheek.

Some have said that Jesus was setting aside capital punishment because of His actions in John 8 since He did not call for the woman caught in adultery to be stoned. But the Pharisees were trying to catch Jesus in a trap between the Roman law and the Mosaic Law. If He said they should stone her, they would break the Roman law. Or if He refused to allow them to stone her, He would break the Mosaic Law (Lev. 20:10; Deut. 22:22). Jesus' answer avoided the conflict: He said that he who was without sin should cast the first stone. Since He did suggest that a stone be thrown (John 8:7), He was not abolishing the death penalty.

The New Testament includes other examples of the principle of capital punishment being reinforced. Romans 13:1–7, for example, teaches that human government is ordained by God and that the civil magistrate is a servant of God. People are to obey the government because it does not bear the sword in vain. The fact that the apostle Paul used the image of the sword (v. 4) further supports the idea that capital punishment was to be used by government in the New Testament age as well. Rather than abolish the idea of the death penalty, Paul used the emblem of the Roman sword to reinforce the idea of capital punishment. The Greek word for "sword" refers not to the weapon the emperor carried as a symbol of the authority of his office, but to the one worn in Roman provinces by the magistrates who had authority to execute criminals.

Paul taught in Romans 13 that government has the right and responsibility to take the life of a criminal under certain circumstances; this continues the principle of capital punishment first stated in Genesis 9:6. Paul's attitude toward capital punishment is seen in Acts 25:11. While standing before Festus, he stated that if "I am guilty of doing anything deserving death, I do not refuse to die." Paul acknowledged that if he had indeed committed a capital crime, then he would not seek to escape capital punishment. Therefore, one can conclude that the New Testament does not abolish the death penalty; instead, it reinforces the principle of capital punishment found in the Old Testament.

CAPITAL PUNISHMENT AND DETERRENCE

Is capital punishment a deterrent to crime? At the outset it should be acknowledged that the answer to this question should not change one's perspective on this issue. Although it is an important question, it should not be the basis for one's view on this issue. A Christian's belief on capital punishment should be based on what the Bible teaches, not on a pragmatic assessment of whether capital punishment works.

If anything, the Bible does seem to teach that capital punishment deters crime. When justice is done, "all the people will hear and be afraid, and will not be contemptuous again" (Deut. 17:13). If nothing else, capital punishment will deter the criminal who is executed from repeating another crime.

Opponents of capital punishment argue that it is not a deterrent because in some states where capital punishment is allowed the crime rate goes up. Does this mean then that capital punishment is not a deterrent?

First, it should be recognized that crime rates have been increasing for some time. The United States has become a violent society as the social and moral fabric of society is breaking down. So the increase in the crime rate is most likely due to many other factors, and cannot be correlated with a death penalty that has been implemented sparingly and sporadically.

Second, some evidence exists that capital punishment *is* a deterrent. And even if we cannot be absolutely sure of its deterrence value, it should be implemented. If it is a deterrent, then implementing capital punishment certainly will save lives. If it is not, then we still will have followed biblical injunctions and put convicted murderers to death.

In a sense opponents of capital punishment, who argue that it is not a deterrent, are willing to give the benefit of the doubt to the criminal rather than to the victims. The poet Hyman Barshay put it this way: "The death penalty is a warning—just like a lighthouse throwing its beam out on the water. We hear about shipwrecks but we do not hear about the ships the lighthouse guides safely on its way. We do not have proof of the number of ships it saves, but we do not tear the lighthouse down."[20] If capital punishment is a potential deterrent, that is significant social reason enough to implement it.

Statistical analysis by Isaac Ehrlich of the University of Chicago suggested that capital punishment is a deterrent.[21] Further cross-sectional analysis has confirmed Ehrlich's original conclusions.[22] His research showed that if the death penalty were used in a consistent way, it may deter as many as eight murders for every execution carried out. If these numbers are indeed accurate, they demonstrate that capital punishment could be a significant deterrent to crime in American society.

Certainly capital punishment will not deter all crime. Psychotic and deranged killers, members of the organized crime, and street gangs will no doubt kill whether capital punishment is implemented or not. A person who is irrational or wants to commit a murder will do so regardless of capital punishment. But social statistics as well as logic suggest that rational people will be deterred from murder because capital punishment is part of the criminal code.

OBJECTIONS TO CAPITAL PUNISHMENT

One objection is that in carrying out capital punishment the government is committing murder. Put theologically, does the death penalty violate the sixth commandment, which teaches "You shall not murder" (Ex. 20:13)?

First, the context of this verse must be noted. The verb used in Exodus 20:13, though sometimes translated "to kill," should best be translated "to murder." Used forty-nine times in the Old Testament, it always describes premeditated murder. It is never used of the killing of animals or of enemies in battle. So the commandment does not teach that all killing is wrong; it teaches that murder is wrong.

Second, the penalty for breaking the sixth commandment was the death penalty (Ex. 21:12; Num. 35:16–21). Therefore, when the government took the life of a murderer, it was not itself guilty of murder. Opponents of capital punishment who accuse the government of committing murder when implementing the death penalty fail to see the irony of using Exodus 20 to define murder while ignoring Exodus 21 which specifically teaches that government is to punish murderers.

A second objection to capital punishment questions the validity of applying the Old Testament Law to today's society. After all, was not the Mosaic Law only for the Old Testament theocracy? There are a number of ways to answer this objection.

First, the premise is questionable. There is and should be a relation between Old Testament laws and modern laws. Christians are not subject to the Old Testament

Law, but that does not invalidate God's moral principles set down in the Old Testament. Murder is still wrong. Thus, since murder is wrong, the penalty for murder must still be implemented.

Second, while the Mosaic Law was given specifically and uniquely for the Old Testament theocracy, this does not mean that the death penalty should be abolished. As stated previously, Genesis 9:6 precedes the Old Testament theocracy and its principle is tied to the creation order. Capital punishment is to be implemented because of the sanctity of human life. We are created in God's image. The universally binding principle is that when a murder occurs, the murderer must be put to death.

Third, the New Testament also teaches capital punishment. Romans 13:1–7 specifically states that human government, ordained by God, is to be obeyed; government does not bear the sword in vain. Human governments are given the responsibility to punish wrongdoers, and this includes murderers who are to be given the death penalty.

Fourth, the principle of capital punishment is never specifically removed or replaced in the Bible. While some would argue that the New Testament ethic replaces the Old Testament ethic, there is no instance in which a replacement ethic is introduced. As already seen, Jesus and the disciples never annulled the Old Testament standard of capital punishment. Paul taught that Christians are to express grace to each other, but he also taught that human governments are to be obeyed. Capital punishment is taught in both the Old and New Testaments.

A fifth objection to capital punishment is that innocent people might be put to death. That argument was given greater weight in the political arena when Governor George Ryan of Illinois imposed a moratorium in 2000 on the imposition of the death penalty in Illinois. After examining the evidence in many of these cases, he "commuted the sentences of all 167 inmates on death row to life imprisonment without the possibility of parole."[23] The political debate over capital punishment and the use of evidence will certainly continue. But it is important to note that this objection is not necessarily a reason to reject the death penalty, but it is certainly an argument for the careful implementation of it.

17

DRUGS

THE STATISTICS ON DRUG USE are staggering. The average age of first alcohol use is twelve and the average age of first drug use is thirteen. According to the National Institute on Drug Abuse, 93 percent of all teenagers in the United States have had some experience with alcohol by the end of their senior year of high school and 6 percent drink daily. Almost two-thirds of all American young people try illicit drugs before they finish high school. One out of sixteen seniors smokes marijuana daily and 20 percent have done so for at least a month sometime in their lives.[1] A recent poll found that adolescents listed drugs as the most important problem facing people their age, followed by crime and violence in school and social pressures.[2]

One survey released by the University of Colorado showed that the problem of drug use is not just outside the church. The study involved nearly 14,000 junior high and high school youth and compared churched young people with unchurched young people and found little difference. For example, 88 percent of the unchurched young people reported drinking beer, compared to 80 percent of church young people. When asked how many had tried marijuana, 47 percent of the unchurched young people had done so, compared to 38 percent of the churched youth. For amphetamines and barbiturates, 28 percent of the unchurched had tried them, while 22 percent of the church young people had tried them. And for cocaine use, the percentage was 14 percent for unchurched youths and 11 percent for churched teens.[3]

Fighting drugs often seems futile. When drug dealers are arrested, they are often released prematurely because court dockets are overloaded. Plea bargaining and paroles are standard fare as the revolving doors of justice spin faster. As the casualties mount in this war against drugs, some commentators have begun to suggest that the best solution is to legalize drugs. But a war is not won by surrendering. If drugs were legalized, addiction would increase, health costs would increase, and governments would once again capitulate to societal pressures and shirk their responsibility to establish moral law.

But if legalization is not the answer, then something must be done about the abuse of drugs like alcohol, cocaine, marijuana, heroin, and PCP. The medical cost of drug abuse in the United States $100 billion yearly.[4]

TYPES OF DRUGS

Alcohol

Alcohol is the most commonly used and abused drug by young people as well as adults. Nationwide surveys indicate that about 90 percent of the nation's youth experiment with alcohol—currently the teenagers' drug of choice. An annual survey conducted by the University of Michigan has revealed the extent to which young people drink. Over 65 percent of the nation's seniors currently do so, and about 40 percent reported having a heavy drinking episode within the two weeks prior to the survey.[5]

Alcohol is an intoxicant that depresses the central nervous system and can bring a temporary loss of control over physical and mental powers. The signs of drunkenness are well known: lack of coordination, slurred speech, blurred vision, and poor judgment.

In recent years debate has raged over whether alcoholism is a sin or a sickness.[6] The Bible clearly labels drunkenness as sin in such passages as Deuteronomy 21:20–21; 1 Corinthians 6:9–10; and Galatians 5:19–20. But the fact that the Bible calls drunkenness sin does not mitigate against the growing physiological evidence that certain people's biochemistry makes them more prone to addiction.

Some studies suggest that because of their body chemistry, alcoholics process alcohol differently than do nonalcoholics. Acetaldehyde is the intermediate byproduct of alcohol metabolism. But the biochemistry of some people makes it difficult to process acetaldehyde into acetate. Thus acetaldehyde builds up in the body and begins to affect a person's brain chemistry. The chemicals produced act much like opiates and therefore contribute to alcoholism.[7]

The social costs of alcohol are staggering. Alcoholism is the third largest health problem (following heart disease and cancer). Often medical problems begin before birth. More than forty thousand babies are born at risk each year because their mothers drank alcohol during pregnancy.[8]

An estimated 10 million problem drinkers are in the American adult population and an estimated 3.3 million teenagers are problem drinkers. Half of all traffic fatalities and one-third of all traffic injuries are alcohol-related. Alcohol is involved in two-thirds of all murders and one-third of all suicides.[9]

Alcohol is also a prime contributor to the breakdown the families. A high percentage of family violence, parental abuse and neglect, lost wages, and divorce are tied to the abuse of alcohol in this country.

Since the publication of Janet Geringer Woitiz's book *Adult Children of Alcoholics*, society has begun to understand the long-term effect of alcoholism on future generations. Children of Alcoholics (COAs) exhibit a number of traits including guessing what normal behavior is, having difficulty following a project from beginning to end, judging themselves without mercy, and having difficulty with intimate relationships.[10]

In the fight against drugs people must not ignore the impact alcohol has had on our society. Alcohol is every bit as addictive as other drugs and has had a profound negative affect on individuals, families, and our society.

Marijuana

Marijuana is produced from the hemp plant (*Cannabis sativa*) that grows throughout the world. It has gone from a hidden drug of the counterculture to the drug of choice for young people wanting to "get high." Marijuana has become widely available and openly used, especially in states that have decriminalized its usage.

Marijuana is an intoxicant usually smoked in order to induce a feeling of euphoria that lasts from two to four hours. Many users believe that it is a relatively harmless drug, but mounting scientific evidence demonstrates how dangerous marijuana can be. The short-term effects of marijuana include impairment in learning, memory, perception, judgment, and complex motor skills. Marijuana can also cause difficulty in speaking, listening effectively, thinking, retaining knowledge, problem-solving, and forming concepts.

An article in the *Journal of the American Medical Association* noted that marijuana users had "55 percent more industrial accidents, 85 percent more injuries and 78 percent increase in absenteeism."[11] In one study of reckless drivers who were not obviously drunk from alcohol, 59 percent tested positive for cocaine or marijuana.[12]

Marijuana also causes many medical complications. Because most marijuana users inhale unfiltered smoke and hold it in their lungs for as long as possible, the lungs and pulmonary system are damaged. Marijuana smoke also has more cancer-causing agents than tobacco smoke.

A study in the journal *Cancer* found that children of women who smoke marijuana are eleven times more likely to contract leukemia.[13] Mothers who smoke marijuana also contribute to a low birth weight and developmental problems for their children. Also, the risk of abnormalities similar to those caused by fetal alcohol syndrome increases by as much as 500 percent.[14]

Since the 1970s, more than 10,500 scientific studies have demonstrated the adverse consequences of marijuana use.[15] Many of these studies were done when most of the marijuana was less potent and less addictive than it is today. The former drug czar Lee Brown estimated that marijuana on the streets today is up to ten times more potent than a generation ago.[16] Carlton Turner, the former National Institute on Drug Abuse director and head of the Marijuana Research Project at the University of Mississippi, concluded, "There is no other drug used or abused by man that has the staying power and broad cellular actions on the body that *cannabis* [marijuana] does."[17]

Marijuana is not a safe drug. It damages brain and lung cells, and adversely affects reproduction in women and fertility in men. It also adversely affects concentration. And most importantly, marijuana has been considered a "gateway drug" because of its potential in leading young people to experiment with stronger drugs such as cocaine and heroin.

Cocaine

Cocaine occurs naturally in the leaves of coca plants and was reportedly chewed by natives in Peru as early as the sixth century. It became widely used in beverages (like Coca Cola) and medicines in the nineteenth century, but was restricted in 1914 by the Harrison Narcotics Act. Today cocaine users range from Wall Street lawyers taking it from fourteen-carat gold spoons to teenage junkies in back alleys smoking it in "crack" pipes.

Cocaine is a stimulant and an ego builder. Along with increased energy omes a feeling of personal supremacy—the illusion of being smarter, sexier, and more competent than anyone else. And while the cocaine confidence makes a person feel indestructible, the crash from coke leaves him or her depressed, paranoid, and searching for more.

In recent years snorting cocaine has given way to smoking it. Snorting cocaine limits the intensity of the effect because the blood vessels in the nose are constricted. Smoking cocaine delivers a much more intense euphoric feeling. The smoke goes directly to the lungs and then to the heart. On the next heartbeat it is on the way to the brain.

Anna Rose Childress of the University of Pennsylvania noted that people "can become compulsively involved with snorted cocaine. We have many Hollywood movie stars without nasal septums to prove that." But when cocaine is smoked, "it seems to have incredibly powerful effects that tend to set up a compulsive addictive cycle more quickly than anything that we've seen."[18]

Until recently, people speaking of cocaine dependence never called it an addiction. Cocaine's withdrawal symptoms are not physically wrenching like those of heroin and alcohol. Yet cocaine involves compulsion, loss of control, and continued use in spite of the consequences. Frequently cocaine sniffers burn a hole in their nasal septum and eventually constrict their nasal passages so that they can no longer snort it. All this suggests that cocaine is indeed addicting.

Cocaine users sucked in by its siren charms describe its effect in sexual terms. Cocaine's intense and sensual effect makes it a stronger aphrodisiac than sex itself. Research at the University of California at Los Angeles with apes given large amounts of cocaine showed that they preferred the drug to food or sexual partners and were willing to endure severe electric shocks in exchange for large doses.[19]

Cocaine has been accorded symbolic status that makes it all the more dangerous. It is perceived as chic, cozy, and clean. Friends snort coke with other friends and rationalize it by asking, "Whom is it hurting?" But the cocaine trade is anything but cozy and clean; it is dirty and dangerous. Cocaine users implicitly acquiesce to hundreds of cocaine-related murders and gang killings each year.

The cocaine problem in the United States has been made worse by the introduction of "crack," which is ordinary cocaine mixed with baking soda and water, and then heated. This material is then dried and broken into tiny chunks that resemble rock candy. Users usually smoke these crack rocks in glass pipes.

Crack (so-called because of the cracking sound it makes when heated) has become the scourge of the drug business. A single hit of crack provides an intense, wrenching rush in a matter of seconds. Unlike normal cocaine, which penetrates the mucous membranes slowly and circulates to the brain in minutes, crack is absorbed rapidly through the lungs and hits the brain within seconds in a dangerously concentrated form. It is the most hazardous form of cocaine and also the most addicting.

Another major difference between ordinary cocaine and crack is the cost. According to Mark Gold, founder of the nationwide cocaine hotline, the cost to an addict using crack is one-tenth the cost he would have paid for the equivalent in cocaine powder just a decade ago.[20] Since crack costs much less than normal cocaine, it is particularly appealing to adolescents. About one in five twelfth-graders have tried cocaine, and that number will probably continue to increase because of the price and availability of crack.

Hallucinogens

Another category of drugs is hallucinogens. The drug of choice during the 1960s was LSD. People looking for the "ultimate trip" would take LSD or perhaps peyote and experience bizarre illusions and hallucinations.

In the last few decades these hallucinogens have been replaced by PCP, often known as "angel dust" or "killer weed." First synthesized in the 1950s as an anesthetic, PCP was discontinued because of its side effects, but it is now manufactured illegally and sold to thousands of teenagers.

PCP is often sprayed on cigarettes or marijuana and then smoked. Users report a sense of distance and estrangement. PCP creates body image distortion, dizziness, and double vision. The drug distorts reality in such a way that the ensuing drug state can resemble mental illness. Because the drug blocks pain receptors, violent PCP episodes may result in self-inflicted injuries. Suicides, drowning, and self-mutilation are all common occurrences for PCP users.

Chronic PCP users have persistent memory problems and speech difficulties. Mood disorders such as depression, anxiety, and violent behavior have also been reported. High doses of PCP can produce a coma, which can last for days or weeks.

Synthetic Drugs

So-called "designer drugs" have also had an impact on society. Manufactured in clandestine laboratories, these drugs mimic the effects of commonly abused drugs. Since they were not even anticipated when current drug laws were written, they often have existed in a legal limbo while the extent of their use has been increasing.

One drug is MDMA, also known as "ecstasy." Called "the LSD of the 1980s and 1990s," it gives the user a cocaine-like rush with a hallucinogen euphoria. Ecstasy was sold legally for a few years despite the National Institute on Drug Abuse fears that it could cause brain damage. In 1985, the Drug Enforcement Agency outlawed MDMA, although it is still widely available.[21]

Designer drugs have become a growth industry in the 1990s. Creative drug makers in clandestine laboratories can produce these drugs for a fraction of the cost of smuggled drugs and with much less hassle from law enforcement officers. In the end these drugs may pose the greatest threat to our society in the future.

HOW TO FIGHT DRUGS

Society must fight America's drug epidemic on five major fronts.[22] The first battlefront is at the nation's borders. Federal agents must patrol the 8,426 miles of deeply indented Florida coastline and the 2,067-mile border with Mexico. This is a formidable task, but vast distances are not the only problem.

The smugglers that the federal agents are up against have almost unlimited funds and some of the best equipment available. Fortunately, the federal interdiction forces (namely, Customs officers, Drug Enforcement Agency, and the Immigration and Naturalization Service) are improving their capabilities. Customs forces have enlisted more personnel and are getting more sophisticated equipment.

The second battlefront is law enforcement at home. Police must crack down with more arrests, more convictions, longer sentences, and more seizures of drug dealers' assets. Unfortunately law enforcement successes pale when compared to the volume of drug traffic. Even the most effective crackdowns seem to do little more than move drugs from one location to another. An effective weapon on this battlefront is a 1984 law that makes it easier to seize the assets of drug dealers before they are convicted. In some cities police have even confiscated the cars of suburbanites who drive into the city to buy crack.

But attempts to deter drug dealing have been limited by flaws in the criminal justice system. A lack of jail cells prevents significant prosecution of drug dealers. And even if this problem were alleviated, the shortage of judges would still result in the quick release of drug pushers.

A third battlefront is drug testing. Many government and business organizations are implementing testing of present and prospective employees on a routine basis. The theory is simple. Drug testing is a greater deterrent to drug use than the remote possibility of going to jail. People who know they will have to pass a urine test in order to get a job will be much less likely to dabble in drugs.

But drug testing is not without its opponents. Civil libertarians feel this deterrent is not worth the loss of personal privacy. Some unions believe that random testing in the workplace would violate the Fourth Amendment's prohibition against unreasonable searches.

A fourth battleground is drug treatment. Those who are addicted to drugs need help. But the major questions are: Who should provide the treatment? And who should pay the cost of such treatement? Private hospital programs are now a $4 billion-a-year business with a daily cost of as much as $500 per bed per day. This treatment is clearly out of the reach of many addicts whose employers or insurance companies cannot pick up the costs.

A fifth battleground is education. Teaching children the dangers of drugs can be an important step in helping them learn to say no to drugs. The National Institute on Drug Abuse estimated that 72 percent of the nation's elementary and secondary school children are being given some kind of drug education.[23]

SHOULD WE LEGALIZE DRUGS?

Those weary of the war on drugs have suggested drugs be decriminalized. For years, an alliance of liberals and libertarians have promoted the idea that legalizing drugs would reduce drug costs and drug crimes in America. But would it? The following are some of the arguments for drug legalization.

"Legalization will take the profit out of the drug business."

Surprising as it may sound, relatively few drug dealers actually earn huge sums of money. Most in the crack business are low-level runners who make very little money. Many crack dealers smoke more crack than they sell. Drug cartels are the ones making the big profits.

Would legalizing drugs affect large drug dealers or drug cartels in any appreciable way? No. Drug cartels would still control price and supply even if drugs were legalized. If the government set the price for legalized drugs, criminals could undercut the price and supply whatever drugs the government did not supply.

Addicts would not be significantly affected by legalization. Does anyone seriously believe their behavior would change just because they were using legal drugs instead of illegal drugs? They would still use theft and prostitution to support their habits.

Proponents also argue that legalizing drugs would reduce the cost of drugs and thus would reduce the supply of drugs flowing to this country. Recent history suggests that just the opposite will take place. When cocaine first hit the United States, it was expensive and difficult to obtain. But when more was dumped into this country and readily available in less expensive vials of crack, drug addiction rose and drug-related crimes rose.

"Drug legalization will reduce drug use."

Proponents argue that legalizing drugs will make them less appealing—they will no longer be "forbidden fruit." However, logic and social statistics suggest that decriminalizing drugs will actually increase drug use.

Those arguing for the legalization of drugs often point to Prohibition as a failed social experiment. But was it a failure? When Prohibition was in effect, alcohol consumption declined by 30 to 50 percent and death from cirrhosis of the liver fell dramatically.[24] One study found that suicides and drug-related arrests also declined by 50 percent.[25] After the repeal of the Eighteenth Amendment in 1933, alcoholism rose and so did alcohol-related crimes and accidents. If anything, Prohibition proves the point. Decriminalization increases drug use.

Comparing alcohol and drugs actually strengthens the argument against legalization since many drugs are even more addictive than alcohol. For example, alcohol has an addiction rate of approximately 10 percent, while cocaine has an addiction rate as high as 75 percent.[26]

Many drugs are actually "gateway drugs" to other drugs. A 1992 article in the *Journal of Primary Prevention* found that marijuana is essentially a "necessary" condition for the occurrence of cocaine use. Other research shows that (a) involvement with illicit drugs is a developmental phenomenon, (b) increased experimentation correlates with increasing age, and (c) cigarette and alcohol use precedes the use of marijuana.[27]

Robert DuPont, former director of the National Institute on Drug Abuse, argued that the potential market for legal drugs can be compared to the number of Americans who now use alcohol (140 million persons). If his analysis it correct, then approximately 50 million Americans would eventually use cocaine if it were a legal drug.[28]

Great Britain's experiment with drug legalization has been a disaster. Between 1960 and 1970, the number of British heroin addicts increased thirtyfold. And during the 1980s, it increased by as much as 40 percent each year. By contrast the number of heroin addicts in this country today is about the same as it was fifteen years ago.

But the real question is not whether drugs are worse than alcohol. The real question is whether both alcohol and drugs should be legalized. Legalized alcohol currently leads to 100,000 deaths annually and costs $99 billion each year.[29] Drugs should not be legalized, too!

"Legalizing drugs will reduce social costs."

"We are losing the war on drugs," say drug legalization proponents, "so let's cut the costs of drug enforcement by decriminalizing drugs."

The United States spends over ten billion dollars annually to combat drug-related crime. If drugs were made legal, some crime-fighting costs might drop, but many social ills, including other forms of crime (to support drug habits), drug-related accidents, and welfare costs, would certainly increase.

Statistics from states that have decriminalized marijuana demonstrate this concern. In California, within the first six months of decriminalization of drugs, arrests for driving under the influence of drugs rose 46 percent for adults and 71.4 percent for juveniles.[30] Marijuana use doubled in Alaska and Oregon when it was decriminalized in those states.[31]

Crime would certainly increase. Justice Department figures show that approximately one-third of inmates used drugs prior to committing their crimes.[32] And juvenile crime would no doubt increase as well. A study published in the *Journal of Drug Issues* found a strong association between the severity of the crime and the type of substance used the more intoxicating the substance, the more serious the incident.[33]

Meanwhile, worker productivity and student productivity would decrease. The Drug Enforcement Administration estimates that drug decriminalization will cost the United States more than alcohol and tobacco combined, perhaps between $140 billion and $210 billion a year in lost productivity and job-related accidents.[34]

Government services would no doubt need to be expanded to pay for additional drug education and treatment for those addicted to legal drugs. And child protective services would no doubt have to expand to deal with child abuse. Patrick Murphy, a court-appointed lawyer for 31,000 abused and neglected children in Chicago, said that more than 80 percent of the cases of physical and sexual abuse of children now involve drugs. Legalizing drugs will not reduce these crimes; it would make the problem worse.[35]

"The government should not dictate moral policy on drugs."

Libertarians who promote drug legalization value personal freedom. They believe government should not dictate morals, and they fear that citizens' civil liberties may be threatened by a tougher policy against drugs.

The true threat to individual freedoms comes from the drug cartels in foreign countries, drug lords in this country, and drug dealers in our streets. Legalizing drugs would send the wrong message to society.

Obviously some people are going to use drugs whether they are legal or illegal. Keeping drugs illegal maintains criminal sanctions that persuade most people their lives are best lived without drugs. Legalization, on the other hand, would remove the incentive to stay away from drugs and would certainly increase drug use.

William Bennett said, "I didn't have to become drug czar to be opposed to legalized marijuana. As Secretary of Education I realized that, given the state of American education, the last thing we needed was a policy that made widely available a substance that impairs memory, concentration, and attention span. Why in God's name foster the use of a drug that makes you stupid?"[36]

BIBLICAL PERSPECTIVE

Some people may believe the Bible has little to say about drugs, but this is not so. First, the Bible says much about the most common and most abused drug, namely, alcohol. Ephesians 5:18 admonishes Christians not to be drunk with wine. In many places in Scripture drunkenness is called a sin (Deut. 21:20–21; Amos 6:6; 1 Cor. 6:9–10; Gal. 5:19–20). The Bible also warns of the dangers of drinking alcohol in Proverbs 20:1; Isaiah 5:11; and Habbakuk 2:15–16. If the Bible warns of the danger of alcohol, then by implication it is also warning of the dangers of taking other kinds of drugs.

Second, drugs were an integral part of many ancient near East societies. For example, the pagan cultures surrounding Israel used drugs as part of their religious ceremonies.[37] Both the Old and New Testaments condemn sorcery and witchcraft. The Greek word translated "witchcraft" (Gal. 5:20), "magic arts" (Rev. 9:21), or "magic spell" (Rev. 18:23) is *pharmakeia*, from which come the English words "pharmacy" and "pharmaceutical." In ancient times drugs were prepared by a witch or shaman.

Pagan worshipers used drugs to induce an altered state of consciousness that allowed demons to take over the minds of the users. Drug use was involved in sorcery. In our day many use drugs merely for so-called "recreational" purposes, but the occult connection cannot be discounted.

Galatians 5:19–21 says, "The acts of the sinful nature are obvious: sexual immorality, impurity and debauchery, idolatry and witchcraft [which includes the use of drugs]; hatred, discord, jealousy, fits of rage, selfish ambition, dissensions, factions, and envy; drunkenness, orgies, and the like. I warn you, as I did before, that those who live like this will not inherit the kingdom of God."

The New American Standard Bible translates the word witchcraft as "sorcery" in reference to drugs. This involvement in witchcraft associated with drugs is a sin. The nonmedical use of drugs is considered one of the acts of a sinful nature. Using drugs, whether to "get a high" or to tap into the occult, is one of the acts of a sinful nature whereby users demonstrate their depraved and carnal nature.

The psychic effects of drugs should not be discounted. A questionnaire designed by Charles Tate and sent to users of marijuana documented some disturbing findings. In his article in *Psychology Today* he noted that one-fourth of the marijuana users who responded to his questionnaire reported that they were taken over and controlled by an evil person or power during their drug induced experience. And over half of those questioned said they have experienced religious or "spiritual" sensations in which they meet spiritual beings.[38]

Many proponents of the drug culture have linked drug use to spiritual values. During the 1960s, Timothy Leary and Alan Watts referred to the "religious" and "mystical" experience gained through the use of LSD (along with other drugs) as a prime reason for taking drugs.[39]

No doubt drugs are dangerous, not only to the body but to the spirit. Christians must warn their children and their society of the dangers of drugs.

HOW TO KEEP CHILDREN OFF DRUGS

Drugs pose a threat to children, but parents can protect them from much of this threat by working on the following preventive measures. First, build up your child's self-esteem. Children with a positive self image stand a better chance against peer pressure to use drugs. Children need to know they are a special creation of God (Ps. 139:13–16) and thus are worthy of dignity and respect (Ps. 8.5–8). Children need to be taught the fallacy of trying to conform to some group's standards by going along with their drug habits. Drugs are dumb and dangerous, not chic and cool, despite what some people might say.

Second, parents should monitor their child's friendships. Before allowing a child to spend too much time with another child, the parents should get to know the family. Does the child go home after school to an empty house? Is there adult supervision of the children's activities?

A third thing parents can do is to promote alternatives to drugs. These alternatives include everything from "Just Say No" clubs and programs to alternative activities such as sports, school clubs, the arts, and hobbies.

Fourth, parents need to teach children about drugs. Drug education should not be left to the schools. Parents must be personally involved, letting their children know that drugs will not be tolerated. Parents should be educated about drugs and drug paraphernalia.

Fifth, parents must set a good example. Parents who are drug-free have a much better chance of rearing drug-free children. If a parent is using drugs, he or she should stop immediately. The unconditional message to their children must be that drugs are wrong and that they will not be tolerated in their home.

WHAT TO DO IF YOUR CHILD IS ON DRUGS

All the preventive measures in the world cannot assure that children will avoid experimenting with drugs. If an adult suspects his or her child is already using drugs, these practical suggestions should be followed.

First, parents should not deny their suspicions. Drug addiction takes time, but it occurs must faster with a child than with an adult. Some of the newer drugs (like crack) can quickly lead to addiction. Denial may waste precious time. A child's life may be in danger.

Second, parents must learn to recognize the symptoms of drug abuse. Some readily noticeable physical symptoms include a pale face, imprecise eye movements, and neglect of personal appearance. Some less noticeable symptoms involving social interaction include diminished drive or reduced ambition, a significant drop in the quality of schoolwork, reduced attention span, impaired communication skills, and less care for the feelings of others.

Third, parents must be consistent. Having clear rules regarding curfew, accountability for an allowance, and knowing where one's teen spends his or her time are important. Consistent parental guidelines allow for less opportunity to stumble into sin of any kind.

Fourth, parents should open up lines of communication. Asking probing questions and becoming informed about the dangers of drugs are strong means for offsetting drug use.

Finally, parents must be tough. Fighting drugs takes patience and persistence. Unconditional love is a potent weapon against drugs.

WHAT CAN THE CHURCH DO?

The church can provide much-needed answers and help to those addicted to alcohol and other drugs. Here are just a few suggestions of how the church can help substance abusers.

First, the pastor and staff must be educated about drug abuse. Substance abuse is a medical problem, a psychological problem, and a spiritual problem. The church staff should be aware of how these various aspects of the problem interrelate.

Pastoral staff members should also know the causes, effects, and treatments. They must be aware of the responses of both dependents and codependents. Sometimes the abuser's family prevents recovery by continuing to deny the problem exists.

The church staff can obtain helpful drug information through local libraries and various local agencies. Fortunately more Christians are writing good material on this issue, so local Christian bookstores are also a source of help.

Second, congregations must be educated. The church should know the facts about substance abuse. This is a worthy topic for sermons and Sunday school lessons. Ignorance puts young people in particular and the congregation in general at risk. Christians must be armed with the facts to combat this scourge on our nation.

Third, a program of prevention must be put in place. The best way to fight drug abuse is to stop it before it starts. A program that presents the problem of substance abuse and shows the results is vital. It should also provide a biblical framework for dealing with the problem of drugs in society and the church.

Fourth, churches might consider establishing a support group. The success of non-church-related groups like Alcoholics Anonymous point to the need for substance abusers to be in an environment that encourages acceptance and accountability. Ideally these should be within the church and should be taught from Christian principles. Offering support can be a primary way of "bearing one another's burdens" as Christians.

18

GAMBLING

GAMBLING used to be what a few unscrupulous people did with the aid of organized crime. But gambling fever now seems to affect nearly everyone as more and more states are legalizing various forms of gambling.

Thirty years ago, gambling was a relatively rare phenomenon with casinos operating only in the distant Nevada desert and a few states with lotteries or pari-mutuel betting. Today, legalized gambling is permitted in forty-seven states and the District of Columbia. More Americans are gambling than ever before, and they are also gambling more money.[1] The momentum seems to be on the side of those who want legalized gambling as a way to supplement state revenues. But these states and their citizens often ignore the costs that are associated with legalized gambling.

TYPES OF GAMBLING

Gambling comes in many forms. Perhaps the most popular type of gambling is state-sponsored lotteries, which would include the weekly lottery games, as well as the daily lottery numbers and scratch-off ticket games. A second type of gambling would be casinos. Gambling in this venue would include jackpot slot machines, video card game machines, various casino card games such as poker and blackjack, and other casino games such as roulette.

Sports betting is a third type of gambling. Someone can bet on the outcome of a sporting event or a particular part of a sporting event. Usually, bets are placed on a bookmaker's odds so that the actual bet is against the point spread. Sports betting would also include illegal office pools and even weekend golfers who bet dollars or cokes for each hole.

Pari-mutuel betting (horse racing, dog racing, and jai-lai) is another form of sports gambling. Horse racing is legal in forty-three states, with over 150 racetracks in the United States.

Convenience gambling (also called retail gambling) is a fourth type of gambling. Such gambling includes stand-alone slot machines, video poker, video keno, and other games that are usually found in bars, truck stops, and convenience stores.

Online gambling represents a new frontier in the spread of gambling. The availability and accessibility of Internet gambling appears to have greatly increased the number of people gambling on a regular basis.

BAD SOCIAL POLICY

Legalized gambling is bad social policy. At a time when Gamblers Anonymous estimates that there are at least 12 million compulsive gamblers, it does not make a lot of sense to have the state promoting gambling. State sponsorship of gambling makes it harder, not easier, for the compulsive gambler to reform. Since about 96 percent of those gamblers began gambling before the age of fourteen,[2] we should be especially concerned about the message such a policy sends to young people.

The economic costs that gamblers themselves incur are significant. The average compulsive gambler has debts exceeding $80,000.[3] And this figure pales in comparison with other social costs that surface because of family neglect, embezzlement, theft, and involvement in organized crime. Compulsive gamblers affect the lives of family, friends, and business associates. Some of the consequences of gambling are marital disharmony, divorce, child abuse, substance abuse, and suicide attempts.

Society also incurs heavy costs from gambling. Proponents argue that state lotteries are an effective way to raise taxes painlessly. But the evidence shows that legalized gambling often hurts those who are poor and disadvantaged. A national task force on gambling found that those in the lowest income bracket lost more than three times as much money to gambling (as a percentage of income) as those at the wealthiest end of the spectrum.[4] One New York lottery agent reported that "seventy percent of those who buy my tickets are poor, black, or Hispanic."[5] And a National Bureau of Economic Research study showed "that the poor bet a much larger share of their income."[6] The study also found that "the less education a person has, the more likely he is to play the lottery."[7]

A major study on the effect of the California lottery came to the same conclusions. The Field Institute's California poll found that 18 percent of the state's adults bought 71 percent of the tickets. These heavy lottery players (who bought more than twenty tickets in the contest's first forty-five days) were "more likely than others to be black, poorer and less educated than the average Californian."[8]

Studies also indicate that gambling increases when economic times are uncertain and people are concerned about their future. Joseph Dunn, director of the National Council on Compulsive Gambling, observed, "People who are worried about the factory closing take a chance on making it big. Once they win anything, they're hooked."[9]

The social impact of gambling is often hidden from the citizens who decide to legalize gambling. But later these costs show up in the shattered lives of individuals and their families. One study in *The Journal of Social Issues* found that as gambling increases, there is an increase in "(a) proportion of divorce and separation; (b) disagreement about money matters with one's spouse; (c) lack of understanding between marital partners; and (d) more reported problems among children of gamblers."[10]

The psychologist Julian Taber warned, "No one knows the social costs of gambling or how many players will become addicted . . . the states are experimenting with the minds of the people on a massive scale."[11] Families are torn apart by strife, divorce, and bankruptcy. In their book *When You Gamble—You Risk More Than Your Money*, Boydon Cole and Sidney Margolius concluded, "There is no doubt of the destructive effect of gambling on the family life. The corrosive effects of gambling attack both the white-collar and blue-collar families with equal vigor."[12]

The impact on crime is also significant. The crime rate in gambling communities is nearly double the national average.[13] Researchers calculated that for every dollar the state received in gambling revenues, it costs the state at least three dollars in increased social costs for criminal justice and social welfare.[14]

BAD GOVERNMENTAL POLICY

Legalized gambling is also bad governmental policy. Government should promote public virtue, not seduce its citizens to gamble in state-sponsored vice. Government is supposed to be servant of God, according to Romans 13, but its moral stance is compromised when it enters into a gambling enterprise.

Citizens would be outraged if their state government began enticing its citizens to engage in potentially destructive behavior, such as taking drugs. But those same citizens see no contradiction when government legalizes and even promotes gambling. Instead of being a positive moral force in society, government contributes to the corruption of society.

Ross Wilhelm, professor of business economics at the University of Michigan, said,

> State lotteries and gambling games are essentially a "rip-off" and widespread legalization of gambling is one of the worst changes in public policy to have occurred in recent years. . . . The viciousness of the state-run games is compounded beyond belief by the fact that state governments actively advertise and promote the games and winners.[15]

The corrosive effect legalized gambling has on government itself is also a cause for concern. As one editorial in *New York Times* noted, "Gambling is a business so rich, so fast, so powerful and perhaps inevitably so unsavory that it cannot help but undermine government."[16]

LEGAL AND ILLEGAL GAMBLING

One of the standard clichés proponents of legalized gambling use is that by instituting legal gambling, illegal gambling will be driven out. This argument makes a number of faulty assumptions. First, it assumes that people are going to gamble anyway; therefore, the state might as well get a piece of the action. Second, the argument assumes that given the choice, people would rather gamble in a state-sponsored program because it will be regulated. The state will make sure that the program is fair and that each participant has an equal chance of winning. Third, the argument assumes that if the state enters the gambling arena, it will eliminate illegal gambling because it will be a more efficient competitor for gamblers' dollars.

Although the arguments seem sound, they are not. First, although some people do gamble illegally, most citizens do not. Legalized gambling entices people to gamble who normally would not gamble at all. Duke University researchers found that the lottery is a "powerful recruiting device" because one-fourth of those who otherwise would not gamble at all do bet on lotteries.[17]

Second, legal gambling does not eliminate illegal gambling. If anything, just the opposite is true. As legalized gambling comes into a state, it provides additional momentum for illegal gambling. The Organized Crime Section of the Department of Justice found that "the rate of illegal gambling in those states which have some legalized form of gambling was three times as high as those states where there was not a legalized form of gambling."[18] And one national review found that,

> In states with different numbers of games, participation rates increase steadily and sharply as the number of legal types of gambling increases. Social betting more than doubles from 35 percent in states with no legal games to 72 percent in states with three legal types; the illegal gambling rate more than doubles from nine percent to 22 percent; and commercial gambling increases by 43 percent, from 24 to 67 percent.[19]

Legalized gambling in various states has been a stimulator of illegal gambling, not a competitor to it.

The reasons for the growth of illegal gambling in areas where legalized gambling exists are simple. First, organized crime syndicates often use the free publicity of state lotteries and pari-mutuel betting to run their own numbers games. The state actually saves them money by providing publicity for events involving gambling. Second, many gamblers would rather bet illegally than legally. When they work with a bookie, they can bet on credit and do not have to report their winnings to the government, two things they cannot do if they bet on state-sponsored games. This explains why illegal gambling thrives in states with legalized gambling.

Another important issue is the corrupting influence legalized gambling can have on society. First, legalized gambling can have a very corrupting influence on state government. In the last few years there have been numerous news reports of corruption and fraud in state lotteries. Second, there is the corrupting influence on the citizens themselves. Gambling breeds greed. Research revealed that the number of compulsive gamblers increases between 100 and 550 percent when legalized gambling is brought into an area.[20] Every day otherwise sane people bet large amounts of money in state lotteries because they hope that they will win the jackpot. Moreover, states and various gambling establishments produce glitzy ads that appeal to people's greed in order to entice them to risk even more than they can afford.

Government should be promoting positive social values like thrift and integrity rather than negative ones like greed and avarice. It should be promoting the public welfare rather than seducing citizens to engage in state-sponsored vice.

ECONOMIC COSTS

Legalized forms of gambling (state lotteries, pari-mutuel betting, and casinos) are often promoted as good economic policy. Proponents say that such forms of gambling are painless ways of increasing billions of dollars in state revenue. But there is another economic side to legalized gambling.

First, the gross income statistics for legalized gambling are much higher than the net income. State lotteries are one example. Although about half the states have lotteries and the figures vary from state to state, we can work with some average figures. Generally, the cost of management, advertising, and promotion is approximately sixty cents of each dollar. In other words, for every dollar raised in a lottery, only forty cents goes to the state budget. By contrast, direct taxation of the citizens costs only about one cent on the dollar, so that for every dollar raised by taxes, ninety-nine cents goes to the state.

Second, gambling adversely affects a state economy. Legalized gambling depresses businesses because it diverts money that could have been spent in the capital economy into gambling that does not stimulate the economy. Boarded-up businesses surrounding casinos are a visible reminder of this, but the effect on the entire economy is even more devastating than may be at first apparent. Money that could be invested, loaned, and recycled through the economy is instead risked in a legalized gambling scheme.

Legalized gambling also siphons off billions of dollars from the economy. More money is wagered on gambling than is spent on elementary and secondary education ($286 billion versus $213 billion in 1990).[21] The historian John Ezel concluded in his book *Fortune's Merry Wheel*, "If history teaches us anything, a study of over 1,300 legal lotteries held in the United States proves . . . they cost more than they brought in if their total impact on society is reckoned."[22]

SPORTS GAMBLING

Although sports gambling is illegal in almost every state, gambling proponents have sought over the last few years to legalize it. One concern is how sports gambling has affected the integrity of the game. Illegal gambling has already adversely affected sports; legalizing it would simply make matters worse.

One issue revolves around how sports betting is carried out. Betting is done against a point spread. A team is picked to win by so many points. The point spread has become a large part of the game. At some sporting events people in the stands are disappointed when their team does not beat the point spread. Even though the team won, some of the fans are upset that their team did not defeat its opponent by enough points to cover the spread.

True fans are concerned if the team wins or loses. Gamblers, however, are concerned with whether the team was able to beat the point spread. Winning by one point is not enough if the point spread was three.

Sportswriters and sports broadcasters routinely announce that a team is favored by a certain number of points. They argue that reporting such information is appropriate because it is relevant to the game. But is it? When the headline of a newspaper article states, for example, "Denver Broncos Favored By Six Points," sports writers have gone far beyond merely reporting about a sporting event and are actually promoting sports gambling.

Sports gambling has affected sports by introducing organized crime into the sporting arena. Past scandals at Boston College and Tulane University illustrate how gambling has adversely affected the integrity of athletes, coaches, and colleges. Players have been involved in point-shaving scandals, and the problem could only become worse in an environment in which sports gambling is legalized.

Another area of concern is how government would become involved in sports gambling. Once sports gambling is legalized, the possibility of governmental investigation is opened up. A wise sports decision might be questioned by a government oversight body. Suppose a football team was picked to win by more than three points and was leading by one point with less than a minute left. Even if the team was on its opponent's twenty-yard-line, the coach might decide not to kick a field goal, for doing so would risk the possibility of a blocked kick. A wise coach would tell his team to sit on the ball and let the clock run out. The team would win, but not beat the point spread. Citizens who lost money would certainly call for an investigation to see if fraud was involved.

Obviously sports gambling takes place, even though it is illegal. But good reasons argue against legalizing it. It is bad social policy, it is bad economic policy, and it is bad governmental policy. Sports gambling is bad not only for these reasons but also because it could adversely affect the integrity of the game.

BIBLICAL PERSPECTIVE

Even though the Bible does not directly address gambling, we can derive a number of principles from Scripture. First, the Bible emphasizes a number of truths that conflict with gambling. The Bible, for example, emphasizes the sovereignty of God (Matt. 10:29–30). Gambling, however, is based on chance. The Bible admonishes people to work creatively and for the benefit of others (Eph. 4:28), while gambling fosters a something-for-nothing attitude. The Bible condemns materialism (Matt. 6:24–25), while gambling promotes it.

Gambling breeds a form of covetousness, whereas the Tenth Commandment (Ex. 20:17) admonishes people not to covet. Coveting, greed, and selfishness are the base emotions that entice individuals to gamble. Christians should be concerned about gambling if for no other reason than the effect it has on the "weaker brother" and how it will affect the compulsive gambler. State-sponsored gambling makes it more difficult for compulsive gamblers to reform. Legalized gambling becomes an institutionalized form of greed.

Second, gambling destroys the work ethic. Two key biblical passages deal with the work ethic. In Colossians 3:23–24 the apostle Paul wrote, "Whatever you do, work at it with all your heart, as working for the Lord, not for men, since you know that you will receive an inheritance from the Lord as a reward. It is the Lord Christ you are serving." And in 2 Thessalonians 3:7, 10, he stated, "For you yourselves know how you ought to follow our example. . . . For even when we were with you, we gave you this rule: 'If a man will not work, he shall not eat.' "

The Twentieth Century Fund research group commented, "Gambling's get-rich-quick appeal appears to mock capitalism's core values: Disciplined work habits, thrift, prudence, adherence to routine, and the relationship between effort and reward."[23] These core values of the work ethic are all part of the free enterprise system and are part of the Christian life. Gambling corrupts these values and replaces them with greed and selfishness. Rather than depending on hard work, gamblers depend on luck and chance.

Third, gambling destroys families. Gambling is a major cause of family neglect. Many of the social costs associated with gambling come from a get-rich-quick mindset. As people get caught up in a gambling frenzy, they begin to neglect their families. Money spent on lottery tickets or at racetracks is frequently not risk capital but is income that should be spent on family needs. According to 1 Timothy 5:8 a person who refuses to care for his family is worse than an unbeliever. Parents must provide for their children (2 Cor. 12:14) and eat the bread of their labors (2 Thess. 3:12). Legalized gambling causes people to neglect their God-mandated responsibility to care for their families, and many of those families then often end up on welfare.

Fourth, gambling is a form of state-sponsored greed. Romans 13:4 teaches that government is to be a servant of God, providing order in society and promoting public virtue. Legalized gambling undercuts government's role and subverts the moral fabric of society through greed and selfishness promoted by a state-sponsored vice.

Since gambling undermines the moral foundations of society and invites corruption in government, Christians must stand against attempts to legalize gambling.

19

RACE AND RACIAL ISSUES

RACE has divided people in our world for millennia, and the prejudice of racism is still with us today. So in this chapter we are going to focus on some important aspects of race and racial issues.

At the outset we should acknowledge that, although we will use the term "race" throughout this discussion, it is not a very precise term. First, the Bible really only talks of one race: the human race. Superficial differences in skin color, hair color, hair texture, or eye shape may provide physiological differences between people groups, but the Bible does not provide any justification for treating people differently simply because of these physical differences.

The Bible teaches that God has made "from one blood every nation of men" (Acts 17:26, KJV). Here Paul taught the Athenians that they came from the same source in the creation as everyone else. We are all from one blood. In other words, no superior or inferior races exist. We are all from the same race: the human race.

Race is also an imprecise term in large part because it is not based upon scientific data. People of every race can interbreed and produce fertile offspring. It turns out that the so-called differences in the races is not very great. A study of human genetic material of different races concluded that the DNA of any two people in the world would differ by just 2/10ths of one percent.[1] And of this variation, only six percent can be linked to racial categories. The remaining 94 percent is "within race" variation. In other words, all the racial differences that have been so important to people for generations are statistically insignificant from a scientific point of view. These differences are trivial when you consider the 3 billion base pairs of human DNA.

Another reason the term "race" also lacks precision is because of interracial marriage. While it is probably true that the so-called races of the world were never completely divided, it is certainly true that the lines are becoming quite blurred today. Take the golfer Tiger Woods as one example. His heritage is Thai, black, white, Chinese, and Native American.

It is ironic that at a time when racial lines are blurring more and more each generation, the government still collects data that requires individuals to check one box that represents their racial or ethnic heritage. A growing number of people are finding it hard to classify themselves by checking just one box.

THE CURSE ON HAM

One of the most destructive false teachings supposedly based on the Bible is the so-called "curse on Ham." Ham was one of Noah's three sons (along with Shem and Japheth) (Gen. 9:18–27).

In the past, certain cults and even some orthodox Christian groups believed that the skin color of black people was due to a curse on Ham and his descendents. Unfortunately, this false teaching has been used to justify racial discrimination and even slavery.

One group said, "We know the circumstances under which the posterity of Cain (and later Ham) were cursed with what we call Negroid racial characteristics."[2] Another group argued that "The curse which Noah pronounced upon Canaan was the origin of the black race."[3]

In response to the preceding claims, all we have to do is study the so-called "curse on Ham." First, the Bible nowhere teaches that God cursed people with black skin. The origin of the black race or of black racial characteristics is not a result of any curse.

Second, Canaan, one of Ham's sons, was cursed, not Ham (Gen. 9:25). And if only one of Ham's four sons was cursed, how could all black people be cursed? As it turns out, the curse on Canaan has unfolded in history. The descendents of Canaan were perhaps one of the most wicked people to live on earth. For example, they were the inhabitants of Sodom and Gomorrah.

Third, even if a curse is given, the Bible clearly places limitations on curses to three or four generations. In Exodus 20:5–6 God said, "You shall not bow down to them or worship them; for I, the LORD your God, am a jealous God, punishing the children for the sin of the fathers to the third and the fourth generations of those who hate me, but showing love to thousands who love me and keep my commandments."

Notice that this passage seems to teach that curses based upon disobedience are reversed when people repent and turn back to obedience. So not only is a curse limited; obedience to God's principles can break it.

Fourth, the Bible teaches that the fulfillment of the curse on Canaan occurred with Israel's defeat and subjugation of Canaan (Josh. 9:23; 1 Kin. 9:20–21). This had nothing to do with placing black people under a permanent curse.

Although the idea of "the curse on Ham" has been dying a well-deserved death, it is still important to remember that not so long ago people misinterpreted a biblical passage to justify their racism and discrimination. No one race or people group is inferior to any other. In fact, the Bible teaches that preferences based upon race, class, or ethnic origin are sinful and subject to God's judgment (James 2:9–13). All of us are created in God's image (Gen. 1:27) and have value and dignity.

RACISM IN SOCIETY

Racism has no doubt been the scourge of humanity. It usually surfaces from generalized assumptions made about a particular race or cultural group. While it is wrong and unfair to assign particular negative characteristics to everyone within a racial group, it is done all the time. The bitter result of these racial attitudes is intolerance and discrimination.

Often racism goes beyond just individual attitudes. These racial attitudes can become the mindset of a particular people group who may use cultural as well as legal means to suppress another race. These cultural norms and laws can be used by the majority race to exploit and discriminate against the minority race.

Although racism has existed throughout the centuries, it gained an unexpected ally in the scientific realm in the nineteenth century. In 1859, Charles Darwin published his famous work *The Origin of Species by Means of Natural Selection of the Preservation of Favored Races in the Struggle for Life*. The last part of this title undoubtedly furthered some of the ideas of racial superiority that flourished during Darwin's time.

It is not at all clear that Darwin meant to apply the concept of favored races in this particular book to human beings. In fact, he did write more on this subject later, but the provocative nature of the subtitle was enough to fuel discussions about racial superiority and inferiority. Later Darwinists took the concept far beyond what Charles Darwin intended.

So why do people hold racist attitudes? Three reasons are: feelings of pride, feelings of inferiority, and feelings of fear. Pride and arrogance fuel racism. When we are proud of who we are, we can easily look down upon those who are different from us and do not manifest the same characteristics that we do. We can start believing we are superior to another person or race.

Racism, however, can come from the opposite end of the emotional spectrum: inferiority. We may not feel good about ourselves. So in order to feel good about ourselves, we disparage another person or race.

Racism also results from fear. We fear what we do not understand. We fear what is strange and foreign. Racial and cultural differences may even seem dangerous to us. Racial attitudes can surface if we do not seek to know and understand those who are different from us.

BIBLICAL PERSPECTIVE ON RACE

We have already noted that the Bible really only talks of one race: the human race. Superficial differences in anatomy and physiology do not provide any justification for treating people differently simply because of these physical differences. The Bible teaches that God has made "of one blood all nations of men" (Acts 17:26 KJV).

The Bible also teaches that Christians should not feel superior to anyone. In Philippians 2, Paul admonished the Christians to live in harmony with one another. They were to have a gentle spirit toward one another, and to let this gentle spirit be known to others.

Christians are also admonished to refrain from using class distinctions within the church. In James 2:1–13, believers are told not to make class distinctions between various people. They are not to show partiality within the church. Showing favoritism is called sin, and the one showing favoritism is convicted by the law. Surely these commands would also apply to holding views of racial superiority and inferiority.

Likewise, Paul instructed Timothy (1 Tim. 5:21) to keep his instructions "without partiality and to do nothing out of favoritism." This command would also exclude making racial distinctions based on a view of racial superiority.

Finally, we see that Paul taught the spiritual equality of all people in Christ. For example, he taught in Colossians 3:11 that "there is no Greek or Jew, circumcised or uncircumcised, barbarian, Scythian, slave or free, but Christ is all, and is in all." This passage is significant because it shows that Christ has removed four kinds of distinctions: national distinctions (Greek or Jew), religious distinctions (circumcised or uncircumcised), cultural distinctions (barbarian or Scythian), and economic distinctions (slave or free).

A similar passage is Galatians 3:28: "There is neither Jew nor Greek, slave nor free, male nor female, for you are all one in Christ Jesus." In Christ, our human distinctions lose their significance. No one is superior to another. A believing Jew is not superior to a believing Greek. A believing slave is of no higher rank than a believing free person.

Racism and racist attitudes are wrong. Christians should work to remove such ideas and attitudes from society.

BECOMING CULTURALLY SENSITIVE

Following are some suggestions on how to become more sensitive to differences in race and culture.

First, take an accurate assessment of ourselves. Often our assumptions and predispositions affect the way we perceive and even treat others. A person who says that he or she has no prejudices is probably in denial. All of us perceive the world differently and find it easier to accept people who are like us and harder to understand people who are different from us.

Our cultural worldview affects how we perceive others. It affects how we evaluate what others think and what others do. So an important first step in becoming more racial and culturally sensitive is to evaluate ourselves.

Second, try to empathize with others. We must start learning how to look at life and our circumstances from the viewpoint of others. Instead of trying to make others think like us, we should strive to begin to begin to think like them. That advice does not mean we have to agree with their viewpoint, but it does mean that becoming empathetic will be helpful in bridging racial and cultural barriers.

Third, learn to withhold judgment. Tolerance (in the biblical sense of the word) is a virtue we should cultivate. We should be willing to put aside our critical thinking and judgment until we know someone better. Taking the time to listen and understand the other person will help build bridges and dismantle barriers that often separate and isolate races and cultures.

Fourth, do not consider yourself superior to another. One of the root causes of racism is a belief in racial superiority. Paul wrote in Romans 12:3 that you should "not think of yourself more highly than you ought." Differences in race and culture should never be used to justify feelings of racial superiority which can lead to racist attitudes.

Fifth, develop cross-cultural traits. Missionaries who go overseas must learn to develop personal traits that will make them successful in a new and different culture. Likewise, we should develop these traits so that we can reach across a racial and cultural divide. Friendliness and open communication are important. Flexibility and open-mindedness are also important. Developing these traits will enhance our ability to bridge a racial and cultural gap.

Finally, take a stand. We should not tell (or allow others to tell) racial and ethnic jokes. These jokes are demeaning to others and perpetuate racism and racial attitudes. Instead, we should be God's instrument in bringing about racial reconciliation. We should seek to build bridges and close the racial and cultural divide between people groups and reach out with the love of Jesus Christ.

20

TECHNOLOGY
AND THE ENVIRONMENT

TECHNOLOGY is the systematic modification of the environment for human ends. Often it is a process or activity that extends or enhances a human function. A microscope, for example, extends man's visual perception. A tractor extends one's physical ability. A computer extends a person's ability to calculate. Technology also includes devices that make physical processes more efficient. The many chemical processes we use to make products fit this description of technology.

BIBLICAL PERSPECTIVE ON TECHNOLOGY

The biblical mandate for developing and using technology is stated in Genesis 1:28. God gave mankind dominion over the land, and we are obliged to use and manage these resources wisely in serving the Lord. God's ideal was not to have a world composed exclusively of primitive areas. Before the Fall Adam was to cultivate and keep the Garden of Eden (Gen. 2:15). After the Fall the same command pertains to the application of technology to this fallen world, a world that "groans" in travail (Rom. 8:22). Technology can benefit mankind in exercising proper dominion, such as curing disease, breeding livestock, or growing better crops, and thus remove some of the effects of the Fall.

Technology is neither good nor evil. The worldview behind the particular technology determines its value for good or evil. In the Old Testament, technology was used both for good (the building of the ark, Genesis 6) and for evil (the building of the Tower of Babel, Genesis 11). Therefore, the focus should not be so much on the technology itself as on the philosophical motivation behind its use. Here are three important principles that should be considered.

First, technology should be seen as a tool, not as an end in itself. Technology is not sacred. Unfortunately Western culture tends to rely on it more than is appropriate. If a computer, for example, proves a particular point, people have a greater tendency to believe it than if the answer was a well-reasoned conclusion given by a person. If a machine can do the job, employers are prone to mechanize, even if human labor does a better or more creative job. Often our society unconsciously places machines over man. Humans become servants to machines rather than the other way around.

People have a tendency to look to science and engineering to solve problems that really may be due to human sinfulness (wars, prejudice, greed), the fallenness of the world (death, disease), or God's curse on Adam (finite resources). In Western culture especially, we tend to believe that technology will save us from our problems and thus we use technology as a substitute for God. Christians must not fall into this trap, but instead must exhibit their ultimate dependence on God. Christians must also differentiate between problems that demand a technological solution and ones that can be remedied by a social or spiritual one.

Second, technology should be applied in different ways, according to specific instructions. For example, there are distinctions between man and animal that, because we are created in God's image (Gen. 1:26–27), call for different applications of medical science. Using artificial insemination to improve the genetic fitness of livestock does not justify using it on human beings. Christians should resist the idea that just because we *can* do something we *should* do it. Technological ability does not grant moral permission.

Another important aspect of this principle is to recognize the diversity of cultural and social contexts. American farmers may use a high-energy, green revolution type of agriculture (using fertilizers, herbicides, and pesticides), but that does not mean it is the best form of agriculture to export worldwide.

Many commentators, most notably E. F. Schulmacher, have focused on the notion of appropriate technology.[1] In Third World countries, for example, sophisticated energy-intensive and capital-intensive forms of agriculture may be inappropriate for a culture as it presently exists. Industrial advance often brings social disruption and increasing havoc to a society. Developing countries must use caution in choosing the appropriate steps to industrialize, lest they be greatly harmed in the process.

Third, ethics rather than technology must determine the direction of our society. Jacques Ellul expressed the concern that technology moves society instead of vice versa.[2] Our society today seems all too motivated by a technological imperative in our culture. The technological ability to do something is not the same as a moral imperative to do it. Technology should not determine ethics.

Though scientists may possess the technological ability to be gods, they nevertheless lack the capacity to act like gods. Too often, man has tried to use technology to become God. He uses it to work out his own physical salvation, to enhance his own evolution, or even to attempt to create life. Christians who take seriously human fallenness will humbly admit that we often do not know enough about

God's creation to use technology wisely. The reality of human sinfulness means that society should be careful to prevent the use of technology for greed and exploitation.

Technology's fruits can be both sweet and bitter. C. S. Lewis wrote in the *Abolition of Man*, "From this point of view, what we call Man's power over Nature turns out to be power exercised by some men over men with Nature as its instrument. . . . There neither is nor can be any simple increase of power on Man's side. Each new power won *by* man is a power *over* man as well. Each advance leaves him weaker as well as stronger. In every victory, besides being the general who triumphs, he is also the prisoner who follows the triumphal car."[3]

Christians must bring strong biblical critique to each technological advance and analyze its impact. The goal should be to liberate the positive effects of technology while restraining negative effects by setting up appropriate constraints against abuse.

ENVIRONMENTAL PROBLEMS

How has technology affected the environment? Given the diverse nature of environmental issues, it is helpful to have a framework for discussing the extent of these problems. Calvin DeWitt developed such a framework of seven degradations of the creation. Presented in his book *The Environment and the Christian*,[4] these concepts were later adapted by the Evangelical Declaration on the Care of Creation. Though not without controversy, DeWitt's framework provides a brief but comprehensive survey of the extent of environmental problems facing mankind.

The first degradation is *land conversion and habitat destruction*. Approximately two billion acres of natural lands in the United States have been converted to human uses in addition to the more than three billion acres of cropland. While much of this land conversion has been beneficial to mankind (in planting crops and irrigating desert regions), some has been detrimental. Examples of detrimental effects would be the building of homes on prime farm land, draining wetland areas, and tropical deforestation.

In the past few centuries, pioneers in America cleared the land for farming, thus making a positive contribution to society and the environment. Today's destruction of habitat and conversion of land far exceeds any environmental action that preceded it and may impact the long-term sustainability of the environment and mankind. The current situation is reminiscent of Isaiah's warning, "Woe to you who add house to house and join field to field till no space is left and you live alone in the land" (Is. 5:8).

The second degradation is *species extinction*. How many species go extinct? Unfortunately the answer to that question is elusive. Harvard biologist Edward Wilson has published varying claims that 4,000 or 50,000 species become extinct every year.[5] Al Gore apparently picked that highest figure when he said in his book *Earth in the Balance* that 100 species become extinct every day.[6] Many scientists feel these estimates for species extinction are much too high. Estimating the extinction rate is made more difficult since scientists are uncertain as to how many millions of species actually exist on this planet. The revitalization of certain species in the United States (alligators and bald eagles) should not obscure the fact that many other species worldwide are becoming extinct. Reasons for extinction are many, including destruction of habitat, over-harvesting (as in hunting and fishing), and the introduction of new species into an environment.

Third is *land degradation*. Much of what was formerly tall grass prairie in the United States is today known as the corn belt. Agronomists estimate that two bushels of topsoil are lost for every bushel of corn produced.[7] Green revolution agriculture has made it possible to plant corn (or any crop) year after year on the same land. The principles of crop rotation used by previous generations have been largely abandoned. Intensive forms of agriculture (single crops, cattle feedlots) have dramatically altered the land, destroying the natural fauna and creating an ecological desert. Earthworms are less abundant on farmland, and birds have diminished by the removal of fencerows and hedgerows. Contrast the current state of agriculture with God's command to obey a sabbath rest for the land: "When you enter the land I am going to give you, the land itself must observe a sabbath to the LORD. For six years sow your fields, and for six years prune your vineyards and gather their crops. But in the seventh year the land is to have a sabbath of rest, a sabbath to the LORD. Do not sow your fields or prune your vineyards" (Lev. 25:2–4). While Christians are not under the Mosaic Law, these conservation principles should be considered

A fourth degradation is *resource conversion and waste and hazard production*. Scientific experiments and industrial processes have produced approximately seventy thousand different kinds of chemicals. The biological impact of these chemicals on the flora and fauna of this planet can be devastating. The products and by-products of industrial manufacture have polluted the air and water. Some chemicals designed to destroy one form of life, such as herbicides and pesticides, may have unintended consequences in other parts of the environment. Various gases produced in manufacturing—carbon dioxide, methane, ozone, and chlorofluorocarbons (CFCs)—affect the air and may even alter the earth's energy exchange and global temperature. Ezekiel 34:18 raises questions about the impact of degradation from one part of the environment to another part: "Is it not enough for you to feed on the good pasture? Must you also trample the rest of your pasture with your feet? Is it not enough for you to drink clear water? Must you also muddy the rest with your feet?"

A fifth degradation is *global toxification*. Weather and the physical systems (rivers, oceans) on the earth are dynamic not static. Chemical substances (whether toxic or not) are transported thousands of miles from their origin so that it is becoming more difficult to talk about a *local* polluter of a *local* environment. Pesticides have been found in the fat of antarctic animals. Toxic wastes leach into groundwater. Pollutants can be measured in the upper atmosphere. In essence, environmental problems have become a global problem.

Sixth is *alteration of planetary exchange.* The earth is in a dynamic balance of light and energy within the solar system. The earth's temperature is merely the sum of energy coming from the sun minus the energy radiated back into outer space. Changing that energy equation will change the temperature of the earth.

Many scientists warn that the production of certain greenhouse gases (like carbon dioxide) will alter the earth's energy equation, leading to catastrophic results, such as melting of polar ice caps or other climate modifications, while skeptics question the assumptions of the climatic models that lead to such predictions. Others warn that certain chemicals, like CFCs, may be destroying the earth's ozone layer, which provides protection from harmful ultraviolet radiation. While it is beyond the scope of this chapter to consider all the scientific evidence for and against such threats, these concerns do remind us of the human potential for disrupting the earth's energy exchange with the biosphere.

Seventh is *human and cultural degradation.* Cultures that have lived in harmony with the land have been affected by social pressures and environmental problems. In the United States, the Amish and Mennonite farming communities face social, economic, and political pressures that force some to abandon their farms and alter their three-hundred-year-old communities. Many tropical cultures are wiped off the land because of deforestation, mining, or the use of political force. Thus, rich cultural heritages disappear and vital information is lost (the use of various tropic plants for medicinal purposes).

These seven environmental degradations illustrate the possible extent of the current environmental crisis. A creation that God pronounced as good (Gen. 1:31) fell into decay at the Fall. Although man was given dominion over the world (Gen. 1:28), benevolent stewardship of the earth has not always been practiced and an environmental crisis has developed.

THE ENVIRONMENT AND HUMAN SINFULNESS

Environmentalists trying to discover the reason for our current environmental crisis have pointed to various culprits of the environmental crisis. Many blame the modern industrial mindset that allows companies virtually to rape the resources. These critics call for a paradigm shift and the adoption of a pantheistic view of the world that views nature is a living organism. James Lovelock, for example, rejected the biblical concept of God and replaced it with a pagan worldview centered on Gaia.[8] In essence, he and other environmentalist are calling for worship of Gaia (or some version of the idea of mother earth) by becoming one with nature.

Other critics have been willing to lay the blame on Christianity. Lynn White, in his 1967 classic essay in *Science* magazine, argued that Christianity established a "dualism of man and nature" that allowed mankind to exploit the environment. He claimed that the ecological crisis would continue "until we reject the Christian axiom that nature has no reason for existence save to serve man."[9]

The proper biblical response is to understand that God is both transcendent (apart from nature) and immanent (involved with the creation). God is both the Creator and the Sustainer of the creation. Nature should not be worshiped, nor should technology be used to destroy the environment. God's command to humankind to "subdue" the earth does not mean to exploit it for selfish gain.

The root of the environmental crisis is human sinfulness. Those looking to assess blame should remember the Pogo cartoon that said, "We have met the enemy and he is us." Francis Schaeffer said that human sinfulness manifests itself in the environmental crisis in two ways: greed and haste. He used the example of strip-mining to illustrate his point:

> If the strip-miners would take bulldozers and push back the topsoil, then rip out the coal, put back the soil, and replace the topsoil, in ten years after the coal was removed there would be a green field, and in fifty years a forest. But, as it stands, for an added profit above what is reasonable in regard to nature, man turns these areas into deserts— and then cries out that the topsoil is gone, grass will not grow, and there is no way to grow trees for hundreds of years![10]

He pointed out that "if you treat the land properly, you have to make two choices." Treating the land properly costs more money and takes more time. Ultimately, he said that the question is, "Are we going to have an immediate profit and an immediate savings of time, or are we going to do what we really should do as God's children?" He concluded that the Christian community must "refuse men the right to ravish the land, just as we refuse them the right to ravish our women."[11] A proper Christian response comes from proper Christian theology concerning the environment.

BIBLICAL PERSPECTIVE ON ECOLOGY

A Christian view of ecology strikes a balance between naturalistic and pantheistic extremes. A naturalistic view is wrong because it alienates humans from nature so that we deny our link with the rest of creation. When people are estranged from nature, any action can be justified and environmental exploitation results. Progress becomes the highest goal, thereby unleashing a wholesale rape of the resources.

A pantheistic view is wrong because it too closely and exclusively identifies people with nature. Humans are not to abuse the environment, but they are to use it responsibly. Pantheists often see killing animals or cutting down trees as improper since they believe humanity must become one with nature.

What is a Christian understanding of the environment? The natural beginning point is with God. He is the Creator and Sustainer of the world. God brought the universe and earth into existence. He gave Adam dominion over the creation, but also commanded him to till the earth and keep the garden (Gen. 1:28; 2:15). The following principles demonstrate how God's creation of man and the world applies to ecology.

First, God is the Owner of the world. Psalm 24:1 says, "The earth is the LORD's, and everything in it, the world, and all who live in it." God owns all of the creation, and man merely is the steward of that creation. To illustrate that point, God said to Job, "Everything under heaven belongs to me" (Job 41:11). In another passage, the Lord declared, "I have no need of a bull from your stall or of goats from your pens, for every animal of the forest is mine, and the cattle on a thousand hills. I know every bird in the mountains, and the creatures of the field are mine. If I were hungry I would not tell you, for the world is mine, and all that is in it" (Ps. 50:9–12).

Second, God is the Sustainer of the world. His Son is "sustaining all things by his powerful word" (Heb. 1:3). Colossians 1:17 says that Christ "is before all things, and in him all things hold together." Besides being active in the origin of the world, God is also continually active in the operation of the world as well.

Although the forces of nature operate according to physical laws affected by the Fall, Scripture nevertheless identifies God's influence within this force. For example, His hand is seen in the storms, the thunder, and the rain (Ps. 77:17–18). He causes the wind and the darkness (Amos 4:13). He is the Sustainer of life and all the forces within the world.

Third, God has a covenant with the world. After the Flood in Noah's day, God made a covenant with "all living creatures" (Gen. 9:16). This covenant was made not just with mankind, but with all animals: "This is the sign of the covenant I am making between me and you and every living creature with you, a covenant for all generations to come: I have set my rainbow in the clouds, and it will be the sign of the covenant between me and the earth. Whenever I bring clouds over the earth and the rainbow appears in the clouds, I will remember my covenant between me and you and all living creatures of every kind. Never again will the waters become a flood to destroy all life" (9:12–15).

Fourth, human beings are to exercise dominion over the creation. God placed man in the garden to take care of it (Gen. 2:15). He further charged mankind with the responsibility of exercising dominion. God said, "Be fruitful and increase in number; fill the earth and subdue it. Rule over the fish of the sea and the birds of the air and over every living creature that moves on the ground" (Gen. 1:28). Two words are important in understanding the concept of dominion: subdue and rule. The Hebrew word for "subdue" (*kabas*) means to tread down or bring into bondage. This word describes the image of a conqueror and implies that mankind is to have control over nature. The Hebrew word for "rule" (*rāda*) means to prevail over. This word also describes the idea of being victorious.

Mankind is also to care for the environment. "The LORD God took the man and put him in the Garden of Eden to work it and take care of it" (Gen. 2:15). The Hebrew word for "care" (*samar*) means to keep or preserve. Having dominion over the creation is not a license to rape the resources, it is a solemn responsibility to keep and care for the environment.

Fifth, God gave specific commands for exercising stewardship of the environment. In the Old Testament theocracy God commanded Israel to care for the land (Lev. 25:1–12), to treat domesticated animals properly, and to respect wildlife (Deut. 25:4; 22:6). The Hebrews were also to conserve trees (20:19–20) and bury their wastes (23:13). God also judged those who misused the land (Is. 5:8–10).

Sixth, God promised to restore the land when humans are obedient. Deuteronomy 28:1–4 says, "If you fully obey the LORD your God and carefully follow all his commands I give you today. . . . the fruit of your womb will be blessed, and the crops of your land and the young of your livestock—the calves of your herds and the lambs of your flocks." God honors faithful obedience to His principles. God also brought worldwide restoration of all the earth's creatures. Noah was commanded to preserve the earth's creatures in the Flood (Genesis 6—7). Therefore, if Christians are faithful to God's principles toward creation, God will bring about restoration.

ACTION STEPS FOR ENVIRONMENTAL STEWARDSHIP

Christians must be good stewards of the creation. The following are a few suggestions for individuals and churches in responding to environmental concerns.

First, Christians should study what the Bible says about stewardship of resources. Often the environment has been a neglected area of study for the Christian community. One Yale University study found that "knowledge of the creatures, respect for the creation and understanding ecological relationships was inversely related to the frequency of church attendance."[12] In other words dedicated Christians were the least likely to be interested in ecological issues.

Why do Christians seem to be so apathetic toward the environment? Two reasons seem possible. One reason is that Christians often see the world as evil and corrupted by sin. Often they are hesitant to enter the political arena for this reason. Perhaps they believe that the world is not worth protecting, especially since a Christian's ultimate destiny is in heaven. This belief, however, clearly contradicts God's direct command for mankind to care for the environment. Another reason is that some Christians may fear the prevailing pantheistic influence on the environmental movement. But New Age thinking in environmentalism may be due in large part to the withdrawal of Christians from this arena. When Christianity did not fill this void, pantheism and other worldviews filled it instead.

Second, churches should integrate biblical concepts about creation in preaching and teaching. Some churches steer away from discussing creation because they do not want to engage in a debate about evolution. This attitude not only leaves the congregation confused about the issue of origins, but it also keeps them from learning vital truths about a Christian's responsibility toward the creation.

Third, parents should see that their children are educated properly about the environment. Many schools do teach ecology but often from a pantheistic perspective. Parents should check the curricula to see if it teaches about Gaia, mother earth, or globalism. Often a good place for Christian-based environmental education is at Christian camps that often provide extensive outdoor education programs.

Fourth, Christians should practice sound ecological principles, including such things as recycling, which helps reduce the amount of trash. People in their occupations and in the homes should develop practices which help the environment. Applying these principles will make a positive impact on the environment as Christians seek to be good stewards of God's creation.

21

THE MEDIA
AND ENTERTAINMENT

THE MODERN MEDIA are so much a part of our lives that it is hard to remember that they are a relatively recent addition to society. Today the various forms of media are ubiquitous. Television is but one example. More homes have TV sets (98 percent) than have indoor plumbing. In the average home the television set is on for more than six hours a day.

The positive aspects of media are significant. They broaden viewers' horizons and bring them in contact with a broad array of events and cultures. Marshall McLuhan envisioned the emergence of a "global village" into which all mankind would be brought together through electronic circuitry.[1] In a sense that global village has been ushered in by the vast number of electronic outlets (radio, television, satellites, the Internet). The media also unify the nation and even the world around major events (presidential inaugurations, Super Bowl football games, Olympic games). Finally, they provide educational input and is a powerful tool for dispensing news and information.

The media also have negative effects that can influence our thinking and shape our worldview. By the selection of programs, scripts, and news events, we see only part of the picture. Christians must therefore make sure they are not conformed to this media image but instead are transformed by the renewing of their minds (Rom. 12:1–2).

The media have also replaced the home as a socializing unit. Cultural values used to be passed down from one generation to the next through the home, school, and church. Electronic communication began to change that. In his book *The Disappearance of Childhood* Neil Postman said that this changed with the first form of electronic communication (the telegraph) and continues today with television and other forms of electronic media. According to Postman, "The maintenance of childhood depended on the principles of managed information and sequential learning. But the telegraph began the process of wrestling control of information from the home and school. It altered the kind of information children could have access to, its quality and quantity, its sequence, and the circumstances in which it would be experienced."[2]

Today the media are *the* socializing unit. Many (perhaps most) social values are transmitted by the popular culture through the media. Values are no longer learned while sitting at the feet of grandpa rocking on the front porch; they are learned in front of a television screen, movie screen, or computer screen. And many American holidays, such as Thanksgiving and the Fourth of July, are celebrated with television rather than just with the family.

The amount of media exposure continues to increase every year. Recent studies of media usage reveal that people spend more than double the time with the media than they think they do. This amounts to nearly 12 hours a day total. And because of media multitasking, summing all the media use by medium results in a staggering 15 hours per day.[3]

The amount of media consumed by teenagers is significant. "Young people today live media-saturated lives, spending an average of nearly 6.5 hours a day with media."[4] Sixty percent of adolescents have television sets in their bedrooms.[5] The *Journal of the American Medical Association* estimates that the average teenager listens to 10,500 hours of music during their teen years.[6]

Student use of the Internet has been increasing to all-time levels. A study done at the University of Massachusetts at Amherst found the following:[7]

- Nearly 90 percent of the students accessed the Internet every day.

- Students spent over 10 hours per week using Instant Messenger.

- Those same students spent over 28 hours per week on the Internet.

- Nearly three-fourths spent more time online than they intended.

Christians should not only analyze the medium; they should also analyze its message. First, the media frequently presents an unreal view of the world. As will be documented in detail later, frequent viewers of the media tend to overestimate their likelihood of being involved in a crime, overestimate the number of people involved in white-collar occupations, and overestimate the percentage of Americans in relation to the rest of the world. The world of television and film is not the real world, and frequent viewers often have false perceptions of the world.

Second, the media presents an oversimplified view of life. The predictable plots of characters in television and film hardly mirror reality. Life for them is relatively easy, and they are unhindered by the difficulties of life or their problems are readily involved. Their world is less ambiguous and complex than reality.

Third, the media often desensitizes its viewers. Yesterday's sensation can become tomorrow's ho-hum. Television and film producers reach for bigger, better, more explicit scenes to build and keep audiences. Over time, viewers become desensitized to the sex and violence in the media. What was shocking ten years ago is generally accepted fare today.

SEX IN THE MEDIA

Is there too much sex on television and in film? Many American people seem to think so. One survey found that 75 percent of Americans felt that television had "too much sexually explicit material." Moreover, 86 percent believed that television had contributed to "a decline in values."[8] And no wonder. Scanning the ads for movies or channel surfing through the television reveals plots celebrating premarital sex, adultery, and even homosexuality. Sexual promiscuity in the media appears to be at an all-time high. A study of adolescents (ages 12–17) showed that watching sex on TV influences teens to have sex. Youths were more likely to initiate intercourse as well as other sexual activities.[9]

The chapter on pornography should have provided ample warning about the dangerous effects of sex, especially when linked with violence. Neil Malamuth and Edward Donnerstain documented the volatile impact of sex and violence in the media: "There can be relatively long-term, anti-social effects of movies that portray sexual violence as having positive consequences."[10]

In a message given by Donnerstein, he concluded with this warning and observation: "If you take normal males and expose them to graphic violence against women in R-rated films, the research doesn't show that they'll commit acts of violence against women. It doesn't say they will go out and commit rape. But it does demonstrate that they become less sensitized to violence against women, they have less sympathy for rape victims, and their perceptions and attitudes and values about violence change."[11]

It is important to remember that these studies are applicable not just to hardcore pornography. Many of the studies used films that are readily shown on television (especially cable television) any night of the week. And many of the movies shown today in theaters are much more explicit than those shown just a few years ago.

The social commentator Irving Kristol asked this question in a *Wall Street Journal* column: "Can anyone really believe that soft porn in our Hollywood movies, hard porn in our cable movies and violent port in our 'rap' music is without effect? Here the average, overall impact is quite discernible to the naked eye. And at the margin, the effects, in terms most notably of illegitimacy and rape, are shockingly visible."[12] Sexual images and violent images in the media have an impact.

VIOLENCE IN THE MEDIA

Violence has always been a part of the human condition because of our sin nature (Rom. 3:23), but modern families are exposed to a level of violence never seen before. Any night of the week, the average viewer can see levels of violence exceeding those found in the Roman gladiator games.

Does this have an effect? The Bible teaches that "as a man thinks in his heart, so is he" (Prov. 23:7, KJV). What we view and what we think about affect our actions. And while this is true for adults, it is especially true for children. They grow up in a scary world of violence. The daily news is rife with reports of child molestations and abductions as well as nightly tallies of murder, rape, and robbery. An article in *Newsweek* magazine concluded:

> It gets dark early in the Midwest this time of year. Long before many parents are home from work, the shadows creep up the walls and gather in the corners, while on the carpet a little figure sprawls in the glow emanating from an anchorman's tan. There's been a murder in the Loop, a fire in a nightclub, an indictment of another priest. Red and white lights swirl in urgent pinwheels as the ambulances howl down the dark streets. And one more crime that never gets reported, because there's no one to arrest. Who killed childhood? We all did.[13]

Some in the entertainment industry argue that violence in the media has no effect on its viewers. They contend that televised imagery does not make people violent nor does it make people callous to suffering. But if televised imagery does not affect human behavior, then the TV networks should refund billions of advertising dollars to TV sponsors.

In essence, TV executives are talking out of both sides of their mouths. On the one hand, they try to convince advertisers that a thirty-second commercial can influence consumer behavior. And on the other hand, they deny that a one-hour program wrapped around the commercials can influence social behavior. Obviously there is a contradiction, especially when there is so much documentation for the harmful affects of violence in the media. Violence in film and television have a devastating impact.

Violence in the Movies

The level of violence in movies has reached an all-time high. Who would have imagined just a few years ago that the top dollar-grossing films would be replete with blood, gore, and violence? No wonder some film critics now say that the most violent place on earth is the Hollywood set.

In one sense violence has always been a part of movie-making, but until recently really violent movies were only seen by the fringe of mass culture. Violence now has gone mainstream. Bloody films are being watched by more than just punk rockers. Family station wagons and vans pull up to movie theaters showing R-rated slasher films. And middle America watches these same programs a few months later on cable television or on video. Many of the movies seen at home would not have been shown in theaters ten to twenty years ago.

The brutal imagery of movies should concern all of us. Even if the appalling assault on our senses is not concern enough, we should at least wonder if these visual images contribute to an increasingly dangerous society.

Nevertheless, most Americans show an ambivalent attitude toward violence. Apparently there is a contradiction between their walk and talk. They talk about the potential danger of violence in the media. One Gallup poll, for example, showed that 40 percent of Americans think movie violence is a "very great" cause of real violence and an additional 28 percent see it as a "considerable" factor.[14] However, many of those same people who express concern will nevertheless stand in block-long lines to see the latest violent action film or horror film.

Movie violence these days is louder, bloodier, and more anatomically precise than ever before. When a bad guy was shot in a black-and-white Western, the most that the audience saw was a puff of smoke and a few drops of fake blood. Now the sights, sounds, and special effects are often more jarring than the real thing. Slow motion, pyrotechnics, and a penchant for leaving nothing to the imagination all conspire to make movies and TV shows more gruesome than ever.

Movie thrillers used to emphasize the deductive powers of the investigator. These types of movies have now given way to plots about police investigators or action heroes with quick fingers who track down villains that have become increasingly psychotic and demonic.

Children especially confront an increasingly violent world with few limits. When, for example, was the last time a child was turned away from a theater for being under age? Moreover, what is to prevent a child from buying a ticket for a PG-rated film and then walking into an R-rated film?

Children are seeing increasingly violent films at younger and younger ages. Glenn Sparks, a researcher at Purdue University, surveyed five- to seven-year-old children in suburban Cleveland. He found that 20 percent said that they had seen "Friday the 13th" and 48 percent had seen "Poltergeist."[15]

Violence on Television

Children's greatest exposure to violence comes from television. TV shows, movies edited for television, and video games expose young children to a level of violence unimaginable just a few years ago. The American Psychological Association said that the average child watches eight thousand televised murders and one hundred thousand acts of violence before finishing elementary school.[16] That number more than doubles by the time he or she reaches age eighteen.

One study by the Washington-based Center for Media and Public Affairs claimed that television was "considerably more violent" than it was just two years before. The study found that television violence increased "across the board" for cable and broadcast networks alike in both fiction and nonfiction programming.[17] Network executives disputed the study because it looked at all programs including news and promotional ads rather than focusing on just the content of network programming. But their criticism actually makes the point. It is the totality of the TV programming that affects families and especially young children.

The violent content of television includes more than just the twenty-two-minute programs produced by the networks. At a very young age, children are seeing a level of violence and mayhem that in the past may have been seen only by a few police officers and military personnel. TV brings hitting, kicking, stabbings, shootings, and dismemberment right into homes on a daily basis.

The impact on behavior is predictable. Over 1,000 studies (including reports from the Surgeon General's office and the National Institute of Mental Health) "point overwhelmingly to a causal connection between media violence and aggressive behavior in some children."[18]

Long-term studies are even more disturbing. Leonard Eron, a psychologist at the University of Illinois, studied children at age eight and then again at eighteen. He found that television habits established at the age of eight influenced aggressive behavior throughout childhood and adolescent years. The more violent the programs preferred by boys in the third grade, the more aggressive their behavior, both at that time and ten years later. Thus, he concluded that "the effect of television violence on aggression is cumulative."[19]

Twenty years later Eron and Rowell Huesmann found the pattern continued. Eron and his researchers found that children who watched significant amounts of TV violence at the age of eight were consistently more likely to commit violent crimes or engage in child or spouse abuse at thirty.[20] They concluded "that heavy exposure to televised violence is one of the causes of aggressive behavior, crime and violence in society. Television violence affects youngsters of all ages, of both genders, at all socioeconomic levels and all levels of intelligence."[21]

Since the Eron and Huesmann report in the 1980s, MTV has arrived with even more troubling images. Adolescents already listen to an estimated 10,500 hours of rock music between the seventh and twelfth grades. Now they also spend countless hours in front of MTV seeing the visual images of rock songs that depict violence, rebellion, sadomasochism, the occult, drug abuse, and promiscuity. MTV reaches 57 million cable households, and its video images are even more lurid than the ones shown on regular TV.[22] Music videos are filled with sex, rape, murder, and other images of mayhem assault the senses. Critics count eighteen acts of violence on the average in each hour of MTV videos.[23]

PSYCHOLOGICAL IMPACT OF VIOLENT MEDIA

What is the effect of violent programs on children? It turns out that some of the greatest dangers of television are more subtle and insidious. Simply watching television for long periods can manipulate their view of the world.

George Gerbner and Larry Gross, working at the Annenberg School of Communications in the 1970s, found that frequent television-viewers live in a scary world. They reported, "We have found that people who watch a lot of TV see the real world as more dangerous and frightening than those who watch very little. Heavy viewers are less trustful of their fellow citizens, and more fearful of the real world."[24] They defined heavy viewers as those adults who watch an average of four or more hours of television a day. Approximately one-third of all American adults fit that category.

Gerbner and Gross found that violence on prime-time TV exaggerated heavy viewers' fears about the threat of danger in the real world. For example, they were less likely to trust others than light viewers. Heavy viewers also tended to overestimate their likelihood of being involved in a violent crime.

And if this is true of adults, imagine how television violence affects children's perceptions of the world. Gerbner and Gross said, "Imagine spending six hours a day at the local movie house when you were 12 years old. No parent would have permitted it. Yet, in our sample of children, nearly half the 12-year-olds watch an average of six or more hours of television per day." This would mean that a large portion of young people fit into the category of heavy viewers. Their view of the world must be profoundly shaped by TV. Gerbner and Gross therefore conclude, "If adults can be so accepting of the reality of television, imagine its effect on children. By the time the average American child reaches public school, he has already spent several years in an electronic nursery school."[25]

Television violence affects both adults and children in subtle ways. We must not ignore the growing body of data that suggests that televised imagery does affect our perceptions and behaviors.

THE WORLDVIEW OF THE NEWS MEDIA

Of all the forms of media, the news media have become a primary shaper of our perspective on the world. Also the rules of journalism have changed in the last few decades. It used to be assumed that reporters or broadcasters would attempt to look at events with the eyes of the average reader or viewer. It was also assumed that they would not use their positions in the media to influence the thinking of the nation but merely to report objectively the facts of an event. Things have changed dramatically in the news business.

The fact that people in the media are out of step with the American people should be a self-evident statement. But for anyone who does not believe it, there is abundant empirical evidence to support it.

Probably the best-known research on media bias was first published in the early 1980s by professors Robert Lichter and Stanley Rothman. Their research, published in the journal *Public Opinion*[26] and later collected in the book *The Media Elite*,[27] demonstrated that reporters and broadcasters in the prestige media differ in significant ways from their audiences. They surveyed 240 editors and reporters of the media elite—*New York Times, Washington Post, Time, Newsweek*, ABC, NBC, and CBS. Their research confirmed what many suspected for a long time. The media elite are liberal, secular, and humanistic.

People have always complained about the liberal bias in the media. But what was so surprising is how liberal members of the media actually are. When asked to describe their own political persuasion, 54 percent of the media elite described themselves as left of center. Only 19 percent described themselves as conservative. When asked whom they voted for in presidential elections, more than 80 percent of them always voted for the Democratic candidate.

Media personnel are also secular in their outlook. Lichter and Rothman's survey found that 86 percent of the media elite seldom or never attend religious services. In fact 50 percent of them have no religious affiliation at all.

This bias is especially evident when the secular press tries to cover religious events or religious issues. Most of them do not attend church, nor do they even know people who do. Instead, they live in a secularized world and therefore tend to underestimate the significance of religious values in American lives and to paint anyone with Christian convictions as a "fundamentalist."

The media elite is also humanistic in its outlook on important moral issues. For example, only 15 percent of the media elite felt that adultery is morally wrong. Thus, they rarely cover the adulterous affair of a prominent politician except when the issue can no longer be ignored, such as in the cases of Wilbur Mills, Gary Hart, or Bill Clinton.

On the issue of abortion 90 percent of the media elite supports a woman's so-called "right to an abortion." No wonder pro-life groups have such a difficult time getting their message to the American people. Usually the issue is framed in terms of whether government has the right to infringe on a woman's right to privacy.

And on the issue of homosexuality the media elite also differ from the general population. Only 24 percent of the media elite agreed or strongly agreed that "homosexuality is wrong," and that percentage has probably dropped significantly since then. Favorable and extensive coverage of gay issues and the AIDS issue are examples of this bias.

For a time, members of the media elite argued against studies that portrayed them negatively. They suggested that the statistical sample was too small. But when Lichter began to enumerate the 240 members of the news media interviewed, that tactic was quickly set aside. Others tried to argue that, though the media might be liberal, secular, and humanistic, it did not affect the way the press covered the news. Later studies by a variety of media watchdogs began to erode the acceptance of that view.

A second significant study on media bias was a 1996 survey conducted by the Freedom Forum and the Roper Center.[28] Their survey of 139 Washington bureau chiefs and congressional correspondents showed a decided preference for liberal candidates and causes. The journalists were asked for whom they voted in the 1992 election. The results were these: 89 percent said Bill Clinton, 7 percent George Bush, 2 percent Ross Perot. But in the election 43 percent of Americans voted for Clinton and 37 percent voted for Bush.

Another question they were asked was, "What is your current political affiliation?" Fifty percent said they were Democrats, 4 percent Republicans. In answer to the question, "How do you characterize your political orientation?" 61 percent said they were liberal or moderately liberal, and 9 percent were conservative or moderately conservative.

The reporters were also asked about their attitudes toward their jobs. They said that they see their coverage of news events as a mission. Ninety-two percent agreed with the statement, "Our role is to educate the public." And 62 percent agreed with the statement, "Our role is sometimes to suggest potential solutions to social problems."

A more recent survey by the Pew Research Center further confirmed the liberal bias in the media. The center interviewed 547 media professionals (print, TV, and radio) and asked them to identify their political perspective. They found that 34 percent were liberal and only 7 percent were conservative. These percentages compare to 20 percent of American who identify themselves as liberal and 33 percent who define themselves as conservative.[29]

It is also worth questioning whether a majority of media professionals who labeled themselves as moderate in the survey really deserve that label. John Leo, writing for *U.S. News and World Report*, said that it has been his experience "that liberal journalists tend to think of themselves as representing the mainstream, so in these self-identification polls, moderate usually translates to liberal. On the few social questions asked in the survey, most of the moderates sounded fairly liberal."[30]

More recent academic studies of media bias further confirm these earlier studies. For example, a systematic analysis of news outlets found that all of them (except Fox News' Special Report and the *Washington Times*) received a score to the left of the average member of Congress.[31] The researchers also found "that journalists, as a group, are more liberal than almost any congressional district in the country."[32]

How Does Bias Show Up?

Bias in the news usually results from the different perspectives of most secular news people. People in the news business tend to be more liberal, more secular, and more humanistic than the rest of the nation and their stories and programs reflect that orientation.

How does bias show up? While reading an article or watching a program, people need to be aware of the media's "tricks of the trade." Although these might seem like subtle, insignificant issues, they can change the whole perspective of a story.

The most important tool is language. The power of words and labels is compelling. Abortionists are called pro-choice advocates, abortion providers, or family planning consultants. Pro-lifers are instead given labels such as antiabortionists, militant moralists, or "self-proclaimed soldiers in God's army."

Frequently the media will allow the liberal cause to label itself but will deny the conservative cause the same right. Thus the press uses the labels "pro-choice" and "antiabortion" (rather than pro-life). In countries attempting to win liberation, military forces fighting for freedom are rarely called "freedom fighters." Instead, they are referred to as rebels, insurgents, or Contras.

Another tool of journalists and broadcasters is inclusion and/or exclusion. By continuously reporting some incidents, the press increases the perceived importance of some issues and decreases the importance of others. If the press extensively covers a feminist march or an environmental protest, then those causes appear to be more important. If they ignore a pro-life rally or a march against pornography, those causes seem less important.

Another journalistic tool is placement. Even when journalists and broadcasters attempt to give fair treatment, editors can change the perception of a story. A front-page story with a headline or the lead story in a broadcast is considered more important. A story buried in the back of the paper or given a single sentence later in the broadcast is perceived as less important.

Interviewing is another tool. When reading a story or watching a broadcast, individuals need to be aware that only a small part of the interview appears in the final story. Key comments may have preceded the quote that was printed or broadcast. The interviewers may have even asked the same question five times before they got the answer they were looking for.

Reporters and broadcasters may have interviewed only people with whom they agree. In fact good reporters usually know the answers they will get from most of the people they interview before they interview them. Thus, by interviewing people they agree with, they can turn what is supposed to be an objective story into a platform for their own views.

Still another tool is the use of experts. Often in controversial stories, a reporter will interview a spokesperson from one side and then a spokesperson from the other. Then many stories will end with an "expert." This person is called in to resolve the issue or set the record straight. But the expert may have a bias too, even if he or she is a professor at a major university or works at a prominent think tank.

BIAS IN OTHER MEDIA

Although bias is easier to spot in news reporting, it is also prevalent in other forms of media. When Lichter and Rothman interviewed people in the news media, they also interviewed prominent people in television and film. They interviewed 104 of Hollywood's most influential television writers, producers, and executives.[33] Many of these individuals had been honored with Emmy Awards and a few were considered household names. As with the news media, Lichter and Rothman found that those working in television were very different from the rest of the public.

Most of the respondents were white (99 percent) and male (98 percent); they were also affluent and bicoastal. Lichter and Rothman found that 63 percent had an annual income over $200,000 and that 82 percent grew up in large metropolitan areas. Few made the fabled journey from small-town America to Hollywood. And 73 percent came from California or the Boston-Washington corridor.

The respondents were also extremely liberal. Seventy-five percent described themselves as left of center, compared to only 14 percent who placed themselves to the right of center. Like the news media, at least 80 percent always voted for the Democratic candidate for president.

The respondents were also secular. Nearly all (93 percent) had a religious upbringing (including 59 percent who were brought up in the Jewish faith) in their childhood. But 45 percent currently claimed no religious affiliation, and 93 percent said they seldom or never attend religious services.

The values of those in television were similar to those in the news media, but even more significant was their attitude toward television. For example, when asked if there is too much sex on TV, only 30 percent agreed or strongly agreed. When asked if TV is too critical of traditional values, only 12 percent agreed or strongly agreed.

A similar pattern emerged for those making major motion pictures. Lichter and Rothman interviewed 149 writers, producers, and directors from the fifty top money-grossing films from 1965 through 1982.[34] Sixty-four percent of those contacted completed the questionnaire and were among the most successful of Hollywood's moviemakers. Most were white (99 percent), male (99 percent), and from metropolitan (81 percent) sectors of society. Most were from the West Coast or the Northeast (73 percent), and nearly two-thirds (64 percent) had an annual income over $200,000. They were also very secular, with 55 percent claiming no religious affiliation and 96 percent admitting that they seldom or never attend religious services.

The conclusion should be self-evident. When reading a newspaper or newsmagazine, listening to radio, or watching television or a movie, people must be aware that the potential for bias is present. Those who make up the media elite (in news, television, and film) have a worldview that differs from the average American and is often contrary to biblical principles. Thus, Christians must read, listen, and watch with discernment.

SUGGESTIONS FOR DEALING WITH THE MEDIA

Christians must address the influence of the media in society because they can be a dangerous influence that can conform us to the world (Rom. 12:2). Therefore, we should do all we can to protect against its influence and to use the media for good. Christians should strive to apply the following two passages to their lives as they seek discernment concerning the media. Philippians 4:8 says, "Finally, brothers, whatever is true, whatever is noble, whatever is right, whatever is pure, whatever is lovely, whatever is admirable—if anything is excellent or praiseworthy—think about such things." Colossians 3:2–5 admonishes Christians, "Set your minds on things above, not on earthly things. For you died, and your life is now hidden with Christ in God. When Christ, who is your life, appears, then you also will appear with him in glory. Put to death, therefore, whatever belongs to your earthly nature: sexual immorality, impurity, lust, evil desires and greed, which is idolatry." The following are suggestions for action.

First, control the quantity and quality of media input. Parents should set down guidelines and help select television programs at the start of the week and watch only those. Parents should also set down guidelines for movies, music, and other forms of media. Families should also evaluate the location of their television set so that it is not so easy to just sit and watch TV for long hours.

Second, watch TV with children. One way to encourage discussion with children is to watch television with them. The plots and actions of the programs provide a natural context for discussion. The discussion could focus on how cartoon characters or TV characters could solve their problems without resorting to violence. What are the consequences of violence? TV often ignores the consequences. What are the consequences of promiscuous sex in real life?

Third, set a good example. Parents should not be guilty of saying one thing and doing another. Neither adults nor children should spend long periods of time in front of a video display (television, video game, computer). Parents can teach their children by example that there are better ways to spend time.

Fourth, work to establish broadcaster guidelines. No TV or movie producer wants to unilaterally disarm all the actors on their screens for fear that viewers will watch other programs and movies. Yet many of these TV and movie producers would like to tone down the violence, even though they do not want to be the first to do so. National standards would be able to achieve what individuals would not do by themselves in a competitive market.

Fifth, make your opinions known. Writing letters to programs, networks, and advertisers can make a difference over time. A single letter may not make a difference, but large numbers of letters can even change editorial policy. Consider joining with other like-minded people in seeking to make a difference in the media.

While the media has a tremendous potential for good, it can also have some very negative effects. Christians need wisdom and discernment to utilize the positive aspects of media and to guard against its negative effects.

22

GOVERNMENT
AND CIVIL DISOBEDIENCE

WHAT IS THE FUNCTION OF GOVERNMENT? Should Christians ever disobey government? If so, under what circumstances? These are key questions for Christians who seek to influence society with biblical convictions.

To answer these questions adequately, we must first look at the structure and function of government. Government is not the invention of man, but is a divinely ordained institution to bring order and justice to a fallen world. Biblical obedience is required, but there are exceptions when civil disobedience is permitted.

CHRISTIAN VIEW OF GOVERNMENT

Government affects our lives daily, yet few citizens take time to consider its basic function. What is a biblical view of government? Why do we have government? What kind of government does the Bible allow?

Developing a Christian understanding of government is difficult since the Bible does not provide an exhaustive treatment of government. This vagueness itself is perhaps instructive and provides some latitude for governmental institutions to reflect the needs and demands of particular cultural situations. Because the Bible does not speak directly to every area of political discussion, Christians often hold different views on particular political issues. However, Christians are not free to believe whatever they want. Christians should not abandon the Bible when they begin to think about these issues because much biblical material can be used to judge particular political options.

The Old Testament provides clear guidelines for the development of a theocracy in which God was the head of government. These guidelines, however, were written for particular circumstances involving a covenant people chosen by God.

These guidelines do not apply today because our modern governments are not the direct inheritors of the promises God made to the nation of Israel.

Apart from that unique situation, the Bible does not propose nor endorse any specific political system. The Bible, however, does provide a basis for evaluating various political philosophies because it clearly delineates a view of human nature. Every political theory rests on a particular view of human nature.

The Bible describes two elements of human nature. This understanding is helpful in judging government systems. Because humans are created in the image of God (Gen. 1:26–27), they are able to exercise judgment and rationality. However, humans are also fallen creatures (Genesis 3). This human sinfulness (Rom. 3:23) has therefore created a need to control evil and sinful human behavior through civil government.

Many theologians have suggested that the only reason we have government today is to control sinful behavior because of the Fall. But government probably would have existed even if we lived in a sinless world. For example, some structuring of authority seems to have existed in the Garden (Genesis 2). The Bible also speaks of the angelic host as being organized into levels of authority and function.

In creation God ordained government as the means by which human beings and angelic hosts are ruled. The rest of the created order is governed by instinct (Prov. 30:24–28) and God's providence. Insect colonies, for example, may show a level of order, such order is due merely to genetically controlled instinct.

Human beings, on the other hand, are created in the image of God and thus are responsible to the volitional commands of God. We are created by a God of order (1 Cor. 14:33); therefore, we also seek order through governmental structures.

A Christian understanding of government differs significantly from views proposed by many political theorists. The basis for civil government is rooted in our created nature. We are rational and volitional beings. We are not determined by fate, as the Greeks believed, nor are we determined by our environment, as modern behaviorists say. We have the power of choice. Therefore, we can exercise delegated power over the created order. Thus, a biblical understanding of human nature requires a governmental system that acknowledges human responsibility.

While the source of civil government is rooted in human responsibility, the need for government derives from the necessity of controlling human sinfulness. God ordained civil government to restrain evil (cf. Genesis 9). Anarchy, for example, is not a viable option because all have sinned (Rom. 3:23) and are in need of external control.

Since civil government is necessary and divinely ordained by God (Rom.13:1–7), it is ultimately under God's control. It has been given three political responsibilities: the sword of justice (to punish criminals), the sword of order (to thwart rebellion), and the sword of war (to defend the state).

As citizens, Christians have been given a number of responsibilities. God calls us to render service and obedience to the government (Matt. 22:21). Because it is a God-ordained institution, we are to submit to civil authority (1 Pet. 2:13–17) as we would to other institutions of God. As will be discussed later, Christians are not to give complete allegiance to the secular state. Other God-ordained institutions exist in society alongside the state. Christians' final allegiance must be to God. We are to obey civil authorities (Rom. 13:5) in order to avoid anarchy and chaos, but there may be times when we may be forced to disobey (Acts 5:29).

Because government is a divinely ordained institution, Christians have a responsibility to work within governmental structures to bring about change. Government is part of the creation order and a minister of God (Rom. 13:4). Christians are to be the salt of the earth and the light of the world (Matt. 5:13–16) in the midst of the political context.

Although governments may be guilty of injustice, Christians should not stop working for justice or cease being concerned about human rights. We do not give up on marriage as an institution simply because there are so many divorces, and we do not give up on the church because of many internal problems. Each God-ordained institution manifests human sinfulness and disobedience. Our responsibility as Christians is to call political leaders back to this God-ordained task. Government is a legitimate sphere of Christian service, and so we should not look to government only when our rights are being abused. We are to be concerned with social justice and should see governmental action as a legitimate instrument to achieve just ends.

A Christian view of government should also be concerned with human rights. Human rights in a Christian system are based on a biblical understanding of human dignity. A bill of rights, therefore, does not grant rights to individuals, but instead acknowledges these rights as already existing. The writings of John Locke and the Declaration of Independence captured this idea by stating that government is based on the inalienable rights of individuals. Government based on humanism, however, would not see rights as inalienable, and thus opens the possibility for the state to redefine what rights its citizens may enjoy. The rights of citizens in a republic, for example, are articulated in terms of what the government is forbidden to do. But in totalitarian governments, while the rights of citizens may also be spelled out, power ultimately resides in the government not the people.

A Christian view of government also recognizes the need to limit the influence of sin in society. Limiting sin is best achieved by placing certain checks on governmental authority. These check and balances protect citizens from the abuse or misuse of governmental power which results when sinful individuals are given too much governmental control.

The greatest threat to liberty comes from the exercise of power. History has shown that power is a corrupting force when placed in human hands. In the Old Testament theocracy there was less danger of abuse because the head of state was God. The Bible amply documents the dangers that ensued when power was transferred to a single king. Even David, a man after God's own heart (1 Sam. 13:14; Acts 13:22), abused his power and Israel experienced great calamity (2 Samuel 11—21).

Abuse and misuse of power characterizes human governments. The contribution of modern democratic theory was to recognize human sinfulness and to devise an ingenious method to tame its effects. John Locke, James Madison, and others recognized that since we cannot rid human nature of sinful behavior, the only solution is to use human nature to control itself.

GOVERNMENTAL AUTHORITY

A key question in political theory is how to determine the limits of governmental authority. With the remarkable growth in the size and scope of government in the last century, we must define clearly the lines of governmental authority. The Bible provides some guidelines. However, setting limits or drawing lines is often difficult. As already noted, the Old Testament theocracy differed from our modern democratic government. Although human nature is the same, drawing biblical principles from an agrarian, monolithic culture and applying them to the technological, pluralistic culture requires discernment.

Part of this difficulty can be eased by separating two issues. First, should government legislate morality? We will discuss this in the section on social action. Second, what are the limits of governmental sovereignty? The following are a few general principles helpful in determining the limits of governmental authority.

As Christians, we recognize that God has ordained other institutions besides government which exercise authority in their particular sphere of influence. This recognition contrasts with other political systems that understand the state as the sovereign agent over human affairs, exercising sovereignty over every other human institution. A Christian understanding is different.

The first institution is the church (1 Pet. 2:9–10). Jesus taught that the government should work in harmony with the church and should recognize its sovereignty in spiritual matters (Matt. 22:21).

The second institution is the family (Eph. 5:22–32; 1 Pet. 3:1–7). The family is an institution under God and His authority (Gen. 1:26–28). When the family breaks down, the government often has to step in to protect the rights of the wife (in cases of wife abuse) or children (in cases of child abuse or adoption). The biblical emphasis, however, is not so much on rights as it is on responsibilities and mutual submission (Eph. 5:21).

A third institution is education. Children are not the wards of the state; they belong to God (Ps. 127:3) and are given to parents as gifts from God. Parents must teach their children (Deut. 4:9), although they may also entrust their children to tutors (Gal. 4:2).

In a humanistic system of government, the institutions of church and family are usually subordinated to the state. In an atheistic system, ultimately the state becomes a substitute god and is given additional power to adjudicate disputes and bring order to a society. Since institutions exist by permission of the state, the possibility always exists that a new social contract will allow government to intervene in the areas of church and family.

A Christian view of government recognizes the sovereignty of these spheres. Governmental intervention into the spheres of church and family is necessary in certain cases where there is threat to life, liberty, or property. Otherwise civil governmental should recognize the sovereignty of other God-ordained institutions.

But what should Christians do if government exceeds its authority? Do Christians have a right and responsibility to disobey? Those who would quickly dismiss this question as irrelevant should realize the implications of civil disobedience on Christian discipleship and obedience to God's law. Francis Schaeffer stated that "one either confesses that God is the final authority, or one confesses that Caesar is Lord."[1] If there is never a circumstance under which a Christian would disobey God, then ultimately the state has become god. Therefore, civil disobedience must be permitted. But if civil disobedience is permitted, under what circumstances is it permissible?

CIVIL DISOBEDIENCE

Civil disobedience has a long history in the United States, starting with the American Revolution. Civil disobedience continued through the nineteenth century (the abolition movement protests preceding the Civil War) and surfaced in the latter part of the twentieth century in the civil rights movement, the environmental movement, and the peace movement (including protests against the Vietnam war and protests against nuclear arms). Today civil disobedience surfaces in many ways. In the Pacific Northwest, environmentalists have placed steel spikes in trees. When a high-speed chain saw hits a buried spike, the saw shatters, sending pieces of metal out like shrapnel. In New York, homosexual activists have disrupted church services and blocked access to the churches because of those churches' public stance on homosexuality. Animal rights activists have broken into laboratories to destroy equipment and release animals.

The modern debate on civil disobedience has been heavily influenced by the nineteenth-century writer Henry David Thoreau. Beginning from a humanistic perspective, he set forth a case for disobeying government. Thoreau wrote his famous essay "On the Duty of Civil Disobedience" after spending a night in the Concord, Massachusetts, jail in July 1846.[2] He had refused to pay his poll tax as a protest against a government that supported slavery. During the night someone paid the tax and he was released. His essay grew out of his experience and has influenced many who consider similar actions. For example, Mahatma Gandhi printed and distributed Thoreau's essay and always carried a copy with him during his many imprisonments.

Thoreau challenged the prevailing notion of his day that obedience to government was more important than obedience to conscience. Most citizens would have argued that if a conflict existed between moral law and the government, one should obey government. Thoreau insisted that moral principle should come first and that civil disobedience was required even if it meant refusing to pay taxes or going to jail.

Thoreau's basic principle, however, leaves a question. Who is to decide when to disobey the government? According to Thoreau, each individual should follow his or her innate sense of goodness. Thus, each person must decide what he or she thinks is right and which laws he or she will obey or disobey. This moral anarchy resulted because he did not believe in an absolute standard of right and wrong.

Christians, however, have a transcendent set of standards to follow. The Bible lays out clear biblical principles that should be followed when a believer feels a conflict between God and government.

The best articulation of these biblical principles can be found in Samuel Rutherford's essay *Lex Rex*.[3] Arguing that governmental law was founded on the law of God, he rejected the seventeenth-century idea of the "divine right of kings." The king was not the ultimate authority; God's Law was (hence the title *Lex Rex*, "The law is king"). If the king and the government disobeyed the law, then they were to be disobeyed. Rutherford argued that all men, including the king, were under God's Law and not above it. According to Rutherford, the civil magistrate was a "fiduciary figure" who held his authority in trust for the people. If that trust was violated, the people had a political basis for resistance. Not surprisingly *Lex Rex* was banned in England and Scotland and was seen as treasonous and fomenting political rebellion.

Biblical Examples of Civil Disobedience

The Bible provides a number of prominent examples of civil disobedience. When Pharaoh commanded the Hebrew midwives to kill all male Hebrew babies, they lied to Pharaoh and did not carry out his command (Exodus 1—2).

The Book of Daniel contains a number of instructive examples. For example, when Shadrach, Meshach, and Abed-Nego refused to bow down to Nebuchadnezzar's golden image, they were cast into a fiery furnace (Daniel 3). The commissioners and satraps persuaded King Darius to decree that no one could petition any god or man for thirty days. Daniel nevertheless continued to pray to God three times a day and was cast into the lion's den (Daniel 6).

The most dramatic example of civil disobedience in the New Testament is recorded in Acts 4—5. When Peter and John were commanded not to preach the gospel, their response was, "We must obey God rather than men" (5:29).

These examples each included at least two common elements. First, a direct, specific conflict arose between God's law and man's law. Pharaoh commanded the

Hebrew midwives to kill male Hebrew babies. Nebuchadnezzar commanded his subjects to bow before the golden image. King Darius ruled that no one could pray. And in the New Testament the high priest and the Sanhedrin forbade the apostles from proclaiming the gospel.

Second, in choosing to obey God's higher law, believers paid the normal consequence for disobedience. Although several of them escaped the consequence through supernatural intervention, we know from biblical and secular history of many others who paid for their disobedience with their lives.

Some critics argue that Romans 13:1 clearly prohibits civil disobedience: "Everyone must submit himself to the governing authorities, for there is no authority except that which God has established." Yet even this passage seems to provide a possible argument for disobeying government that has exceeded its authority. The verses following these speak of the government's role and function. The ruler is to be a "servant of God" and government should reward good and punish evil. Government that fails to do so is outside of God's mandated authority and function. Government is not autonomous, it has delegated authority from God. It is to restrain evil and punish wrongdoers. When government does violate God's delegated role and refuses to reward good and punish evil, it has no proper authority.[4]

The apostle Paul called for believers to "be subject" to government, but he did not instruct them to "obey" every command of government. When government commands an unjust or unbiblical injunction, Christians have a higher authority. One can be "subject" to the authority of the state but still refuse to "obey" a specific law which is contrary to biblical standards.

The Pro-Life Example

Although civil disobedience has been debated in various arenas, the primary discussion of its use among Christians has been in the abortion debate. Millions of unborn babies are killed every year, and the political means to redress this evil have often been stymied. Pro-life Christians, therefore, have debated whether civil disobedience is an appropriate action.

Proponents argue that we cannot wait for the political process since unborn babies are currently dying. Therefore, we should "rescue those being led away to death" (Prov. 24:11). They further argue that Christians must follow the dictates of James 4:17: "Anyone, then, who knows the good he ought to do and doesn't do it, sins."

The range of activities proposed under civil disobedience varies depending on the philosophy of the pro-life groups and their leaders. Such action would include picketing abortion clinics and providing sidewalk counseling to women considering abortions. Others propose picketing the homes of abortionists. Some call for physical intervention in the form of blockading clinics and some even call for stronger uses of force.

Critics of the use of civil disobedience usually draw the line with trespassing and the use of physical intervention (blockading clinics). Four criticisms usually surface in their critique of the use of civil disobedience to protest abortion.

First, the law being broken has nothing to do with abortion. Those arrested are not being arrested because they are protesting abortion; they are being arrested for trespassing. Critics note that if certain anti-God protesters blocked the entrance to their church, they would use the same ordinance to have the protestors arrested.

Second, *Roe v. Wade* neither requires nor prohibits abortions, but makes them permissible with certain restrictions. Women who choose to have an abortion are free moral agents responsible before God for their actions, including the exercise of the rights of their innocent, unborn child. The Christian's role is to use moral arguments to save the life of the unborn child, but using physical intervention is not an option.

Third, Christians are not permitted to disobey a just law in order to minimize the effects of other unjust laws. When a clear contradiction exists between God and Caesar, Christians must obey God. But in other cases, Christians should render obedience to civil authority. If they do not, then a state of anarchy would quickly develop in which each person is doing what he feels is right in his own eyes.

Christians must resist our culture's tendency to rebel at the first provocation, especially in light of the numerous scriptural admonitions to obey those in authority. These verses place the burden of proof on those advocating civil disobedience. Those advocating civil disobedience should successfully argue their case for disobeying the law. If they do not or cannot, then we should obey civil authority.

Obedience to government should especially be true in light of our sin nature (Rom. 3:23). All of us have some rebellion in us because of our sin nature, and we want to break the law. A good check on our carnal nature (Rom. 7:14) is to ask if breaking a civil law is biblically required. If not, we should give obedience to the law the benefit of the doubt.

Fourth, opponents have objected to the use of physical force. Is it proper to use physical force? Proponents believe that physical force should be used to restrain the evil of abortion. But this position raises several questions: What are the limits to the use of physical force? If blocking clinics is justified, what about burning them down or blowing them up? Once any form of physical force is justified, how do we define the limits of its use? If physical force can be justified in fighting abortion, what about using physical force in restraining other evils like idolatry or adultery? Should Christians block the entrances to New Age bookstores or pornography shops? Critics are concerned that the use of physical force would lead to unintended consequences and could be used to justify violent actions by Christians protesting all sorts of evil. Christians are not to fight with "the weapons of the world" (2 Cor. 10:4), but instead are to fight social evil with moral persuasion.

Biblical Principles for Civil Disobedience

How should Christians engage in civil disobedience? Here are five principles that should guide an individual's decision about civil disobedience. First, the law or injunction being resisted should clearly be unjust and unbiblical. Christians are not allowed to resist laws merely because they disagree with them. Given our sin nature and our natural tendency toward anarchy, it seems appropriate for Christians to make a strong case for civil disobedience before they act. The burden of proof should be on the person advocating civil disobedience. In a sense, we should be talked into disobedience. If the case is not compelling for civil disobedience, then obedience is required by default.

Second, the means of redress should be exhausted. One of the criteria for a just war is that the recourse to war must be the last resort. Civil disobedience should follow the same rigorous criterion. When all recourse to civil obedience has been exhausted, then and only then can discussion of revolution begin. Even then minimum resistance should be used if it can achieve a just result. If peaceful means can be used, then force should be avoided. Only when all legal channels for change have been closed or exhausted should civil disobedience be seriously considered. The only exception may be when the injustice is so grave and immediate that time for lengthy appeals is impossible.

Third, Christians must be willing to accept the penalty for breaking the law. The various biblical examples mentioned provide a model for Christian behavior in the midst of civil disobedience. Christians should submit to authority even when disobeying government. Such an attitude distinguishes civil disobedience from anarchy. By accepting the punishment, believers can often provide a powerful testimony to nonbelievers and awaken their concern for the injustice.

Fourth, civil disobedience should be carried out in love and with humility. Disobeying government should not be done with an angry or rebellious spirit. Martin Luther King, Jr., taught that "whom you would change you must first love."[5] Bringing about social change requires love, patience, and humility, not anger and arrogance.

A fifth and more controversial principle is that civil disobedience should be considered only when there is some possibility for success. Another criteria for a just war is that there be some reasonable hope of success. In the case of civil disobedience success is not an ultimate criterion, but it should be a concern if true social change is to take place. An individual certainly is free to disobey a law for personal reasons, but any attempt to change a law or social situation should enlist the aid and support of others. Also Christians should prayerfully evaluate whether the social disruption and potential promotion of lawlessness that may ensue is worth the action of civil disobedience. In most cases Christians will be more effective by working within the social and political arenas to affect true social change.

BIBLICAL PERSPECTIVE ON WAR

When it comes to the subject of war and military intervention, Christians have historically adopted one of three positions:

1. *Activism*—it is always right to participate in war.

2. *Pacifism*—it is never right to participate in war.

3. *Selectivism*—it is right to participate in some wars.

The primary positions today are pacifism and the concept of a just war (selectivism).

Pacifism is based upon at least two assumptions. First is the assumption that the conduct of wars in the Old Testament has no bearing on how Christians are to live in the New Testament era. Second is the assumption that the teachings of Jesus on the Sermon on the Mount (Matthew 5) apply not only to individual behavior but social and governmental behavior. Jesus did not advocate a political revolution but instead a spiritual revolution. Christians are not to resist an evil person (Matt. 5:39) but instead are to love your enemies (Matt. 5:44).

The Just War Theory

The just war theory, is a 1,600-year-old Christian doctrine that attempts to answer two questions: When is it permissible to wage war? and What are the limitations on the ways we wage war? This theory was initially articulated by Augustine (354–430), who developed it as a logical extension of Romans 13:1–7:

> Everyone must submit himself to the governing authorities, for there is
> no authority except that which God has established. The authorities
> that exist have been established by God. Consequently, he who rebels
> against the authority is rebelling against what God has instituted, and
> those who do so will bring judgment on themselves. For rulers hold no
> terror for those who do right, but for those who do wrong. Do you
> want to be free from fear of the one in authority? Then do what is right
> and he will commend you. For he is God's servant to do you good. But
> if you do wrong, be afraid, for he does not bear the sword for nothing.
> He is God's servant, an agent of wrath to bring punishment on the
> wrongdoer. Therefore, it is necessary to submit to the authorities, not
> only because of possible punishment but also because of conscience.
> This is also why you pay taxes, for the authorities are God's servants,
> who give their full time to governing. Give everyone what you owe
> him: If you owe taxes, pay taxes; if revenue, then revenue; if respect,
> then respect; if honor, then honor.

Augustine argued that not all wars are morally justified. He said, "It makes a great difference by which causes and under which authorities men undertake the wars that must be waged."[6] This seven-point theory provides a framework for evaluating military action.

A just war will include the following conditions: just cause, just intention, last resort, formal declaration, limited objectives, proportionate means, and noncombatant immunity. The first five principles apply as a nation is "on the way to war" (*jus ad bellum*), while the final two apply to military forces "in the midst of war" (*jus in bello*). Consider these seven points:

1. *Just cause*—All aggression is condemned in just war theory. Participation must be prompted by a just cause or defensive cause. No war of unprovoked aggression can ever be justified.

2. *Just intention*—War must be to secure a just peace for all parties involved. Revenge or conquest is not a legitimate motive.

3. *Last resort*—War must be engaged as a last resort only after diplomacy and economic pressure have been exhausted.

4. *Formal declaration*—War must be initiated with a formal declaration by properly constituted authorities.

5. *Limited objectives*—War must be characterized by limited objectives such as peace. Complete destruction is an improper objective. War must be waged in such a way that once peace is attainable, hostilities cease.

6. *Proportionate means*—Combatants may not be subjected to greater harm than is necessary to secure victory. The types of weapons and amount of force used should be limited to what is needed to repel aggression and secure a just peace.

7. *Noncombatant immunity*—Military forces must respect individuals and groups not participating in the conflict. Only governmental forces or agents are legitimate targets.

Objections to Just War Theory

Two types of objections often surface against the idea of just war theory. First, there is the moral objection. Pacifists argue that it is never right to go to war and often cite biblical passages to bolster their argument. For example, Jesus said that believers should turn the other cheek (Matt. 5:39). He also warned that those who take up the sword shall perish by the sword (Matt. 26:52).

However, the context of the statements is key. In the first instance, Jesus spoke to individual believers in his Sermon on the Mount, admonishing believers not to engage in personal retaliation. In the second instance, He told Peter to put down his sword because the gospel should not be advanced by the sword. But at the same time, Jesus actually encouraged his disciples to buy a sword in order to protect themselves (Luke 22:36).

Two political objections have been cited in recent years against the application of just war theory to our war on terrorism. Critics say that the idea of a just war applies to only to nations and not to terrorists. Even so, that would not invalidate American military actions in Afghanistan or Iraq. But the criticism is incorrect. Christian thought about a just war predates the concept of modern nation-states. So the application of these principles can apply to governments or terrorist organizations. Moreover, the first use of American military force by the newly formed United States was against Barbary Pirates, who were essentially the terrorists of the 18th century.

Critics also argue that since terrorism is an international threat, the concept of just war would require an international declaration of war. This argument is not true. The United States or any other country does not need to get international approval to defend itself. Even so, both President George H. W. Bush and President George W. Bush brought the issue of Iraq to the United Nations for a vote.

BIBLICAL PRINCIPLES FOR SOCIAL ACTION

How then should Christians be involved in the social and political arena? We should be distinctively Christian in our approach, and we should learn from the mistakes of other Christians in the past so that we might be effective without falling into compromise or sin.

First, we must remember that they have a dual citizenship. On the one hand, our citizenship is in heaven and not on earth (Phil. 3:17–21). We must remind ourselves that God is sovereign over human affairs even when circumstances look dark and discouraging. On the other hand the Bible also teaches that Christians are citizens of this earth (Matt. 22:15–22). We are to obey government (Rom. 13:1–7) and work within the social and political circumstances to affect change. We must pray for those in authority (1 Tim. 2:1–4) and to obey those in authority.

Jesus compared the kingdom of heaven to leaven hidden in three pecks of meal (Matt. 13:33). The meal represents the world and the leaven represents the Christian presence in it. We must exercise our influence within the mass of society, seeking to bring about change that way. Though the Christian presence may seem as insignificant as leaven in meal, nevertheless, we are to bring about the same profound change within society.

Second, Christians must remember that God is sovereign. As the Sovereign over the nations, He bestows power on whom He wishes (Dan. 4:17) and He can turn the heart of a king whenever He wishes (Prov. 21:1). Christians have often been guilty of believing that they alone can make a difference in the political process. Christian leaders frequently claim the future of America depends on the election of a particular candidate, the passage of a particular bill, or the confirmation of a particular Supreme Court justice. While it is important for Christians to be involved in social and political affairs, we must not forget that God is ultimately in control.

Third, Christians must use their specific gifts within the social and political arenas. Christians have different gifts and ministries (1 Cor. 12:4–6). Some may be called to a higher level of political participation than others, such as a candidate for school board or for Congress). All have a responsibility to be involved in society, but some are called to a higher level of social service, such as a social worker or crisis pregnancy center worker. We must recognize the diversity of gifts and encourage fellow believers to use our individual gifts for the greatest impact.

Fourth, Christians should channel their social and political activity through the church. We need to be accountable to each other, especially as we seek to make an impact on society. Wise leadership can prevent zealous evangelical Christians from repeating mistakes made in previous decades by other Christians.

The local church should also provide a context for compassionate social service. In the New Testament, the local church became a training ground for social action (Acts 2:45; 4:34). Meeting the needs of the poor, the infirm, the elderly, and widows is a responsibility of the church. Ministries to these groups can provide a foundation and a catalyst for further outreach and ministry to the community at large.

Christians must be the salt of the earth and the light of the world (Matt. 5:13–16). In our needy society, we have abundant opportunities to preach the gospel of Jesus Christ and meet significant social needs. By combining these two areas of preaching and ministry, we can make a strategic difference in society.

ENDNOTES

Chapter 1

[1] "A Biblical Worldview Has a Radical Effect on a Person's Life," *The Barna Update* (Ventura, CA), 1 December 2003, www.barna.org.

[2] "Only Half of Protestant Pastors Have a Biblical Worldview," *The Barna Update* (Ventura, CA), 12 January 2004, www.barna.org.

[3] "The Year's Most Intriguing Findings, From Barna Research Studies," *The Barna Update* (Ventura, CA), 12 December 2000, www.barna.org.

[4] "Americans Are Most Likely to Base Truth on Feelings," *The Barna Update* (Ventura, CA), 12 February 2002, www.barna.org

[5] James Patterson and Peter Kim, *The Day America Told the Truth* (New York: Prentice Hall Press, 1991), 6.

[6] George Barna and Mark Hatch, *Boiling Point* (Ventura, CA: Gospel Light, 2001).

[7] "Research Predicts Mounting Challenges to Christian Church," *The Barna Update* (Ventura, CA), 16 April 2001, www.barna.org.

[8] "Practical Outcomes Replace Biblical Principles as the Moral Standards," *The Barna Update* (Ventura, CA), 10 September 2001, www.barna.org.

[9] Ibid.

[10] "Morality Continues to Decay," *The Barna Update* (Ventura, CA), 3 November 2003, www.barna.org.

[11] "The Year's Most Intriguing Findings, From Barna Research Studies," www.barna.org.

[12] "Research Predicts Mounting Challenges to Christian Church," www.barna.org.

[13] Quoted in John Leo, "A No-fault Holocaust," *U.S. News and World Report*, 21 July 1997, 14.

[14] Quoted in ibid.

[15] "Ethics, Enron, and American Higher Education: An NAS/Zogby Poll of College Seniors," *National Association of Scholars*, July 2002, www.nas.org.

[16] Dan Seligman, "Oxymoron 101," *Forbes*, 28 Oct. 2002, www.forbes.com.

Chapter 2

[1] James W. Sire, *The Universe Next Door* (Downers Grove, IL: InterVarsity, 2004), 9.
[2] Immanuel Kant, *Groundwork of the Metaphysics of Morals,* trans. Mary Gregor (Cambridge: Cambridge University Press, 1997).

Chapter 3

[1] William Graham Sumner, *Folkways* (Boston: Ginn and Company, 1906), 76.
[2] Melville J. Herskovits, *Cultural Relativism* (New York: Random House, 1973), 15.
[3] Ibid., 56.
[4] Anthony Flew, *Evolutionary Ethics* (New York: St. Martin's Press, 1968), 55.
[5] E. O. Wilson, *Sociobiology: The New Synthesis* (Cambridge, MA: Harvard University Press, 1975).
[6] Robert Wallace, *The Genesis Factor* (New York: Morrow and Co., 1979).
[7] Jeremy Bentham, *An Introduction to the Principles of Morals and Legislation*, printed in 1781 and published in 1789 (Batoche Books: Kitchener, ON Canada, 2000), 14.
[8] Ibid.
[9] John Stuart Mill, "Last Stage of Education and First of Self-Education," *Autobiography*, 1873 (New York: P.F. Collier & Sons, 1909–14).
[10] Joseph Fletcher, *Situation Ethics: The New Morality* (Philadelphia: Westminster, 1966).
[11] Ibid., 70.
[12] Ibid., 120.
[13] Ibid., 121.
[14] Ibid., 136.

Chapter 5

[1] "The Ethics of American Youth," *Josephson Institute of Ethics*, 16 October 2000, www.josephsoninstitute.org.
[2] "Americans Are Most Likely to Base Truth on Feelings," *The Barna Update* (Ventura, CA), 12 February 2002, www.barna.org.
[3] Stephen Carter, *Integrity* (New York: HarperCollins, 1996), 7.
[4] James Patterson and Peter Kim, *The Day America Told the Truth* (New York: Prentice Hall Press, 1991).
[5] Ibid., 6.
[6] Ibid., 7.
[7] Ibid., 8.
[8] Ibid., 155.
[9] Ibid,, 25–26.
[10] Marc Marsan, *Who Are You When Nobody's Looking?* (Boston: Element, 1999).
[11] Stephen Carter, *Civility: Manners, Morals, and the Etiquette of Democracy* (New York: HarperCollins, 1998), 11.

[12] Ibid., 28–29.

[13] Ibid., 29.

Chapter 6

[1] S. K. Henshaw, "Unintended pregnancy in the United States," *Family Planning Perspectives* 30 (1998), 24–29.

[2] Aristotle, *Politics*, 1335B.

[3] Josephus, *Apion*, 2.202.

[4] *Didache*, 2.2.

[5] *Epistle of Barnabas*, 19.5.

[6] Athenagoras, *A Plea for Christians*, 35.6.

[7] Clement, *Paedagogus*, 2:10.96.1.

[8] Tertullian, *Apology*, 9.4.

[9] Augustine, *On Marriage*, 1.17.15.

[10] Daniel H. Johnson Jr., M.D., President, American Medical Association, Letter to the Editor, *New York Times*, 26 May 1997, A22.

[11] The Greek word *brephos* used in Luke 1:41, 45 to identify the unborn John the Baptist is the same word used for the already-born Jesus (Luke 2:12, 16) and for babies who received his blessing (Luke 18:15–17). Also the Hebrew word *yeled*, used in the Old Testament to refer to the unborn (Ex. 21:22–25), is the same word used to describe young children.

[12] H. P. Valman and J. F. Pearson, "What the Fetus Feels," *British Medical Journal* (26 January 1980): 233–34.

[13] *Roe v. Wade* (1973) 410 U.S. 113, 93 S.Ct. 705, 35 L.Ed.2d 147.

[14] General Assembly resolution 1386 (14), 20 November 1959.

[15] Paul Ramsey, *The Patient as Person* (New Haven: Yale University Press, 1970); Paul Ramsey, "Reference Points in Deciding About Abortion" in *The Morality of Abortion*, ed. by John T. Noonan, Jr. (Cambridge: Harvard University Press, 1970).

[16] Francis Crick, "Logic of Biology," *Nature*, 2 November 1968, 429–30.

[17] Ashley Montagu, *Sex, Man and Society* (New York: Putnam, 1967).

[18] Joseph Fletcher, *Humanhood: Essays in Biomedical Ethics* (Buffalo, NY: Prometheus, 1979), 135.

[19] Joseph Fletcher, "Indicators of Humanhood: A Tentative Profile of Man," *Hastings Center Report* 2 (November 1972), 1.

[20] James A. Thomson et al., "Embryonic Stem Cell Lines Derived from Human Blastocysts," *Science*, 6 November 1998, 1145–47.

[21] Michael Shamblott et. al., "Derivation of Pluripotent Stem Cells from Cultured Human Primordial Germ Cells," *Proceedings of the National Academy of Sciences of the United States of America*, 95 (November 1998), 13726–31.

[22] Charles Krauthammer, "The great stem cell hoax," *Weekly Standard*, 20–27 August 2001, 12.

[23] Yuehua Jing et al., "Pluripotency of Mesenchymal Stem Cells Derived from Adult Marrow," *Nature* 418 (4 July 2002), 41–49.

[24] H. M. Blau, T. R. Brazelton, and J. M. Weiman, "The Evolving Concept of a Stem Cell: Entity or Function," *Cell* 105 (29 June 2001), 829–41.

[25] David Hamilton and Antonio Regaldo, "Biotech Industry—Unfettered, but Possibly Unfulfilled," *Wall Street Journal*, 13 August 2001, B1.

[26] Michael J. New, "Analyzing the Effects of State Legislation on the Incidence of Abortion During the 1990s," *A Report of the Heritage Center for Data Analysis*, 21 January 2004, 2.

[27] Focus on the Family Crisis Pregnancy Ministry Ultrasound Research: The Impact of Ultrasound Usage on Abortion-Minded Pregnancy Center Clients, average statistical finding, 26 November 2003.

Chapter 7

[1] Plato, *Republic* 3. 405.

[2] Katrine Ames, "Last Rights," *Newsweek*, 26 August 1991, 41.

[3] A further discussion of the care and counseling of dying patients can be found in the author's book *Life, Death, and Beyond* (Grand Rapids: Zondervan Publishing House, 1980).

[4] David Cundiff quoted in Debbie Decker, "Euthanasia is NOT the Answer—A Hospice Physician's View," *Currents in Science, Technology, and Society* 1(1991): 20.

[5] Rita Marker, "What's All the Fuss about Tube Feeding?" *New Covenant*, January 1991, 19.

[6] More information can be found at: www.bioethics.gov/reports/past_commissions.

[7] Susan Moran, "Medical Choices: A Will Doesn't Always Mean a Way," *Insight*, 15 February 1993, 12.

[8] "Question: Who Will Play God," *Time*, 9 April 1984, 68.

[9] R. Finigsen, "The Report of the Dutch Committee on Euthanasia," *Issues in Law and Medicine*, July 1991, 339–44.

[10] Herbert Hendlin, Chris Rutenfrans, and Zbigniew Zylicz, "Physician-Assisted Suicide and Euthanasia in the Netherlands: Lessons from the Dutch," *Journal of the American Medical Association* 277 (4 June 1997): 1720–22.

[11] Interview with Surgeon General C. Everett Koop, "Focus on the Family" radio broadcast, 1986.

[12] "The Hemlock Manuever," *Physician* (March/April 1991), 2.

[13] Interview with Koop, "Focus on the Family" radio broadcast.

[14] Quoted in *Euthanasia: False Light*, produced by IAETF, P.O. Box 760, Steubenville, OH 43952.

[15] Joni Eareckson, *Joni* (Grand Rapids: Zondervan, 1976).

[16] Joni Eareckson, *A Step Further* (Grand Rapids: Zondervan, 1978).

Chapter 8

1 "Three Families, Three Decisions," *USA Today*, 18 August 1997, D1.

2 Eugenics literally means "good birth" or "well born."

3 Quoted in Nicholas Wade, "Gene Splicing: Congress Starts Framing Law for Research," *Science*, 1 April 1977, 39.

4 Michael Crichton, *The Andromeda Strain* (New York: Dell, 1969).

5 "The DNA Furor: Tinkering with Life," *Time*, 18 April 1977, 45.

6 Kenneth Woodward, "Thou Shalt Not Patent!" *Newsweek*, 29 May 1995, 68.

7 Ibid.

8 Testimony by Ethan Singer before the Subcommittee on Health and the Environment, House Committee on Interstate and Foreign Commerce, *Hearings*, 15 March 1977, 79.

9 Quoted in Joseph Fletcher, *The Ethics of Genetic Control* (Garden City, NY: Anchor, 1974), 8.

10 Quoted in George Wald, "The Case against Genetic Engineering," *The Sciences*, May 1976, 10.

11 Nancy McCann, "The DNA Maelstrom: Science and Industry Rewrite the Fifth Day of Creation," *Sojourners*, May 1977, 23–26.

12 Skeptics sometimes argue that fighting disease is the same as fighting against God's will. Albert Camus poses this dilemma for Dr. Reux in *The Plague*. Christians should follow the cultural mandate (Gen. 1:28) and use genetic technology to treat and cure genetic disease.

13 Paul Ramsey, *Fabricated Man* (New Haven: Yale University Press, 1970).

14 Sharon Begley, "Little Lamb, Who Made Thee?" *Newsweek*, 10 March 1997, 55.

15 Ibid.

16 Quoted in *Los Angeles Times*, 17 May 1971, 1.

17 N. N. Glazer, *Hammer on the Rock: A Short Midrash Reader* (New York: Schocken, 1962), 15.

Chapter 9

1 Diane Swanbrow, "Immaculate Conceptions," *New West*, 25 August 1980, 28.

2 Lori Andrews, "Embryo Technology," *Parents*, May 1991, 63–64.

3 Lewis Lord, "Desperately Seeking Baby," *U.S. News and World Report*, 5 October 1987, 58.

4 M. Curie-Cohen, M. Luttrell, and S. Shapiro, "Current Practice of Artificial Insemination by Donor in the United States," *New England Journal of Medicine* 300 (1979): 585–90.

5 Many states have enacted legislation to protect the legal rights of the child. Other state courts are affected by case law concerning AID.

6 "Artificial Insemination by Donor: Survey Reveals Surprising Facts," *Journal of the American Medical Association*, 23 March 1979, 1219.

[7] Karl Ostrom, "Psychological Considerations in Evaluating AID," *Soundings* 54 (Fall 1971): 325–30.

[8] Quoted in Carin Rubenstein "Little Known Hazards of AID: Disease, Inbreeding, Guilt," *Psychology Today*, May 1980, 23.

[9] David Rorvick with Landrum Shettles, *Your Baby's Sex: Now You Can Choose* (New York: Bantam, 1970).

[10] Lisa Busch, "Designer Families, Ethical Knots," *U.S. News and World Report*, 31 May 1993, 73.

[11] Charles Westoff and Ronald Rindfuss, "Sex Preselection in the United States: Some Implications," *Science*, 10 May 1974, 633–36.

[12] Sharon Begley, "Against the Odds: How the Methods Compare," *Newsweek*, 4 September 1995, 41.

[13] Philip Elmer-DeWitt, "Making Babies," *Time*, 30 September 1991, 58.

[14] Paula Mergenbagen DeWitt, "In Pursuit of Pregnancy," *American Demographics*, May 1993, 52.

[15] Sharon Begley, "The Baby Myth," *Newsweek*, 4 September 1995, 40.

[16] "Test to Boost IVF Success Rates," *BBC News*, 17 May 2004, http://news.bbc.co.uk.

[17] Quoted in "Lab Growth of Human Embryo Raises Doubt of Normality," *Washington Post*, 21 March 1971.

[18] Justin M. Norton, "Court Rules Egg Donor Has No Parental Rights," *Law.Com*, 12 May 2004, http://www.law.com.

[19] Quoted in Otto Friedrich, "The New Origins of Life," *Time*, 10 September 1984, 46.

[20] Stephen Budiansky, "The New Rules of Reproduction," *U.S. News and World Report*, 18 April 1988, 67.

[21] Traci Watson, "Sister, Can You Spare an Egg?" *U.S. News and World Report*, 23 June 1997, 44.

[22] Andrews, "Embryo Technology," 69.

[23] Thomas Giles, "Test-Tube Wars," *Christianity Today*, 9 January 1995, 38.

Chapter 10

[1] "American Teens Speak: Sex, Myth, TV and Birth Control," The Planned Parenthood Poll, Lou Harris and Associates, September/October 1986, 13.

[2] David Van Biema, "What You Don't Know About Teen Sex," *People*, 13 April 1987, 110–21.

[3] William Bennett, "Sex and the Education of Our Children," in *School Based Clinics*, Barrett Mosbacker, (Westchester, IL: Crossway, 1987), 159.

[4] Ibid.

[5] Wendy Cole, "How Should We Teach Our Children about Sex?" *Time*, 24 May 1993, 61.

[6] Ibid., 63.

[7] Barbara Dafoe Whitehead, "The Failure of Sex Education," *Atlantic Monthly*, October 1994, 55–80.

[8] Ibid.

[9] Ibid., 57.

[10] Ibid., 69.

[11] Ibid.

[12] Lawrence Criner, "Safer Sex Ads Downplay Risks," *Insight*, 9 May 1994, 22.

[13] Scientific Evidence on Condom Effectiveness for Sexually Transmitted Diseases (STD) Prevention, June 12–13, 2000, Hyatt Dulles Airport, Herndon, VA, www.niaid.nih.gov/dmid/stds/condomreport.pdf.

[14] Criner, "Safer Sex Ads Downplay Risks," 22.

[15] Ibid.

[16] Ibid.

[17] Nicholas Fiumara, "Effectiveness of Condoms in Preventing V.D.," *New England Journal of Medicine*, 21 October, 1971, 972.

[18] Criner, "Safer Sex Ads Downplay Risks," 22.

[19] Asta Kenney, "School-Based Clinics: A National Conference," *Family Planning Perspectives* 18 (January/February 1986): 6.

[20] FDA, *Compliance Policy Guidelines*, chapter 24, guide 7124.21 (10 April 1987), 1.

[21] Criner, "Safer Sex Ads Downplay Risks," 24.

[22] Victor Cline, "Correlating Adolescent and Adult Exposure to Sexually Explicit Material and Sexual Behavior," University of Utah Department of Psychology, National Conference on HIV.

[23] Joseph Olsen and Stan Weed, "Effects of Family Planning Programs on Adolescent Birth and Pregnancy Rates," *Family Perspective*, July 1986.

[24] Douglas Kirby, Speech at the Sixteenth Annual Meeting of the National Family Planning and Reproductive Health Association, 2 March 1988.

[25] Louis Harris poll, "Planned Parenthood Poll," (New York: Lou Harris, 1986).

[26] Report of the Select Committee on Children, Youth, and Families, 99th Congress, *Teen Pregnancy: What Is Being Done? A State By State Look* (Washington, DC: U.S. Government Printing Office, 1986), 375–78.

[27] Deborah Anne Dawson, "The Effects of Sex Education on Adolescent Behavior," *Family Planning Perspectives* 18 (July/August 1986): 166.

[28] Quoted in Josh McDowell, *The Myths of Sex Education* (San Bernardino, CA: Here's Life, 1990), 68.

[29] Charles Donovan, *An Estimate of Federal Spending on Contraceptive "Safe Sex" Services for Adolescents* (Washington, DC: Family Research Council, 1994).

[30] Douglas Kirby, "Sexuality Education: A More Realistic View of Its Effects," *Journal of School Health* (December 1985): 422.

[31] Tom Smith, *Attitudes toward Sexual Permissiveness: Trends, Correlates, and Behavioral Connections* (Chicago: University of Chicago, 1992), 66.

[32] Tom McNichol, "Sex Can Wait," *USA Weekend*, 25–27 March 1994, 4–6.

[33] Robert E. Rector et. al., "What Do Parents Want Taught in Sex Education Programs," *Heritage Backgrounder*, The Heritage Foundation, 28 Jan. 2004.

[34] Alan Guttmacher Institute, *Sex and America's Teenagers* (New York: The Alan Guttmacher Institute, 1994), 19.

[35] Cheryl Wetzstein, "Reported Number of Teen Virgins Rises," *Washington Times*, 22 July 2002, A-3.

[36] M. Howard and J. S. McCabe, "Helping Teenagers Postpone Sexual Involvement," *Family Planning Perspectives* 22 (January/February, 1990): 21–26.

[37] Bennett, "Sex and the Education of Our Children," 164.

[38] Dinah Richard, *Has Sex Education Failed Our Teenagers?* (Pasadena, CA: Focus on the Family, 1990), 59–60.

[39] Larry Withan, "As Washington Pushes Safe Sex, Others Preach Abstinence," *Washington Times*, 3 October 1993, A4.

[40] *Abstinence Programs Show Promise in Reducing Sexual Activity and Pregnancy among Teens* (Washington, DC: Family Research Council, 1994).

[41] Project Respect, *Final Report: Office of Adolescent Pregnancy Programs*, Performance Summary Report, #000816, Title XX, 1985–1990.

[42] John S. Santelli, "Can Changes in Sexual Behaviors Among High School Students Explain the Decline in Teen Pregnancy Rates in the 1990s?" *Journal of Adolescent Health* 35 (2004) 80–90.

[43] Cole, "How Should We Teach Our Children about Sex?", 65.

[44] Andres Tapia, "Abstinence: The Radical Choice for Sex Ed," *Christianity Today*, 8 February 1993, 28.

[45] Robert E. Rector et. al., "Teens Who Make Virginity Pledges Have Substantially Improved Life Outcomes," *Center for Data Analysis Report*, The Heritage Foundation, 21 Sept. 2004.

[46] Joe McIlhaney, *Safe Sex* (Grand Rapids: Baker, 1991), 23.

[47] *The Common Appeal*, 7 Nov. 1988, A-12.

[48] Robert E. Rector et. al., "Sexually Active Teenagers Are More Likely to be Depressed and to Attempt Suicide," *Center for Data Analysis Report*, Washington, DC: The Heritage Foundation, 3 June 2003.

[49] Roper Starch Organization, "Teens Talk about Sex: Adolescent Sexuality in the 90s," April 1994, 25.

[50] Larry Bumpass, James Sweet, and Andrew Cherlin, "The Role of Cohabitation in Declining Rates of Marriages," *Journal of Marriage and Family* 53 (1991): 913–27.

[51] Edward Laumann, John Gagnon, Robert Michael, and Stuart Michaels, *The Organization of Sexuality: Sexual Practices in the United States* (Chicago: University of Chicago Press, 1994), 363–65.

[52] Robert Levin and Amy Levin, "Sexual Pleasure: The Surprising Preferences of 100,000 Women," *Redbook*, September 1975, 51–58.

Chapter 11

[1] Laura Sullivan, "Administration Wages War on Pornography," *Baltimore Sun*, 6 April 2004.

[2] Michael McManus, ed., *Final Report of the Attorney General's Commission on Pornography* (Nashville: Rutledge Hill, 1986), 8.

[3] *Miller v. California*, 413 US 15, 47 (1973).

[4] Cheryl Wetzstein, "Porn on the Web Exploding," *Washington Times*, 9 October 2003.

[5] Phillip Elmer-Dewitt, "On a Screen Near You," *Time*, 3 July 1995, 38.

[6] Quoted in Jim Dyar, "Cyberporn Held Responsible for Increase in Sex Addiction," *Washington Times*, 26 January 2000.

[7] Survey cited in Dirk Johnson and Hilary Shenfeld, "Preachers and Porn," *Newsweek*, 12 April 2004, 52.

[8] Edward Donnerstein, "Pornography and Violence against Women," *Annals of the New York Academy of Science* 347 (1980): 277–88.

[9] Edward Donnerstein, "Pornography: Its Effects on Violence against Women," in *Pornography and Sexual Aggression*, ed. Neil Malamuth and Edward Donnerstein (New York: Academic, 1984).

[10] Neil Malamuth, "Rape Fantasies as a Function of Repeated Exposure to Sexual Violence," *Archives of Sexual Behavior* 10 (1981): 33–47.

[11] Daniel Linz, Edward Donnerstein, and Steven Penrod, "The Effects of Multiple Exposures to Filmed Violence against Women," *Journal of Communication* 34 (1984): 130–47.

[12] James Check, "The Effects of Violent and Nonviolent Pornography," Department of Justice, Ottawa, Canada, June 1984.

[13] Dolf Zillman and Jennings Bryant, "Pornography, Sexual Callousness, and the Trivialization of Rape," *Journal of Communication* 32 (1982): 10–21.

[14] Dolf Zillman, Jennings Bryant, and R.H. Carveth, "The Effect of Erotica Featuring Sadomasochism and Beastiality of Motivated Inter-Male Aggression," *Personality and Social Psychology Bulletin* 7 (1981): 153–59.

[15] Dolf Zillman, "Effects of Prolonged Consumption of Pornography," a paper prepared for the Surgeon General's Workshop on Pornography and Public Health, Arlington, VA, 22–24 June 1986.

[16] M. Allen and D. D'Allessio, "A Meta-Analysis Summarizing the Effects of Pornography II: Aggression After Exposure," *Human Communication Research* 22 (1995), 258–283.

[17] Zillman and Bryant, "Pornography, Sexual Callousness and the Trivialization of Rape," 15.

[18] Larry Baron and Murray Strauss, "Legitimate Violence and Rape: A Test of the Cultural Spillover Theory," *Social Problems* 34 (December 1985).

[19] Joseph Scott and Loretta Schwalm, "Rape Rates and the Circulation Rates of Adult Magazines," *Journal of Sex Research* 24 (1988): 240–50.

[20] David Alexander Scott, "How Pornography Changes Attitudes," in *Pornography: A Human Tragedy* (Wheaton, Ill.: Tyndale House Publishers, 1986).

[21] Victor Cline, *Where Do You Draw the Line?* (Provo, UT: Brigham Young University Press, 1974).

[22] Victor B. Cline, *Pornography's Effects on Adults and Children* (New York: Morality in Media, 1990), 11.

[23] J. L. McGaugh, "Preserving the Presence of the Past," *American Psychologist*, February 1983, 161.

[24] Kimberley Young, Paper presented to 1997 convention of the American Psychological Association. A full treatment can be found in Kimberley Young, *Caught in the Net: How to Recognize the Signs of Internet Addiction—and a Winning Strategy for Recovery* (New York: John Wiley & Sons, Inc. 1998).

[25] Quoted in Kenneth Kantzer, "The Power of Porn," *Christianity Today*, 7 February 1989, 18.

[26] Gary R. Brooks, *The Centerfold Syndrome: How Men Can Overcome Objectification and Achieve Intimacy with Women* (San Francisco, CA: Jossey-Bass, 1996), 2.

[27] Berl Kutchinsky, "The Effect of Easy Availability of Pornography on the Incidence of Sex Crimes: The Danish Experience," *Journal of Social Issues* 29 (1973): 163–81.

[28] Dolf Zillman, "Pornography Research and Public Policy," in *Pornography: Research Advances and Policy Considerations*, ed. Dolf Zillman and Jennings Bryant (New York: Academic, 1989), 387–88.

[29] Deborah Baker, "Pornography Isn't Free Speech," *Dallas Morning News*, 17 March 1989.

[30] Testimony by John B. Rabun, deputy director of the National Center for Missing and Exploited children, before the Subcommittee on Juvenile Justice of the Senate Judiciary Committee, 12 September 1984.

[31] W. Marshall, "Pornography and Sex Offenders," in *Pornography: Research Advances and Policy Considerations*.

[32] *The Men Who Murdered*, FBI Law Enforcement Bulletin, August 1985.

[33] Cass R. Sunstein, "Pornography and the First Amendment," *Duke Law Journal*, September 1986, 595.

[34] Karen Thomas, "Inconsistency Plagues Net Filters," *USA Today*, 15 February 2001, 3D.

Chapter 12

[1] At recent United Nations Conferences, some participants proposed that five genders be recognized: male heterosexual, female heterosexual, male homosexual, female homosexual (lesbian), and bisexual.

[2] Two prominent pro-homosexual commentators are Sherwin Bailey, *Homosexuality and the Western Christian Tradition* (London: Longmans, Green, 1955; repr., Hamden, CT: Shoestring Press, 1975), and John Boswell, *Christianity, Social Tolerance, and Homosexuality* (Chicago: University of Chicago Press, 1980).

[3] Bestiality was common in the ancient Near East. Canaanites were guilty of both homosexuality and bestiality (Lev. 18:23–29).

[4] Ralph Blair, *An Evangelical Look at Homosexuality* (Chicago: Moody, 1963), 3.

[5] Letha Scanzoni and Virginia Ramey Mollenkott, *Is the Homosexual My Neighbor?* (San Francisco: Harper & Row, 1978), 60–61.

[6] Sherwood Cole, "Biology, Homosexuality, and Moral Culpability," *Bibliothecra Sacra* 154 (July–September 1997): 355.

[7] Simon LeVay, "A Difference in Hypothalamic Structure Between Heterosexual and Homosexual Men," *Science*, 30 August 1991, 1034–37.

[8] David Gelman, "Born or Bred?" *Newsweek*, 24 February 1992, 46.

[9] Michael Bailey and Richard Pillard, "A Genetic Study of Male Sexual Orientation," *Archives of General Psychiatry* 48 (1991): 1089–96.

[10] Joe Dallas, *Desires in Conflict* (Eugene, OR: Harvest House, 1991), 90.

[11] Quoted in Gelman, "Born or Bred?" 46.

[12] Paul Cameron, "Twins Born Gay," *Family Research Report*, January–February, 1992, 3.

[13] Quoted in Gelman, "Born or Bred?" 46.

[14] Dean Hamer et. al., "A linkage between DNA markers on the X chromosome and male sexual orientation," *Science*, 16 July 1993, 321–27.

[15] "Study Links Homosexuality to Genetics," *Dallas Morning News*, 16 July 1993, 1A.

[16] Cole, "Biology, Homosexuality, and Moral Culpability," 357.

[17] Dallas, *Desires in Conflict*, 96.

[18] Ibid.

[19] John Money, *Gay, Straight, and In-Between* (Baltimore: Johns Hopkins University Press, 1988), 117.

[20] Glenn Wood and John Dietrich, *The AIDS Epidemic: Balancing Compassion and Justice* (Portland, OR: Multnomah, 1990), 238.

[21] Ruben Fine, *Psychoanalytic Theory, Male and Female Homosexuality: Psychological Approaches* (New York: New York Center for Psychoanalytic Training, 1987).

[22] Robert L. Spitzer, "Can Some Gay Men and Lesbians Change Their Sexual Orientation?" *Archives of Sexual Behavior* 32, no. 5 (October 2003): 403–17.

[23] Laura Sessions Stepp, "Partway Gay? For Some Teen Girls, Sexual Preference is a Shifting Concept," *Washington Post*, 4 January 2004, D-1.

[24] Lisa Diamond, "Was it a Phase? Young Women's Relinquishment of Lesbian/Bisexual Identities over a 5-year period." *Journal of Personality and Social Psychology*, 84 (2003): 352–364.

[25] William Masters and Virginia Johnson, *Homosexuality in Perspective* (Boston: Little, Brown and Co., 1979), 402.

Chapter 13

[1] David Popenoe and Barbara Dafoe Whitehead, "Should We Live Together? What Young Adults Need to Know about Cohabitation before Marriage," The National Mar-

riage Project, the Next Generation Series, Rutgers, the State University of New Jersey, January 1999, 1–20.

2 P. G. Jackson, "On Living Together Unmarried," *Journal of Family Issues* 4 (1983): 39.

3 U. S. Bureau of the Census, Current Population Reports, Series P20-537; America's Families and Living Arrangements: March 2000 and earlier reports.

4 Larry L. Bumpass, James A. Sweet, and Andrew Cherlin, "The Role of Cohabitation in the Declining Rates of Marriage," *Journal of Marriage and Family* 53 (1991): 914.

5 Ibid., 926

6 George Barna, *The Future of the American Family* (Chicago: Moody Press, 1993), 131.

7 Jerald G. Bachman, Lloyd D. Johnston, and Patrick M. O'Malley, *Monitoring the Future: Questionnaire Responses from the Nation's High School Seniors, 2000* (Ann Arbor, MI: Institute for Social Research, University of Michigan, 2001), 173–174.

8 Linda Waite and Maggie Gallagher, *The Case for Marriage: Why Married People Are Happier, Healthier and Better Off Financially* (New York: Random House, 2000).

9 R. E. L. Watson, "Premarital Cohabitation vs. Traditional Courtship: The Effects of Subsequent Marital Adjustment," *Family Relations* 32 (1981): 139–147.

10 Popenoe and Whitehead, "Should We Live Together?", 1–20.

11 Alfred DeMaris and K. Vaninadha Rao, "Premarital Cohabitation and Subsequent Marital Stability in the United States: A Reassessment," *Journal of Marriage and Family* 54 (1992): 178–190.

12 Stephen Nock, "A Comparison of Marriages and Cohabiting Relationships," *Journal of Family Issues* 16 (1995): 53–76.

13 Michael D. Newcomb and P. M. Bentler, "Assessment of Personality and Demographic Aspects of Cohabitation and Marital Success," *Journal of Personality Assessment* 44 (1980): 11–24.

14 Jan E. Stets, "The Link Between Past and Present Intimate Relationships," *Journal of Family Issues* 14 (1993): 236–60.

15 Catherine L. Cohan and Stacey Kleinbaum, "Toward A Greater Understanding of the Cohabitation Effect: Premarital Cohabitation and Marital Communication," *Journal of Marriage and Family* 64 (2002): 180–92.

16 Lee Robins and Darrel Reiger, *Psychiatric Disorders in America* (New York: Free Press, 1990), 72.

17 Andrew Greeley, *Faithful Attraction* (New York: Tom Doherty, 1991), 206.

18 Jan E. Stets, "Cohabiting and Marital Aggression: The Role of Social Isolation," *Journal of Marriage and Family* 53 (1991): 669–80.

19 Todd K. Shackelford, "Cohabitation, Marriage and Murder," *Aggressive Behavior* 27 (2001), 284–91.

20 Elizabeth Thompson, T. L. Hanson, and S. S. McLanahan, "Family Structure and Child Well-Being: Economic Resources versus Parental Behaviors," *Social Forces* 71(1994): 221–42; Rachel Dunifon and Lori Kowaleski-Jones, "Who's in the House? Effects of Family Structure on Children's Home Environments and Cognitive Outcomes," *Child Development* 73 (July/August 2002): 1249–64.

Chapter 14

1 Samuel Janus and Cynthia Janus, *The Janus Report on Sexual Behavior* (New York: John Wiley and Sons, 1993), 169.

2 Joannie Schrof, "Adultery in America," *U.S. News and World Report*, 31 August 1998, 31.

3 Frank Pittman, *Private Lies: Infidelity and the Betrayal of Intimacy* (New York: Norton, 1989), 117.

4 Ibid., 13.

5 Annette Lawson, *Adultery: An Analysis of Love and Betrayal* (New York: Basic Books, 1988).

6 Lorraine Ali and Lisa Miller, "The Secret Lives of Wives," *Newsweek*, 12 July 2004, 48.

7 Carol Travis and Susan Sadd, *The Redbook Report on Female Sexuality* (New York: Delacorte Press, 1977).

8 "Infidelity Survey," *New Woman*, October–November 1986.

9 Philip Blumstein and Pepper Schwartz, *American Couples* (New York: William Morrow, 1983).

10 Maggie Scarf, *Intimate Partners* (New York: Ballantine, 1996).

11 Trish Hall, "Infidelity and Women: Shifting Patterns," *New York Times*, 1 June 1987, B8.

12 Kenneth Woodward, "Sex, Morality and the Protestant Minister," *Newsweek*, 28 July 1997, 62.

13 Survey done by Jeff Seat and reported in the *The Journal of Pastoral Care* (Winter 1993): 364.

14 "How Common Is Pastoral Indiscretion?" *Leadership*, vol. 17 (Winter 1988): 12ff.

15 In this poll Americans were asked: "What is your opinion about a married person having sexual relations with someone other than his or her spouse? Their answers: 79 percent answered "always wrong" and another 11 percent answered "almost always wrong." See "Attitudes on Adultery," *USA Today/CNN/*Gallup Poll, 1997.

16 Willard Harley, *His Needs, Her Needs: Building an Affair-Proof Marriage* (Grand Rapids, MI: Fleming H. Revell, 1994).

17 Pittman, Private Lies, 122.

18 Bonnie Eaker Weil, *Adultery: The Forgivable Sin* (Norwalk, CT: Hastings House, 1994), 9.

19 Pittman, *Private Lies*, 37.

20 Ibid., 53.

21 Statistic cited at www.doctorbonnie.com.

22 Quoted in Karen Peterson, "Spouses Browse Infidelity Online," *USA Today*, 6 July 1999, 1D.

23 Ibid.

24 Linda Wolfe, *Playing Around: Women and Extramarital Sex* (New York: William Morrow, 1975).

[25] "Reducing the risks of a wandering eye," *USA Today*, 6 July 1999, 10D.

[26] Lawson, *Adultery*.

[27] Jan Halper, Quiet Desperation: The Truth About Successful Men (New York: Warner-Books, 1988).

[28] Pittman, *Private Lies*, 247.

[29] William Allman, "The Mating Game," *U.S. News and World Report*, 19 July 1993, 57–63.

Chapter 15

[1] Diane Medved, *The Case Against Divorce* (New York: Donald I. Fine, 1989), 1–2.

[2] "Advance Report of Final Divorce Statistics, 1983," *NCHS [National Center for Health Statistics] Monthly Vital Statistics Report*, 26 December, 1985, Table 1.

[3] Dennis Ahlburg and Carol DeVita, "New Realities of the American Family," *Population Bulletin* 47 (August 1992): 15.

[4] Landon Jones, *Great Expectations: America and the Baby Boom Generation* (New York: Ballantine, 1980), 215.

[5] David Popenoe, *Disturbing the Nest: Family Change and Decline in Modern Societies* (New York: de Gruyter, 1988), 223.

[6] Norval Glenn and Michael Supancic, "The Social and Demographic Correlates of Divorce and Separation in the United States," *Journal of Marriage and Family* 46 (1984): 566.

[7] William Mattox, "Split Personality," *Policy Review* 73 (Summer 1995): 51.

[8] The pollster Louis Harris first used this phrase in the 1980s to illustrate his concern over the misuse of the statistic that one out of every two marriages end in divorce.

[9] Cheryl Russell, *100 Predictions for the Baby Boom* (New York: Plenum, 1987), 107.

[10] Judith Wallerstein and Sandra Blakeslee, *Second Chances: Men, Women and Children a Decade after Divorce* (New York: Ticknor and Fields, 1989).

[11] Robert H. Coombs, "Marital Status and Personal Well-Being: A Literature Review," *Family Relations* 40 (1991): 97–101.

[12] Edward Beal and Gloria Hachman, *Adult Children of Divorce: Breaking the Cycle and Finding Fulfillment in Love, Marriage, and Family* (New York: Delta, 1991), 27–28.

[13] Paul Amato and B. Keith, "Parental Divorce and Well-Being of Children: A Meta-Analysis," *Psychological Bulletin* 110 (1991): 26–46.

[14] Paul Amato and B. Keith, "Parental Divorce and Adult Well-Being: A Literature Review," *Journal of Marriage and Family* 53 (1991): 43–48.

[15] Sheila Fitzgerald Klein and Andrea Beller, *American Demographics*, March 1989, 13.

[16] Sara McLanaghan and Gary Sandefur, *Growing Up with a Single Parent: What Hurts, What Helps* (Cambridge, MA: Harvard University Press, 1994), 103.

[17] Bureau of the Census, *Statistical Abstract of the United States, 1992* (Washington, DC: U.S. Government Printing Office, 1993), Table 719.

[18] William Dunn, "I Do, Is Repeat Refrain for Half of Newlyweds," *USA Today*, 15 February 1991, A-1.

[19] "Families: neo-nukes," *Research Alert*, 17 August 1990, 6.

[20] "When the Family Will Have a New Definition," *What the Next 50 Years Will Bring*, a special edition of *U.S. News and World Report*, 9 May 1983, A3.

[21] Arland Thornton and Deborah Freedman, "The Changing American Family," *Population Bulletin* 38 (1983): 10.

[22] Lynn K. White and Alan Booth, "The Quality and Stability of Remarriages: the Role of Stepchildren," *American Sociological Review* 50 (October 1985): 689–98.

[23] John Leland, "Tightening the Knot," *Newsweek*, 19 February 1996, 73.

[24] Quoted in Elizabeth Schoenfeld, "Drumbeats for Divorce Reform," *Policy Review* 77 (May–June 1996): 8.

[25] Quoted in Martin King Whyte, *Dating, Mating, and Marriage* (New York: de Gruyter, 1990), 1.

[26] Maggie Gallagher, *The Abolition of Marriage* (Washington, DC: Regnery, 1996), 135.

[27] Frank Furstenberg and Andrew Cherlin, *Divided Families: What Happens to Children When Parents Part* (Cambridge, MA: Harvard University Press, 1991), 22.

[28] G. J. Wenham, "Gospel Definitions of Adultery and Women's Rights," *Expository Times* 95 (1984): 330.

Chapter 16

[1] U.S. crime statistics for 1990, United States Justice Department 1990 report.

[2] "Cost of Crime: $674 Billion," *U.S. News and World Report*, 17 January 1994, 40–41.

[3] Daniel Patrick Moynihan, "Defining Deviancy Down," *American Scholar* 62 (Winter 1993): 17–30.

[4] William Bennett, *The Index of Leading Cultural Indicators* (Washington, DC: Empower America, 1993), 2.

[5] "Killer Teens," *U.S. News and World Report*, 17 January 1994, 26.

[6] Ibid.

[7] James Wooten, "Lessons of Pop Jordan's Death," *Newsweek*, 13 September 1993, 12.

[8] Eugene Methvin, "Mugged by Reality," *Policy Review* 84 (July–August 1997): 33.

[9] John DiIulio, "Getting Prisons Straight," *American Prospect* 1 (Fall 1990).

[10] Morgan Reynolds, "Why Does Crime Pay?" *National Center for Policy Analysis Backgrounder*, No. 110 (1990).

[11] Morgan Reynolds, "Crime Pays, But So Does Imprisonment," *National Center for Policy Analysis Policy Report*, No. 149 (March 1990).

[12] Mortimer Zuckerman, "War on Crime, By the Numbers," *U.S. News and World Report*, 17 January 1994, 67–68.

[13] Ben Wattenberg, "Crime Solution-Lock 'em Up," *Wall Street Journal*, 17 December 1993.

[14] Edwin Zedlewski, *Making Confinement Decisions*, (National Institute of Justice Research in Brief, 1987); Edwin Zedlewski, *New Mathematics of Imprisonment: A Reply to Zimring and Hawkins*, 35 (1989) Crime and Delinquency 171.

[15] Ed Rubenstein, "The Economics of Crime," *IMPRIMIS*, journal of Hillsdale College 24 (August 1995).

[16] Bureau of Justice Statistics, National Corrections Reporting Program, 1988.

[17] Frank Graham, *Prison Chapels Make Safer Texas* (Dallas: Chapel of Hope Ministries, 1995).

[18] Cal Thomas, "Programs of the Past Haven't Reduced Crime," *Los Angeles Times*, 13 January 1994.

[19] U. Cassuto, *A Commentary on the Book of Genesis, Part 2* (Jerusalem: Magnes, 1964), 127.

[20] Quoted in Ernest van den Haag, "On Deterrence and the Death Penalty," *Journal of Criminal Law, Criminology and Police Science* 60 (1969).

[21] Isaac Ehrlich, "The Deterrent Effect of Capital Punishment: A Question of Life and Death," *American Economic Review* 65 (June 1975), 397–417.

[22] Isaac Ehrlich, "The Deterrent Effect of Capital Punishment: Reply," *American Economic Review* 67 (June 1977) 452–458; Isaac Ehrlich, "Fear of Deterrence—A Critical Evaluation of the Report of the Panel on Research on Deterrent and Incapacitative Effects," *Journal of Legal Studies* 6 (June 1977).

[23] William Raspberry, "Mugged by the Reality of Injustice," *Washington Post*, 20 January 2003, A23.

Chapter 17

[1] Elizabeth Tener, "You Can Help Kids Resist Drugs and Drinking," *McCall's*, August 1984, 92.

[2] "Survey Links Drugs to TV," Associated Press story, 29 June 1995.

[3] Ibid.

[4] Craig Horowitz, "Drugs Are Bad: The Drug War is Worse," *New York* magazine, 5 Feb. 1996, 22–33.

[5] David Lynn, "The Church's Drug of Choice," *Eternity*, November 1988, 20.

[6] Russ Pulliam, "Alcoholism: Sin or Sickness?" *Christianity Today*, 18 September, 1981, 22–24.

[7] James R. Milan and Katherine Ketcham, *Under the Influence* (New York: Bantam, 1982), 34–37.

[8] Wayne Roques, *Legalization: An Idea Whose Time Will Never Come*, U.S. Drug Enforcement Administration, Miami Field Division: U.S. Department of Justice, 27 December 1994.

[9] L. J. West, D. S. Maxwell, E. P. Noble, and D. H. Solomon, *Annals of Internal Medicine* 100 (1984): 405–16.

[10] Charles Leerhsen, "Alcohol and the Family," *Newsweek*, 18 January 1988, 62–68.

[11] Quoted in "Marijuana Research Review," *Drug Watch Oregon*, 1 (July 1994).

[12] Daniel Brookoff et al., "Testing Reckless Drivers for Cocaine and Marijuana," *The New England Journal of Medicine*, 25 August 1994, 518–22.

[13] Leslie Robison, "Maternal Drug Use and Risk of Childhood Nonlymphoblastic Leukemia Among Offspring," *Cancer* 63 (1989): 1904–11.

[14] "Drug Legalization: Myths and Misconceptions," U.S. Department of Justice, Drug Enforcement Administration, Seattle, WA, 12 May 1994, 43.

[15] *Marijuana Research Review*, July 1994.

[16] "National Survey Finds Teen Drug Use Up: 13% of 9th-Graders Have Used Marijuana," *St. Louis Post-Dispatch*, 13 December 1994, A-1.

[17] Quoted in Peggy Mann, "Reasons to Oppose Legalizing Illegal Drugs," *Drug Awareness Information Newsletter*, September 1988.

[18] Quoted in Tom Seigfried, "Pleasure, pain: Scientists focus on cocaine's highs to unlock mysteries of addiction," *Dallas Morning News*, 11 April 1989, A-12.

[19] Kurt Anderson, "Crashing on Cocaine," *Time*, 11 April 1983, 25.

[20] Dan Sperling, "But we are not winning on addiction," *USA Today*, 1 August 1989, 2A.

[21] Ronald Taylor, "America On Drugs," *U.S. News and World Report*, 28 July 1986, 50.

[22] The basic outline of this section is adapted from the article by Evan Thomas, "Battle Strategies: Five Fronts in a War of Attrition," *Time*, 15 September 1986, 69–73.

[23] Ibid., 73.

[24] Mark Gold, *The Good News about Drugs and Alcohol* (NY: Viliard, 1991), 245.

[25] "Drug Legalization: Myths and Misconceptions," 39.

[26] Ibid., 43.

[27] Richard Clayton and Carl Leukefeld, "The Prevention of Drug Use Among Youth: Implications of Legalization," *Journal of Primary Prevention* 22 (Spring 1994).

[28] Morton M. Kondracke, "Don't Legalize Drugs," *The New Republic*, 27 June 1988.

[29] "Substance Abuse: The Nation's Number One Health Problem," (Princeton, NJ: Institute for Health Policy, Brandeis University for the Robert Wood Foundation), October 1993, 16.

[30] Peggy Mann, *"Reasons to Oppose Legalizing Drugs"* Committees of Correspondence Newsletter (Danvers, MA, September 1988), 3.

[31] Wayne Roques, "Decriminalizing Drugs Would Be a Disaster," *Miami Herald*, 20 Jan. 1995.

[32] "Poll Says One-third of Inmates Used Drugs before Committing Crimes," *Dallas Times Herald*, 21 August 1983, A-3.

[33] J. E. Fagan, J. Weis, and Y. Cheng, "Delinquency and Substance Abuse Among Inner-City Students," *Journal of Drug Issues* 20 (1993) 351–99.

[34] "Drug Legalization: Myths and Misconceptions," 32.

[35] Don Feder, "Legalizers Plan Harvard Pot Party," *Boston Herald*, 19 May 1994.

[36] William Bennett, "How Intellectuals Have Failed in the Drug War," *Human Events*, 6 January 1990, 10–11.

[37] Merrill Unger, *Demons in the World Today* (Wheaton, IL: Tyndale, 1971), 10–13, 75–76.

[38] Charles Tate, "Work with Marijuana: II. Sensations," *Psychology Today* (May 1971): 41–44.

[39] Alan Watts, *The Joyous Cosmology* (New York: Vintage, 1962), 18–19.

Chapter 18

[1] *Report of the National Gambling Impact Study Commission*, (Washington, DC: U.S. Govt. Printing Office, 1999) 1.

[2] "Gambling in America," *Gambling Awareness Action Guide* (Nashville: Christian Life Commission, 1984), 5.

[3] Sylvia Porter, "Economic Costs of Compulsive Gambling in U.S. Staggering," *Dallas Morning News*, 4 January 1984, 6C.

[4] *The Final Report of the Commission on the Review of the National Policy toward Gambling* (Washington, D.C.: U.S. Govt. Printing Office, 1976) 65.

[5] Quoted in Charles Colson, "The Myth of the Money Tree," *Christianity Today*, 10 July 1987, 64.

[6] Gary Becker, "Higher Sin Taxes: A Low Blow to the Poor," *Business Week*, 5 June 1989, 23.

[7] J. Emmett Henderson, *State Lottery: The Absolute Worst Form of Legalized Gambling* (Atlanta, GA: Georgia Council on Moral and Civil Concerns, n.d.), 11.

[8] Brad Edmonson, "Demographics of Gambling," *American Demographics*, July 1986, 40–41.

[9] Quoted in Curt Suplee, "Lotto Baloney," *Harper's*, July 1983, 19.

[10] T. Dielman, "Gambling: A Social Problem?" *Journal of Social Issues* 35, no. 3 (1979): 39.

[11] Julian Taber, "Opinion," *USA Today*, 14 August 1989, 4.

[12] Borden Cole and Sidney Margolis, *When You Gamble—You Risk More Than Your Money* (New York: Public Affairs Pamphlet, 1964), 12.

[13] Joseph Shapiro, "America's Gambling Fever," *U.S. News and World Report*, 15 January 1996, 58.

[14] John Warren Kindt, statement before a hearing of the U.S. House of Representatives Committe on Small Business, 21 September 1994.

[15] Quoted in "State Lotteries and Gambling—Results Have Not Equaled Expectations," *USA Today*, April 1979, 1.

[16] *New York Times*, 9 February 1980.

[17] Charles Clotfelter and Philip Cook, *Selling Hope: State Lotteries in America* (Cambridge, MA: Harvard University Press, 1991), 105.

[18] Henderson, *State Lottery*, 26.

[19] *The Final Report of the Commission on the Review of National Policy toward Gambling*, 1976, 71.

[20] John Warren Kindt, "The Economic Aspects of Legalized Gambling Activities," *Duke Law Review* 43 (1994): 59.

[21] David Neff and Thomas Giles, "Feeding the Monster Called More," *Christianity Today*, 25 November 1991, 20.

[22] Quoted in William Petersen, *What You Should Know about Gambling* (New Canaan, CT: Keats, 1973), 37.

[23] Quoted in James Mann, "Gambling Rage: Out of Control," *U.S. News and World Report*, 30 May 1983, 30.

Chapter 19

[1] J. C. Gutin, "End of the Rainbow," *Discover*, November 1994, 71–75.

[2] Bruce McConkie, "Apostle of the Mormon Council of 12," in *Mormon Doctrine* (Salt Lake: Bookcraft, 1958), 554.

[3] "The Golden Age," *The Watchtower*, 24 July 1929, 702.

Chapter 20

[1] E. F. Schumacher, *Small Is Beautiful* (London: Abacus, 1973).

[2] Jacques Ellul, *The Technological Society* (New York: Vintage, 1964).

[3] C. S. Lewis, *The Abolition of Man* (New York: Macmillan, 1947), 68–69, 71 (italics his).

[4] Calvin DeWitt, "Seven Degradations of Creation," in *The Environment and the Christian*, ed. Calvin DeWitt (Grand Rapids: Baker, 1991), 15–22.

[5] Stephen Budiansky, "The Doomsday Myths," *U.S. News and World Report*, 13 December 1993, 82.

[6] Al Gore, *Earth in the Balance: Ecology and the Human Spirit* (New York: Houghton Mifflin, 1992), 28.

[7] DeWitt, "Seven Degradations of Creation,"16.

[8] James Lovelock, *The Ages of Gaia: A Biography of Our Living Earth* (New York: Norton, 1988), 208–12.

[9] Lynn White, "The Historical Roots of Our Ecological Crisis," *Science*, 10 March 1967, 1203–7.

[10] Francis Schaeffer, *Pollution and the Death of Man: The Christian View of Ecology* (Wheaton, IL: Tyndale, 1970), 83.

[11] Ibid., 83–84.

[12] Glenn Schicker, "Tending the Garden as God's Stewards," *Eternity*, September 1988, 68.

Chapter 21

[1] Marshall McLuhan, *Understanding Media* (New York: New American Library, 1964).

[2] Neil Postman, *The Disappearance of Childhood* (New York: Vintage Books, 1994), 72.

[3] Robert A. Papper et. al., "Middletown Media Studies," *International Digital Media & Arts Association Journal* 1, no. 1 (Spring 2004): 5.

[4] "Generation M: Media in the Lives of 8-18 Year Olds," Kaiser Family Foundation Study, March 2005, www.kff.org/entmedia/entmedia030905pkg.cfm.

[5] E. H. Woodard and N. Gridina, *Media in the Home: The Fifth Annual Survey of Parents and Children 2000* (Philadelphia, PA: The Annenberg Public Policy Center of the University of Pennsylvania, 2000),www.appcpenn.org/inhome.pdf.

[6] Elizabeth F. Brown and William R. Hendee, "Adolescents and Their Music: Insights Into the Health of Adolescents," *The Journal of the American Medical Association* 262 (22–29 September 1989): 1659.

[7] Gary D. Malaney, "Student Internet Use at U. Mass Amherst," *Student Affairs Online*, 5, no. 1, January 2004, www.studentaffairs.com/ejournal/Winter_2004/StudentInternet Use.html.

[8] *National Family Values: A Survey of Adults* conducted by Voter/Consumer Research (Bethesda, MD, 1994).

[9] Rebecca Collins et. al., "Watching Sex on Television Predicts Adolescent Initiation of Sexual Behavior," *Pediatrics* 114, no. 3 (September 2004), 280–289.

[10] Neil Malamuth and Edward Donnerstain, *Pornography and Sexual Aggression* (New York: Academic, 1984).

[11] Edward Donnerstein, "What the Experts Say," a forum at the Industry-wide Leadership Conference on Violence in Television Programming, 2 August 1993, in *National Council for Families and Television Report*, 9.

[12] Irving Kristol, "Sex, Violence and Videotape," *Wall Street Journal*, 31 May 1994.

[13] Jerry Adler, "Kids Growing Up Scared," *Newsweek*, 10 January 1994, 49.

[14] Peter Plagen, "Violence in Our Culture," *Newsweek*, 1 April 1991, 48.

[15] Ibid., 51.

[16] John Johnston, "Kids: Growing Up Scared," *Cincinnati Enquirer*, 20 March 1994, E01.

[17] Elizabeth Jensen, "One-Day Study Finds Rise in Violence on TV, but Research Method Is Disputed," *Wall Street Journal*, 5 August 1994.

[18] Joint Statement on the Impact of Entertainment Violence on Children, *American Academy of Pediatrics*, 26 July 2000.

[19] Quoted in Leo Bogart, "Warning: The Surgeon General Has Determined that TV Violence Is Moderately Dangerous to Your Child's Mental Health," *Public Opinion* 36 (Winter 1972–73): 504.

[20] Plagen, "Violence in Our Culture," 51.

[21] Quoted in ibid.

[22] Mark Robichaux, "MTV Is Playing a New Riff," *Wall Street Journal*, 9 February 1993.

[23] Stewart Powell, "What Entertainers Are Doing to Your Kids," *U.S. News and World Report*, 28 October 1985, 46–50.

[24] George Gerbner and Larry Gross, "The Scary World of TV's Heavy Viewer," *Psychology Today*, April 1976, 41.

[25] Ibid.

[26] S. Robert Lichter and Stanley Rothman, "Media and Business Elites," *Public Opinion* (October–November 1981): 42–46.

[27] S. Robert Lichter, Stanley Rothman, and Linda S. Lichter, *The Media Elite* (New York: Adler and Adler, 1986).

[28] S. Robert Lichter, "Consistently Liberal: But Does It Matter?" *Media Critic* (Summer 1996): 26–39.

[29] "Survey: Liberals dominate news outlets: Far higher number in press than in general population," *WorldNetDaily*, 24 May 2004, www.worldnetdaily.com/news/article.asp?ARTICLE_ID=38628.

[30] John Leo, "Liberal media? I'm shocked!" *U.S. News and World Report*, 7 June 2004, 12.

[31] Tim Groseclose and Jeff Milyo, "A Measure of Media Bias," December 2004, www.polisci.ucla.edu/faculty/groseclose/Media.Bias.8.htm.

[32] Ibid. "For instance, in the Ninth California district, which includes Berkeley, twelve percent voted for Bush in 1992, nearly double the rate of journalists. In the Eighth Massachusetts district, which includes Cambridge, nineteen percent voted for Bush, approximately triple the rate of journalists." Similar patterns can be found for the 1996 and 2000 presidential elections.

[33] Linda Lichter, S. Robert Lichter, and Stanley Rothman, "Hollywood and America: The Odd Couple," *Public Opinion* (December 1982–January 1983): 54–58.

[34] Stanley Rothman and S. Robert Lichter, "What Are Moviemakers Made Of?" *Public Opinion* (December 1983–January 1984): 14–18.

Chapter 22

[1] Francis Schaeffer, *A Christian Manifesto* (Westchester, IL: Crossway, 1981), 116.

[2] Henry David Thoreau, "On the Duty of Civil Disobedience" (n.p., 1849).

[3] Samuel Rutherford, *Lex Rex or The Law and the Prince* (n.p., 1644).

[4] Schaeffer, *A Christian Manifesto*, 91.

[5] Quoted in Richard John Neuhaus, *Naked Public Square* (Grand Rapids: Eerdmans, 1984), 237.

[6] St. Augustine of Hippo, *Against Faustus the Manichaean*, 22.222.